DISSERTATIONS AND THESES

▪ FROM START TO FINISH ▪

PSYCHOLOGY AND RELATED FIELDS

DISSERTATIONS AND THESES

FROM START TO FINISH

PSYCHOLOGY AND RELATED FIELDS

JOHN D. CONE, UNITED STATES INTERNATIONAL UNIVERSITY AND
SHARON L. FOSTER, CALIFORNIA SCHOOL OF PROFESSIONAL PSYCHOLOGY

...

AMERICAN PSYCHOLOGICAL ASSOCIATION · WASHINGTON, DC

Seventh printing March 1998

Published by the
American Psychological Association
750 First Street, NE
Washington, DC 20002

Copies may be ordered from
APA Order Department
P.O. Box 92984
Washington, DC 20090-2984

In the UK and Europe, copies may be ordered from
American Psychological Association
3 Henrietta Street
Covent Garden
London WC2E 8LU
England

Typeset in Futura and New Baskerville by Easton Publishing Services, Inc., Easton, MD

Printer: Braun-Brumfield, Inc., Ann Arbor, MI
Cover Designer: Grafik Communications, Ltd., Alexandria, VA
Text designer: Enigma Concepts, Inc., Silver Spring, MD
Technical/production editors: Peggy Schlegel and Susan Bedford

Library of Congress Cataloging-in-Publication Data
Cone, John D., 1942–
    Dissertations and theses from start to finish: Psychology and related fields / John
  D. Cone and Sharon L. Foster.
      p.   cm.
    Includes bibliographical references and index.
    ISBN 1-55798-194-9 (acid-free paper)
    1. Psychology—Research—Methodology.   I. Foster, Sharon L.
  II. Title.
  BF76.5.C645   1993
  150'.72—dc20   92-38195
                                                          CIP

British Library Cataloguing-in-Publication Data
A CIP record is available from the British Library.

Printed in the United States of America

"Well, a pop-up doctoral dissertation is certainly an original idea..."

Contents

Foreword   *Gregory A. Kimble*   ix

Acknowledgments   xiii

Chapter 1   What Are Dissertations and Theses and
            Why Write a Book About Them?   1

Chapter 2   Starting Out: Assessing Your Preparation
            for the Task Ahead   11

Chapter 3   Topics: How to Find and Refine Them   27

Chapter 4   Time and Trouble Management   45

Chapter 5   Selecting a Chairperson and a
            Committee   61

Chapter 6   Formulating and Communicating Your
            Plans: An Overview of the Proposal 81

Chapter 7   Reviewing the Literature   93

Chapter 8   Methodology (or, How You're Gonna
            Do What You're Gonna Do!)   119

Chapter 9   Measurement   147

Chapter 10 Selecting the Appropriate Statistics 173

Chapter 11 Collecting, Managing, and Analyzing
            the Data   201

Chapter 12   Presenting the Results   219

Chapter 13   Discussing the Results   237

Chapter 14   Managing Committee Meetings:
              Proposal and Oral Defense   255

Chapter 15   Presenting Your Project to the World   277

Epilogue   297

Appendix A   Selected Ethical Standards Relevant to
              the Conduct of Research in Psychology   299

Appendix B   Bibliographic Databases   309

Appendix C   Statistical Software   317

Appendix D   Bibliography for Research Design,
              Measurement, Statistics, and
              Writing Style   319

              References   323
              Index   329
              About the Authors   349

Foreword

An Open Letter to Graduate Students

Greetings!

So you entered graduate school. I've been wondering what happened to you. The decision you have made will often bring great satisfaction, and only now and then regret. Finances may make life difficult, but you and your student colleagues are in the same boat. You will find ways to make poverty seem like fun. Soon you will be making friends who will be your friends forever. You are in a very good department. You will be mastering the skills to help you cure the miseries of the world. Congratulations!

You asked me for advice about your thesis or dissertation, but I am not sure that I can be useful; my degree is more than half a century older than yours will be. On the other hand, I have been in this field for a long time. So, I will take advantage of the lofty perch to which my years of experience have lifted me and pronounce for you the lessons I have learned—about dissertations, theses, and some other things, as well.

Lesson 1. Graduate departments are in the business of advancing a science and profession. Think of your time there as an apprenticeship, preparing you to contribute to that goal. Possibly, your most important contribution to science will be your thesis or dissertation. It may be the biggest research project you ever do. The experience can be rewarding. My next few lessons have to do with that.

Lesson 2. The topic of your dissertation or thesis should match your intellectual style. The social sciences cover a spectrum of exactness—from quantitative rigor to qualitative imprecision. You, in turn, have what psychologists call a certain *tolerance for ambiguity*. This is where a cognitive match becomes important. Choose a topic that is definite enough to make you feel secure but open-ended enough to be exciting.

Lesson 3. Your dissertation or thesis should be part of an established program of research. Your need to be creative may be urging you toward something unique and independent. Not a good idea! You will miss the stimulating interactions that you otherwise would have with faculty and other students working on related problems. You are apt to get inadequate guidance—or none. No faculty member knows enough to supervise everything, and such "unique" dissertations usually add nothing to knowledge. Instead, they exacerbate the worst problem of the discipline: its lack of coherence and integrity.

Lesson 4. The spirit of your relationship with your supervisor should be one of collaboration. When you decide on someone you may want to work with, approach that person and ask for general ideas. Go away with one or two of them and return later with thoughts about research. If things go right, the potential sponsor's reaction will be something like, "I was hoping that you'd be interested in that area, and your project is a good start. Here are a few reprints that describe my work on the topic. Don't you think that we need this control group? That additional condition? Let's work more on this together, and very soon. I'm sure that we can work out something of mutual interest." If you find that you can't relate to a faculty member in this way, look for someone else.

Lesson 5. When it comes to writing your dissertation or thesis, be as brief as they will let you be. At your university, there will be an informal lower limit, established by tradition, on what is acceptable. Almost certainly that limit is more than you will need to tell your story. You won't get away with it these days, but the most successful student I ever supervised did a dissertation that was less than 20 pages long.

Welcome it if your chairperson wants to bother with the details of expression. I learned more about writing from Kenneth Spence when I did my dissertation than from all the English courses that I took in college.

Lesson 6. Realize that the methods you are learning are more important than the subject matter. Most "facts" in social science have a half-life of about 5 years. Research design and methods of analysis are more durable. If *operational definition* is a dirty word in your department, avoid it; but, when you describe your research on "self-concept," "the representation of information in memory," "separation anxiety"—whatever, be sure that you provide the information required for someone else to replicate your study.

Be suspicious of those fascinating incidental findings. They may be just an accident of sampling (Type I error). For years, I have watched the unexpected outcomes of research become parts of a theory being tested. Then, tests of the enriched theory produce their own new insights that the theory embraces—and so on, until the system collapses. Unless you have reproduced them, such revelations deserve, at most, a mention in your dissertation.

Now, three final lessons that are more general.

Lesson 7. Become a socialized member of the community of scholars in your discipline. Go to the departmental colloquia—even those outside your field of interest; often, thinking in another area will clarify your own. Interact with the colloquium speakers. Find out what is happening in their universities and where they think the field is going. If there are opportunities to do so, attend conventions; meet some of the scholars whose work you have been reading. Learn about the national associations in your field, and become a student affiliate member of one or two.

Lesson 8. Start becoming a professional. For the next 5 years—4 if you are lucky—your world is the lab and library, but there is life after graduation. Prepare for it. Learn the folklore and the tricks of the trade you're going into.

Try presenting a paper or a poster at a convention. You will meet the people who will be your colleagues—or maybe even hire you—later on. You will hear about the cutting edge of research and application in your area of interest.

Learn how to prepare an article for publication in your field, and write something for publication (stick to the refereed journals; the others count against you).

Apply for a national fellowship. If you win one, you have tangible recognition of your worth, and your life as a graduate student will be more comfortable. Also, preparing the fellowship request will be practice for writing grant applications later on.

Lesson 9. This is a lesson I hate to have to tell you, but unfortunately life is real. What if you bomb in graduate school? What if you get Cs in your courses and they put you on probation? What if you hate research (or therapy, or teaching), but they insist that you do it? God spare you that predicament but, if you find that you are in it, take stock of your resources and ask yourself two questions.

First, is this the field I really want to be in? The first step toward "making it" in this world is to find something you enjoy so much that you would be happy doing it for nothing; the second step is to find someone to pay you for it. Perhaps this field isn't it.

Second, am I really cut out for this line of work? Be honest. Growing up continues for a lifetime; mostly, it's a matter of more and more accurate self-evaluation. You should be in a profession in which you can be excellent, not just good enough. If candid self-assessment tells you that you can't be excellent where you are, move on to something that suits your talents better.

Lesson 10.   The book that you have in your hands has much useful information. It goes into great detail on the topics of my lessons. You will find the content thoughtful and usually appropriate to your situation. The book raises questions that you'd never think (or dare) to ask and comes to useful answers. You will learn a lot and, if—the best of all possible outcomes—you become an academic, it will help you in your work with your own students.

Again, let me offer congratulations and the hope that your life in graduate school will be a short and happy one!

Sincerely,

Gregory A. Kimble
Professor Emeritus
Duke University

Acknowledgments

A book such as this cannot be produced without the assistance of many people. Students who have heeded our advice over the years and then had the courage to tell us which ideas were pearls and which were dross helped us to refine our thoughts. Their questions also showed us the gaps in graduate education regarding the details involved in conducting independent research for the first time.

We are also grateful to our editors, Julia Frank-McNeil and Mary Lynn Skutley, for seeing the value in bringing a book like this to graduate student audiences. Our production editors, Peggy Schlegel and Susan Bedford, worked tirelessly and cheerfully at keeping the book on schedule and negotiating numerous delicate details. Thomas Cash and Brian Yates provided valuable commentary on an earlier version and helped us make this volume more user-friendly. Constance Dalenberg and Richard Gevirtz provided informative critiques of our statistics chapter. Avid Khorram, Vicky Wolfe, Tom DiLorenzo, and Heidi Inderbitzen kindly allowed us to reproduce portions of their dissertation work to illustrate our points. Sherry Casper-Beliveau and Linda Jansen were sharp-eyed in their proofreading of several sections of the typeset copy. Finally, our spouses graciously endured the inevitable late nights and lost weekends that accompany producing a book such as this. We thank all who assisted and hope the final product reflects those contributions.

What Are Dissertations and Theses and Why Write a Book About Them?

et's answer the second question first. We have written this book to help graduate students in psychology and related fields negotiate the thesis and dissertation process from beginning to end more successfully. We have also written the book to serve as an archival source of the wisdom we have amassed from a combined total of 35 years of supervising students completing theses and doctoral dissertations. Both of us have told graduate students many useful (and some not-so-useful!) things over the years, in an effort to help them through the process. We have never systematized these suggestions, though, and so we, like other faculty members, have had to tell each new thesis and dissertation fledgling everything all over again each time we are approached. We have written this book to compile the best of our suggestions on how to make the process a less mysterious and more exciting educational experience. Although we gear our suggestions primarily toward advanced graduate research in psychology and related fields, many are useful to the first-time researcher, generally.

How This Book Is Organized

The 15 chapters of this book provide the nuts and bolts needed to put together good theses and dissertations. This book cannot do it all, of course. It will be most valuable to the extent that it supplements an already adequate graduate education. For example, we do not explain research design or statistics in detail. Instead, we help you apply what you have already learned in graduate school to the practical conduct of research.

In the present chapter, we talk about what theses and dissertations are, how they came to be, what they look like, and why students do them. Then, we move to chapter 2, in which we ask you to assess your own preparation for the task ahead. Chapter 2 is full of useful suggestions about finding out the local norms concerning the thesis and dissertation process and organizing your life so that you can complete your project successfully. Chapter 3 discusses finding a topic, developing a research question, and formulating testable hypotheses. Chapter 4 helps you estimate the time you will need to finish your project and manage the myriad events that might come along to derail your efforts. Chapter 5 provides valuable tips about selecting a chairperson and committee members and about thesis and dissertation etiquette, in general. Chapter 6 goes into detail about the all-important proposal. Suggestions for developing a literature review (chapter 7) follow. Chapter 8 discusses what to include in a good method section and also covers research design, research ethics, and informed consent. Data collection, data analysis, and results are covered in chapters 9 through 11. Chapter 12 treats the presentation of these results, and chapter 13 deals with their discussion. Chapter 14 reviews strategies for handling your proposal meeting and oral defense. The final chapter discusses adapting the thesis or dissertation for presentation at professional meetings and for eventual submission for publication. Finally, a number of tools useful in the entire process can be found in the appendixes. Among these are the American Psychological Association's (APA's) ethical standards for conducting research, lists of on-line bibliographic databases and statistical software, and an annotated bibliography of publications about research design, measurement, statistics, and writing style.

The topics we cover follow the sequence you would normally encounter in the thesis or dissertation process. We think you will get the most out of the book by reading the relevant chapter as you approach each new phase of your thesis or dissertation. It would also be useful to skim the entire book quickly before starting the process, so you will have some idea of what is included and where to look for something should you need it in a sequence different from the one presented here. At the end of chapters 2 through 15, we provide useful "to do" lists. Taken together, they form a task analysis of the steps needed to complete a dissertation or thesis *and* submit it for publication. Do everything on these lists and you can't help but be successful.

Now, let's go back to the first question posed in this chapter: What are theses and dissertations anyway? First we define them; then we talk a little bit about their history. Finally, we say something about what theses and dissertations in the behavioral sciences actually look like.

Definitions, Distinctions, and Functions

A check of several dictionaries for definitions of *thesis* or *dissertation* shows immediately that there is no universal consensus. *Webster's* defines a dissertation as (1) "discourse; debate; discussion"; (2) "an extended treatment of a subject, especially in writing; a disquisition; an essay; thesis; treatise" (*Webster's New International Dictionary*, 1950, p. 753). Oxford and Random House define dissertations similarly, referring to a spoken or written treatment of a subject in which the subject is discussed at length, a "written essay, treatise or thesis, especially one written for the degree of doctor of philosophy" (*Random House Dictionary of the English Language*, cited in Davinson, 1977, p. 12). As these definitions reveal, there is no clear distinction between the terms *thesis* and *dissertation*. In fact, the *Random House* definition of the former includes the latter! To wit, a thesis is "a dissertation on a particular subject in which one has done original research, as one presented for a diploma or degree, especially a master's degree" (*Random House*, cited in Davinson, 1977, p. 12). Similarly, *Webster's* (1950) defines a thesis as a "dissertation embodying results of original research" (p. 2624).

In universities in the United States, it has become common to distinguish between dissertations and theses by referring to the work done for a master's degree as a thesis and that done for a doctoral degree as a dissertation. This is not a universally accepted distinction by any means, and some schools (e.g., Harvard University and the University of Washington) refer to dissertations as *theses*. Throughout this volume, we will use the term *dissertation* to refer to an original piece of empirical research, done in partial fulfillment of the requirements of doctoral (PhD or PsyD) programs in psychology and related fields. Similarly, *thesis* will refer to empirical research conducted en route to a master's degree.

There is general agreement on the functions of theses and dissertations, however. One major purpose is to reveal the student's skill in conducting independent research that makes an original contribution to knowledge on an important topic. With respect to dissertations, the *Yale University Catalog* asserts that the dissertation reveals whether the student has attained "technical mastery of the field of specialization, is capable of doing independent scholarly work, and is able to formulate conclusions that will in some respect modify or enlarge what has been previously known" (Yale University, 1975, p. 182). Thus, the dissertation process is an examination of your competence to function autonomously as a researcher. The finished product also results in a new and significant contribution to the knowledge base. Theses, too, are expected to contribute in this way. Thesis requirements place less emphasis on originality, however, and candidates are often given more guidance and supervision. Some thesis candidates conduct a systematic replication of already completed research, for example. In addition, thesis candidates rarely operate as independently as dissertation candidates must.

Origins of Theses and Dissertations

In medieval times, as today, it was necessary to obtain a degree from a university in order to teach. In those days, the church controlled the universities, and a diploma or license to teach was a church-dispensed prerogative. From the very earliest times, a graduate student was prepared for this role by a "sponsoring doctor," who stayed with the process until satisfied with the student's preparation (Davinson, 1977). This was, of course, the forerunner of today's thesis and dissertation committee chairperson. The evolution of the form of theses and dissertations and the process of producing them has varied from country to country, but the general apprenticelike nature of the process has remained fairly consistent. In Great Britain, it is common for the doctoral candidate to work with a single faculty member, eventually to be examined on the product of that work by that person and another faculty member within the university. In the United States, the candidate works with a committee of scholars, although primarily with the chair of this committee. The committee conducts an examination of the thesis or dissertation, and this examination is usually open to the entire academic community. This is called a thesis or dissertation *defense.* In some cases, the candidate must also argue the case for conducting the particular research in the first place, usually at a proposal meeting held in advance of formal data collection. We discuss the preparation of the proposal in chapter 6, and the proposal meeting and defense in chapter 14.

Although in this book we assume that your project will involve empirical research, not all theses and dissertations require this. The traditional terminal degree in psychology, the PhD, virtually always requires an empirical project. Some applied psychology programs offer an alternative terminal degree, the PsyD, or doctor of psychology. PsyD programs explicitly prepare students for careers as practitioners, often in clinical psychology. PsyD programs typically require final written scholarly projects that make original contributions to knowledge, which are sometimes called *dissertations*. Many practitioner-oriented schools allow alternatives to the traditional *empirical* dissertation, however. Sanchez-Hucles and Cash (1992) surveyed directors of 40 "Vail-model" (i.e., professional clinical psychology) programs in the United States, which presumably included a significant number of PsyD programs. Seventy-five percent reported that they accept nonempirical alternatives, such as theoretical papers, program evaluations, and clinical case reports. Interestingly, approximately half of the students in these programs elected to conduct empirical research to satisfy their doctoral requirements, however.

Topography (or, What Theses and Dissertations Should Look Like)

You have probably asked yourself a number of questions about the form your thesis or dissertation is supposed to take. How long should it be? What format are you supposed to follow? Are there writing style requirements to follow, and so on. Let's take a look at some of these questions.

As for length, there is a great deal of variability within and between disciplines and within and between universities. Although we do not have objective data on theses, we do know something about the length of dissertations. Davis and Parker (1979) selected a random sample of 400 dissertations in sociology, economics, business, and English literature from *Dissertation Abstracts International* in 1976 and reported a median length of 225 pages. Interdisciplinary differences were not great, ranging from a low for English literature of 206 to a high for sociology of 254. In a random sample of 100 dissertations in psychology selected from *Dissertation Abstracts International* in 1990, we found a median page length of 174, with a range of 59 to 679.[1] Considering that the standard deviation for our sample was 95.4, a safe estimate is that 85% of present-day psychology dissertations fall between 67 and 287 pages, inclusive of text, tables, appendixes, and related items. Our educated guess is that master's theses would average about two thirds of this length, or about 62 pages.

As for format, yes, there is a format you are supposed to follow. This will be dictated by your particular academic institution. We suggest that you get in touch with the person in charge of such matters and learn about your local requirements. These people can be found in the office of the dean of your graduate school or at your library. They will usually

---

1. We are indebted to Katherine Shumaker for collecting and analyzing these statistics.

have written materials to give you that will spell out the acceptable format or formats. In addition, they will probably provide you with other useful information, such as time lines, committee requirements, binding fees, and so on. Theses and dissertations in psychology commonly follow the style and format guidelines set forth in the *Publication Manual of the American Psychological Association* (APA, 1994). This book has been written in that format, and most journals in the behavioral sciences adhere to it. Indeed, we will refer extensively to APA's *Publication Manual* throughout this book. Although this is a frequently followed format, it is not universally accepted, even in schools and departments of psychology. Also, even where it is accepted, there are often local deviations (e.g., in references and in the placement of tables) that you will do well to discover. Our advice is to make learning the local norms one of your first priorities. You will save much time and aggravation later by using a format consistent with the locally accepted one right from the start.

A good place to start would be to examine some theses and dissertations completed by students who have previously worked with the same committee chairpersons you are considering. These will provide excellent concrete examples of what format you can expect to follow. You might also ask faculty members for some suggestions. Completed projects vary in quality, and faculty members might want to direct you to examples that are most relevant to the type of research you are contemplating. (Chapter 5 deals specifically with the selection of committee chairs, so don't worry if you haven't picked one out already.)

What, in general, will your final document contain? It will closely resemble a journal article, but with more detail. It will begin with a table of contents and then launch into a review of the literature. Following this will be your method section, then your results, and finally your discussion. A reference section will contain details on the works cited in the text, and appendixes will provide supplemental material, such as equipment blueprints, consent forms, and data-recording forms.

So, there you have it. You know what theses and dissertations are, something about their place in history, and generally what they look like. Now, let's turn our attention to what is probably the most important question of this chapter.

Motivation (or, Why Do a Thesis or Dissertation in the First Place?)

There are many sound reasons for doing a thesis or dissertation. In the final analysis, you are writing one because the graduate program you are in requires it to obtain a particular degree. You've worked long and hard completing your course work so far. It would be almost unthinkable to throw all that effort away by not completing the last step toward your degree.

There are other good reasons, of course. Some are economic: the dissertation might be your ticket to higher income, an academic or applied job, and the beginning of your professional career. Other reasons are intellectual. Research offers many challenges and opportunities to think about and solve conceptual, methodological, and practical problems. Conducting research is also a way to find out about some psychological or other behavioral science phenomenon about which you are curious. Completing a thesis or dissertation can also provide the personal satisfaction of taking on and mastering a complex and challenging task.

Now that you are at this point in your program, take a moment to consider how you view the specific requirement of a thesis or dissertation. As cognitive–behavior therapists know, the way you think about the major research you are about to undertake will bear on the enjoyment, ease, and speed of the process, as well as the amount you learn from it. If you are filled with curiosity about some aspect of psychology or even about the process of doing research in psychology, good for you! You will probably have the stamina to stick with your project from start to finish. And, you are likely to have some fun along the way.

But what if you don't feel this way right now? It is normal at first to see a thesis or dissertation as a troublesome hurdle to clear on your way to a degree and to want to look for the easiest, quickest way to get beyond it. But it may be more helpful to focus on the benefits of clearing this hurdle that have meaning to you. Can you anticipate gaining useful skills during the project? Can you see it as having any relevance to the work you plan to do after graduation? Is it an opportunity for you to extend research you are already pursuing or to answer questions you have been asking yourself in your course work or field experiences? It can be useful to concentrate on these positive aspects of the project and to view the hurdles you will encounter as challenges rather than obstacles. Remember, you probably haven't got this far if you don't enjoy learning, and doing research, for many, is the ultimate learning experience.

Success (or, Doing What Works)

Before ending this chapter, perhaps a word of warning is in order: Some of the advice we offer may not be useful to you. Not every strategy works well for every student, and not every faculty member and department orchestrates the thesis and dissertation process with the same instruments and score. Rules and traditions differ from place to place. Take what we say with some healthy skepticism and see whether your local situation is different from what we present in this book. Remember, completing a thesis or dissertation is, in some respects, a rite of passage. As with most such rites, some of the process may seem arbitrary and nonfunctional. If you acknowledge this up front and decide to do what works whether it makes complete sense or not, you will succeed much more easily and have a lot more fun along the way.

In other words, don't get too intimidated by the thesis or dissertation process. Yes, it's lengthy. Yes, it's involved. Yes, you may never have done anything quite like this before. Yes, it may be scary at times. And yes, you, like many others, will probably complete the process and earn your degree. Remember, many parts of the project will involve skills that you already have. In addition, your chairperson and committee will be there to help.

A recent student put it very well:

> As I come to the close of my graduate process and the completion of my dissertation, one thought keeps coming back to me—that any goal is possible given two factors: 1) the ability to break things down into tiny steps, and 2) the support of family, friends, and the community. (Dionne, 1992, p. iii)

We know you are motivated or you wouldn't be reading this book. Are you ready to act on this motivation? Let's turn to chapter 2 to examine your preparation in some detail and find out what you might do to be even better equipped for the task before you.

2 Starting Out: Assessing Your Preparation for the Task Ahead

In the previous chapter, we asked you to do a little soul searching and to examine your attitude toward completing a thesis or dissertation. In this chapter, we help you assess your preparation: the skills needed to do a competent job. The material in the following pages should help you gauge your overall readiness to tackle your thesis or dissertation.

Check Your Preparation

In this section, we provide a way of testing reality. You are convinced that you want to undertake a major research project and that you have good reasons for doing it. Are you really prepared, though? A good way to find out is to complete the Research Readiness Checklist that follows. Answer each of the questions as truthfully as you can. Remember, this is a test of just how realistically you are approaching this process. Be honest with yourself. A "no" answer will provide useful material for reflection when we talk about the implications of your responses. Write your answers on a separate sheet of paper and we will discuss how to interpret them in the next section.

Because this checklist is not an empirically validated psychometric measure, don't think of it as providing definitive answers concerning your preparation to navigate a complex research project successfully. Instead, use it as an inventory of the important types of preparation you will need to make the journey a smooth one. Basically, this list is a task analysis of the skills and resources that we believe you will need to complete the project in a smooth and timely fashion. This leads to another word of warning: Do not let a "no" answer be a stimulus for an anxiety attack. A "no" does not mean you will fail to complete your thesis or dissertation.

Exhibit 2.1

Research Readiness Checklist

Yes	No	**How Well Do You Write?**
☐	☐	1. Do you generally write well-organized, logical, coherent papers?
☐	☐	2. Do you use correct grammar?
☐	☐	3. Do you spell correctly?
☐	☐	4. Do you know APA format well enough to write with only occasional checking of the *Publication Manual*?

Yes	No	**Do You Have the Necessary Methodological Preparation?**
☐	☐	5. Have you taken two or more graduate-level statistics courses within the past 3 years?
☐	☐	6. Have you taken a graduate-level course in test construction or measurement theory?
☐	☐	7. Have you taken a course in research design as a graduate student?
☐	☐	8. Have you been required to critique empirical research literature in graduate school?
☐	☐	9. Have you been involved in empirical research as a graduate student?

Yes	No	**General Preparation**
☐	☐	10. Have you talked to at least three other persons about their thesis or dissertation experience?
☐	☐	11. Do you have at least 20 hours per week to spend on the project?
☐	☐	12. Will this time be available for *at least* 12 to 18 months?
☐	☐	13. Do you have the physical space to do uninterrupted writing, data analysis, etc.?
☐	☐	14. Do you have access to adequate bibliographic resources (e.g., libraries and databases)?
☐	☐	15. Do you have access to faculty and advisor input on a regular basis?
☐	☐	16. Do you have the agreement of family and loved ones to support you in this effort?
☐	☐	17. Do you own or have access to a computer?
☐	☐	18. Do you have adequate keyboard skills?
☐	☐	19. Do you have reasonable time management skills?
☐	☐	20. Do you have reasonable interpersonal and political skills?
☐	☐	21. Do you know the formal rules governing the thesis and dissertation process at your school?
☐	☐	22. Do you know the informal rules governing this process?

One of us, for example, would have said no to at least four of the questions before beginning her successfully completed dissertation. Nor does a full complement of yesses mean that you will sail through the project trouble free. Rather, use "no" answers to alert you to potential trouble spots that advance planning and preparation can help you avoid. Below, we provide some tips on what this preparation might involve.

Interpret Your Responses

To analyze your preparation, let's look more closely at some of the categories of items on the checklist.

Writing

Writing and methodology skills are probably the most important skills to have in completing a thesis or dissertation. We'll discuss methodology in a moment. First, let's talk about writing. If you said "no" to Items 1 and 2, you should seriously consider additional preparation before undertaking your project. Organizational skills in writing (Item 1) are an indication of how clearly you think. If you do not organize well, you might have trouble thinking in a linear fashion. And, unfortunately, there are no quick and easy programs to teach this skill. So, if you have reason to believe you do not organize verbal material well, stop and reconsider. You might benefit from specific course work or tutoring in organizing and sequencing written material. Examine offerings in the English department of your school. Have you ever taken a course in logic? If not, look for one in the philosophy department.

Grammatical prowess (Item 2) is somewhat more specific than organization. If you have consistently received input during your university schooling that you have problems with sentence structure and the proper choice of words, give some serious thought to remediating before beginning your thesis or dissertation. Although some schools permit editorial consultation on dissertations, most stop short of allowing the kind of input serious grammatical deficiencies would require. Unless English is not your native language, faculty will expect you to write the document yourself, not have an editor do it.

Several steps can be taken to improve grammatical skills. First, make sure that you have taken a good course in syntax and the rules of grammar and punctuation. If you have a basic foundation in syntax and punctuation, the next step toward grammatical proficiency would be to subject a sample of your writing to one of the several good grammar-checking programs that run in conjunction with your word processor. Among these software programs are Grammatik,™ RightWriter,™ Writes Right,™ and Writer's Tool Kit.™ These should be available at most software stores. Such programs will indicate whether you have violated one or more of hundreds of rules of grammar, made punctuation errors, produced too many long sentences, been too negative, or written in the active or passive voice. Using one of these programs is like hiring a professional copyeditor to review your work. You will be amazed at the thoroughness with which these programs analyze your writing. Even if you have typically been considered a good writer, you will benefit. We all have bad habits that are so automatic we're not even aware of them.

As an example of the type of analysis you will receive from using a grammar-checking program, look at the writing sample in Exhibit 2.2. This is a section from an earlier draft of chapter 3 of this book.

As you can see, RightWriter™ provides a rather detailed analysis of this writing sample. Your writing can be improved considerably by subjecting repeated samples to analyses of this type. You will not get feedback this extensive from your committee chairperson. About all these busy persons will have time to do is to comment that your writing needs improvement. They might point out a few specific split infinitives, verb–subject disagreements, and so on, but their job is to teach research skills, not writing. It is unlikely that any person could provide the comprehensive feedback available from well-constructed software programs. It is just not humanly possible to keep the thousands of rules in one's head and recall them at just the right moment, even if time allowed.

Spelling (Item 3) and style requirements (Item 4) deal with even more specific verbal skills. Happily, although they are important, their absence is not fatal in the budding behavioral scientist. If you have access to a computer, you can put your document through its spell-checking program and catch most of the results of poor spelling skills. If not, you can hire someone to proofread and correct spelling errors for you. The same can be said for APA format. Some computer programs (e.g., Pergamon Press's Manuscript Manager™) actually do most of the formatting work required. If you don't have such a program, get one or hire an editor familiar with APA style. Better yet, buy APA's *Publication Manual* and learn the proper formatting yourself. Anyone competent enough to complete graduate work can master APA style with a little help from this clear and detailed manual. If you are at a school that uses some other style, most likely there is someone who can give you a style sheet or manual that indicates what is acceptable. Ask at your library or dean's office for such a document.

Exhibit 2.2

Sample of Writing Proofread by RightWriter™

Develop the Research Question Next

Assuming you have successfully identified an area of research (e.g., dental phobia, child sexual abuse, depression, AIDS prevention), hopefully in collaboration with a respected faculty member, you next have to frame some sort of researchable question within that area. <<*_G3. SPLIT INTO 2 SENTENCES? *>><<*_S3. LONG SENTENCE: 44 WORDS *>> The *form* such questions should take is fairly specific, as we will see <<*_U11. WORDY: as we will see *>> later. The *source* of such questions is something we want to take up first.

In general, you want to ask questions that the scientific community is interested in having answered. It is *not* a good idea to propose a particular study merely because there is a lack of research on a topic. There might be good reasons why no one has published anything on the question. More important, such a rationale does not inform us as to why the question should be asked in the first place.

In coming up with a researchable question, keep in mind that it should have a place in the literature. That is, you should know how it fits, conceptually and methodologically <<*_U14. IS THIS A WORD? methodologically *>>. After all, science is the cumulative process of knowledge generation. What will answering this question tell us, generally <<*_S17. WEAK: generally *>>? Why is this important? It may be useful to know what percentages of students in a given school show particular cognitive deficits associated with learning disabilities, but this will have little relevance beyond that particular school. <<*_G3. SPLIT INTO 2 SENTENCES? *>><<*_S3. LONG SENTENCE: 32 WORDS *>> Far more generally <<*_S17. WEAK: generally *>> relevant <<*_S19. OVERUSED: relevant *>> to others interested in children would be the correlates of those problems. If you really want to beef up <<*_U1. COLLOQUIAL: beef up *>> the study, you will pick variables that have theoretical relevance for particular approaches to learning disabilities as well. Remember, the purpose of research is to produce generalizable <<*_U1 4. IS THIS A WORD? generalizable *>> knowledge. It will do this best <<*_U9. IS THIS JUSTIFIED? best *>> if it builds on research and theory that has preceded it. We will have more to say about this when we talk about hypothesis formulation later in this chapter.

continued

Exhibit 2.2, continued

RightWriter™ Feedback

<<** SUMMARY **>>
READABILITY INDEX: 10.91

Readers need an 11th grade level of education.

STRENGTH INDEX: 0.54

The strength of delivery is good, but can be improved.

DESCRIPTIVE INDEX: 0.54

The use of adjectives and adverbs is normal.

JARGON INDEX: 0.25

SENTENCE STRUCTURE RECOMMENDATIONS:
1. Most sentences contain multiple clauses.
Try to use more simple sentences.
7. Most sentences begin with pronouns.
Try using other sentence start conditions.

<< WORDS TO REVIEW >>
Review this list for words that may confuse your message.
These include words that are negative, frequently misused,
colloquial, or jargon. As you review each word, think of
its effect on the reader.

abuse	1	(Negative)
collaboration	1	(Possible jargon)
conceptually	1	(Possible jargon)
disabilities	2	(Negative)
formulation	1	(Possible jargon)
generalizable	1	(Possible jargon)
methodologically	1	(Possible jargon)
no	1	(Negative)
not	2	(Negative)
relevant	1	(Often misused)
researchable	2	(Possible jargon)
theoretical	1	(Possible jargon)

<< END OF WORDS TO REVIEW LIST >>

<<** END OF SUMMARY **>>

Methodology

Items 5 through 9 deal with the adequacy and recency of your methodological preparation. It is probably safe to say that Item 5 represents an essential requirement for satisfactory thesis or dissertation completion in most departments. (It is not, of course, if you are in a program in applied behavior analysis in which analyses are largely confined to verbal descriptions of the impact of graphically presented results.) If you are not *currently fluent* in the statistical concepts and tools covered in the usual two-course graduate statistical sequence, you may have to take some remedial steps. Part of the material covered in such courses can be found in chapter 10. Look it over. Does it seem comfortably familiar? Could it be with just a brief review?

A student of ours recently approached the appraisal of her statistical readiness more systematically. She had taken statistics courses many years earlier in graduate school at a prestigious eastern college. Having heard warnings that current statistical fluency was important, she approached one of us and asked to be given a test covering the material commonly included in statistics courses. After reviewing her performance on the test, she decided to rearrange her remaining graduate program so that she could audit the major statistics courses in the department.

Of course, for some, rearranging your schedule to this extent might not be feasible or necessary. If you can identify specific areas in which you need to review, you can map out a self-study program involving reading and periodic consultations with faculty who teach statistics. Perhaps one of them might be willing for you to sit in for a class session or two that covers the material you have targeted for remediation. You might also find another dissertation student who needs to work on a similar review. Like exercise partners who motivate each other by scheduling joint workouts, you can plan the content, structure, and timing of your review sessions together.

Before you statistics phobics abandon the whole idea of a thesis or dissertation, remember that we said "fluent." We did not say that you must be a whiz in statistics or that you should find the material easy. Most students, in our experience, find statistics to be the most challenging and intimidating part of the thesis or dissertation. Nonetheless, with adequate guidance, they master this aspect of the project. The key is obtaining adequate guidance if you have mastered basic statistical concepts and additional training or tutoring if you have not. Thousands of psychologists-in-training have conquered their fear of numbers, and, with some work, you can too.

An affirmative answer to Item 6 (measurement theory) is most important if you are planning a project that will require the construction or development of an individual difference measure of some kind. Are you working in an area with nonexistent or inadequate measures of the variables you will be studying? Are you planning to survey the attitudes of a group of migrant workers? Are you interested in violence in dating relationships but have found there are no good measures of it? If your answer to questions such as these is affirmative, you should be fluent in the concepts covered in a good measure development or test construction course. The intricacies of scale construction and validation are myriad and should not be approached lightly. Even if your research does not involve the actual construction of new measures, it is well to be an educated consumer. To make the most informed choice of instruments for the variables you will be studying requires more than passing familiarity with psychometric concepts. If you are unsure of your preparation in this area, take a look at the material in chapter 9.

Having taken a class in research design (Item 7) is important in understanding how to design studies in ways that minimize internal invalidity while maximizing external validity. If these terms sound like Greek to you, a review of research design principles is strongly recommended.

Another function of design classes is to teach you to speak the language of research, and to speak it correctly. Ill-prepared students, for example, often use the word *confound* when they mean *methodological problem*. Others refer to the reliability of a research design or confuse dependent and independent variables. Correct use of terminology is important in discussing the methodology of your own study as well as others' work. In addition, an incorrectly used term in an oral defense is a signal to committee members that you may not know what you are talking about. This may invite probing and sometimes antagonistic questioning. Fortunately, it is easily prevented if you make sure that you understand research terms and use them precisely.

Which brings us to Item 8—having some experience at reading and evaluating the research literature. All published articles are not equal in terms of their methodological rigor. Part of your job is to sort the good from the mediocre (hopefully the bad never made it into print!) and to make sure that your study is at least as good as the "good" group. In addition, you will need to be appropriately critical of what others have done (in the literature review) and what you yourself have done (in the discussion section). As with most things, practice makes perfect. Experience critically reading and evaluating empirical literature in graduate courses has the added advantage of sharpening your thinking skills, generally.

To some extent, answering affirmatively to Item 9 (research experience) may cover you with respect to the previous four items. If you have been especially active in a program of research that serves as the basis for your own study, you will likely be familiar with the methodology required for conducting that research. If you have been involved less extensively or if your plans have led you to another area, you might not be as ready. In this case, a thorough appraisal of your competence in statistics and measurement might be in order.

In summary, your writing and methodology skills are the most important determinants of your success in the research process. Before moving on, however, let's look at the implications of some of the other items on the Research Readiness Checklist. Consider Items 11 and 12, for example. Some otherwise realistic candidates are amazed that they will need *at least* 10 to 20 hours a week to devote to the effort. And the thought that this might extend over 1 to 2 years completely dumbfounds them! In truth, these are probably conservative estimates—at least for dissertations. In their empirical survey described earlier, Davis and Parker (1979) found that 80% of dissertations require 11 to 19 actual work months to complete. And, these figures are based on 175-hour months! Of course, these estimates are subject to local variation, and that is where Item 10 can be useful. What have others at your school said about the time required to complete their theses or dissertations?

Environmental Support

What about the space to pursue this mammoth undertaking? This is clearly not the time to be eyeing the kitchen table, figuring that you can work around the salt and pepper, the toaster, and the morning paper! You are going to be at this awhile, so you will want to choose your work space carefully. Find some place quiet that will afford uninterrupted privacy for sustained periods of time. Many university libraries provide locked carrels for scholars working on long-term projects.

One of us recently encountered a student who actually rented an office specifically for doing his dissertation. He planned to do no other work in this office. This exemplifies an important behavior management principle. Behavior that is under the control of narrowly defined stimulus conditions will, other things being equal, become increasingly focused. Researchers in self-control have talked about stimulus control for some time (Stuart, 1977). People with weight problems are told to eat only at the dining room table and (sometimes) only with a white place mat in front of them. Insomniacs are told to sleep only in bed and only to sleep in bed, thus bringing sleeping more clearly under the stimulus control of the bed. B. F. Skinner had a special desk in his house for writing. He spent several hours at this desk each day and permitted himself no other activity (e.g., bill paying or personal correspondence) at this desk.

Related to bringing your writing under the stimulus control of a particular location is bringing it under the control of a particular time of day. In his later years, Skinner wrote each day between 5 and 7 a.m. By being consistent in the time you work each day, you bring a whole host of additional temporally related stimuli into controlling your writing. The outside light and sounds are likely to be constant (and thus less distracting), as is your biological state. Although consistency might be, for some, the hobgoblin of little minds, it is more often the godparent of successful theses and dissertations.

You will be much more likely to produce this consistency if you carefully cultivate the support of family and loved ones. Do not neglect these important people. Be up front and realistic with them about your need for sustained periods of molelike behavior. At the same time, arrange occasions when you can be exclusively with them. Children and other family members will be much less likely to interrupt your work if they know that you have committed to spend specific times with them and that you keep your commitments.

Computer Access and Skills

What about access to a computer and having keyboard skills (Items 17 and 18)? Are these really all that important? It is hard to imagine anyone asking these questions in this computer age. Yes, they are important. Computer literacy is not absolutely essential, however, and we all know of dissertations completed successfully even today by people who cannot type. If you are one of these people, in estimating your time requirements (Item 12) you will need to allow considerably more time for typists to prepare your various drafts. If you are starting early in the process, you might have time to learn to type. There are excellent self-teaching computer programs for keyboard skills, so you don't have to enroll in an adult education class at your local high school. The time spent learning will be repaid manyfold over the rest of your life.

If you are not yet computer literate, we strongly recommend purchasing and learning to use this important tool. One of us resisted the cajoling of her more adventurous colleague for years, only to discover that using a computer revolutionized her writing and liberated her from the tyranny of temperamental typists. If you are worried about the expense, compare the cost of a used computer with that of having multiple drafts of proposals (40+ pages) and final documents (80–100+ pages) typed.

Time Management

Chapter 4 has lots to say about time management skills (Item 19), an area in which most of us can improve. We have also discussed some of the elements in successful time management in the material on stimulus control earlier in this chapter.

Interpersonal Skills

Items 20 to 22 are related to just how well you are likely to "get along" with others in your research endeavor. Interpersonal and political skills refer to effective interaction with the key players in this work. The most important, of course, is your chairperson. Do you have the interpersonal skills needed to work effectively with this person? Are you willing to submit innumerable rewrites in response to what may seem to you to be petty criticisms? Often students do not appreciate that multiple revisions are required to make a scientific document clear, coherent, and sufficiently detailed. It is said that Sir Isaac Newton knew well the importance of multiple rewrites. He took great care in revising his papers and would write, cross out, correct, copy all over again, cross out, recorrect, and recopy. When he finished this process, he would start all over again. "Thus, he made at least eight drafts of the *Scholium generale* for the second edition [of *Principia Mathematica*]" (Koyre, 1965, p. 262). Are you ready for a similar level of care?

Do you know how to assert your disagreement with suggestions in positive, constructive ways? Or, do you typically react defensively to suggestions for change? Do you know how to read the relationships between and among committee members? Are you likely to select members whose failure to get along interferes with your thesis or dissertation? Can you recognize grandstanding in committee meetings so that when it happens in yours you handle it effectively? If your project requires the support of people in off-campus agencies, do you have the interpersonal resources to obtain and maintain this support? Can you move in and out of these agencies in effective, nondisruptive ways?

If your interpersonal skills are a bit rough, make a list of those situations in which you have difficulty. You may be able to recruit an assistant to help you with situations that involve contact with agencies. The assistant can actually do most of the interacting, if you are not good at it. With situations you must handle yourself, plan to seek advice from other students or faculty who are good at handling such situations. Rehearse effective approaches with a friend and get feedback on your performance.

Formal and Informal Rules

At all schools, there are both formal and informal rules governing the entire thesis and dissertation process. There are forms to be completed, fees to be paid, deadlines to be met, formats to be followed, and so on. For example, many schools publicize the occurrence of doctoral defenses. These are open meetings to which all members of the academic community are invited. To give notice in a timely way, it is often necessary to impose deadlines for specifying a time and place for the meeting. Is this true at your school? Some schools circulate a form, or "shuttle sheet," among committee members indicating the time and place of the defense. At that time, the committee member is asked to sign the form agreeing to be available and acknowledging receipt of the thesis or dissertation. Does your school do this? What about the time committee members are given to review the proposal before the proposal meeting is convened? Two calendar weeks is not an unusual amount of time for this. Is there a time period such as this at your school? Find out early what the formal rules are. Ask for a copy of them at the office of the chairperson of your department, the dean of the graduate school, or, if there is no graduate school dean, the dean of whatever school you happen to be in.

Then, there are myriad informal rules. Becoming aware of these will make your life go more smoothly. For example, when should you approach a faculty member about chairing your committee? Do faculty expect you to have a well-developed idea and literature to back it up before you contact them? What if you have discussed ideas with several faculty and like the ideas of one best but really want to work with another?

Is it okay to use the ideas provided by one faculty member while choosing another as chair? How complete and carefully proofread do drafts need to be before presenting them to your chair? To your committee? Are there certain "blackout" periods during which proposal meetings generally cannot be scheduled (e.g., during the first or last weeks of the term or during the summer)? Start finding out about these informal rules early in the process. Discover what they are before getting too far down the path. Talk to other graduate students who have nearly completed the journey. Ask your chair or potential committee members what they know about such rules. There will be no published list to obtain from the dean's office. And, although the informal rules are often as important as the formal ones, faculty and more advanced students may not think to mention them unless you ask.

Examine Your Cognitive Ecology

In assessing your overall preparedness, it is useful to identify and dispel some common assumptions that will impede your progress. Mahoney and Mahoney (1976) referred to this process of cleaning up irrational thinking as *cognitive ecology*. The first few irrational thoughts may have to do with estimates of what it will take to get the job done. Even after everything you have read so far, you may be saying to yourself that if you start now, you can expect to be finished with the entire process in 6 months. You might be thinking that the typist can get the final draft prepared in 5 days. Or, you might be saying that you can get all the subjects you will need from two elementary schools and that it will take only 2 weeks to get permission from the principals to contact their teachers. If there is anything close to a Newtonian principle governing research, it is that estimates such as these are almost always wrong. In fact, this is true of research in the behavioral sciences generally. Estimates are so often off that we have found it helpful to invoke the "rule of threes" whenever we make them. Multiply everything you think you'll need by three, and your estimates will be much more on target.

A related irrationality is thinking that everything will run smoothly. It won't. Plan for the unexpected. It is going to happen anyway, and you might as well be ready for it. In addition to needing three times more of just about everything to complete the job, you can expect subjects to break their appointments, equipment to fail, data to be lost, your chair to take another job and leave the university, and so on. Are you ready for these events? Assess the likelihood of each and prepare contingency plans. If the event is significant and its likelihood great (e.g., chair leaving) and you cannot develop a plan for working around it with your particular project, you might want to consider an alternative project.

Another irrational thought is that your study must be the definitive work in the area. We are not saying that there is anything wrong with ambition. The problem is the paralyzing implications of the "Nobel laureate" error. If you think yours has to be *the* definitive study, you are never going to be satisfied that you've researched enough literature, framed the question and hypotheses properly, selected the absolutely best design, controlled all the important variables, and so on. Keep in mind that knowledge grows by increments. Scientific breakthroughs and paradigmatic revolutions (Kuhn, 1970) are rare, and it is even more rare that they are the result of single studies.

The "myth of methodological perfection" is a related collection of thoughts that impedes research progress. Every study has its faults. These may not be recognized until the scientific community has scrutinized the work closely, but the faults are there. At a minimum there are trade-offs, the most common being that between internal and external validity (i.e., between scientific control on the one hand and generalization to the "messy" real world on the other). To expect your study to be different is simply unrealistic. We are not saying that you should strive for anything less than excellence in pursuing your research. But, to insist on methodological perfection when this is unattainable is likely to lead to an unfinished project.

If you still think your research has to be a methodologically perfect, definitive study, analyze the function of such thoughts. What are you gaining? Will they serve to insulate you from your own and other's criticisms of your lack of progress? After all, who could be faulted for wanting to do the perfect study and for refusing to be a part of anything less? Is it keeping the research process deliberately drawn out so that you can stay in school and not have to face the cold cruel world of job seeking and economic self-sufficiency?

Summary

This chapter has been about assessing your preparation for doing a thesis or dissertation. It has dealt with a number of skill and knowledge issues related to completing the task successfully. Some issues deal with things you can more or less readily change. In this category are the irrational beliefs discussed in the preceding section. Other issues concern areas (e.g., measurement and statistics) in which you might need better preparation. This might be accomplished by taking or reviewing additional courses. Finally, some basic skill areas (e.g., coherent, grammatically correct writing) *require* proficiency to complete a major research project. The guidelines in this chapter will be most useful to you if you approach them in an open and honest self-appraising way. Answer the questions on the Research Readiness Checklist as forthrightly as possible. There is no shame in acknowledging areas of needed improvement. If the changes cannot be made, better to discover this now than to struggle along in self-defeating ways.

We hope that you have taken this appraisal seriously. Theses and dissertations are complex projects that require many skills. Remember, you do not have to be perfect to complete yours. It is normal to have to work on areas in which you have less experience or expertise. Most of us muddle through the process one way or another. If you have a history of academic success (and most likely you do), if you apply the skills you have and work on those you lack, you, too, will make it through.

Now that you've completed this self-assessment, you're ready to plunge into the exciting and all-important task of finding a topic for your dissertation. We turn to that subject in chapter 3.

✔ **To Do . . .**

Assessing Your Preparation

☐ Complete Research Readiness Checklist

☐ Interpret your responses

   —Writing skills

   —Methodology skills

   —Environmental support

   —Computer access and skills

   —Time management skills

   —Interpersonal skills

☐ Examine your cognitive ecology

3 Topics: How to Find and Refine Them

Coming up with a researchable idea can be the most challenging step for many graduate students. In part, this is the result of the "rite-of-passage view" of theses and dissertations mentioned in chapter 1. Many of us who have been through this think it is an important initiation rite for all candidates, and coming up with the questions to research is part of that rite. It is also difficult to get an idea because many of us have the mistaken notion that we have to do something that will move science a quantum leap beyond where it is now. If you are thinking Nobel laureate at this stage in your academic career, it is wonderful that you are ambitious. Such thinking may interfere with completing your project, however.

Students contemplating a thesis or dissertation sometimes make one of two errors: the Nobel laureate error just described or the undergraduate research paper error. The first reflects unrealistically grand thinking; the second, unrealistically miniscule thinking. As faculty members chairing these projects, we often prefer the Nobel laureate error. This is because it is easier to trim the fat off a bloated research idea than to build up an anorexic one. Both errors reflect poor reality testing. The first shows the candidate is willing to work, however!

These errors are more common in persons who have not had much firsthand exposure to research. Thus, master's students may have more trouble than doctoral students, unless the doctoral student has been sliding through the program deliberately avoiding research involvement or has been in a program without many faculty who are active researchers. If you have been active in research up to now, you probably already have an idea. It's likely to be a logical extension of some research that you have been collaborating on with faculty and other students. If not, the challenge of coming up with a workable research idea will be a bit more formidable. If you are a master's student, your chairperson might give you a specific idea. Alternatively, you might replicate and extend work already published. If you are a doctoral student, your idea should be original, and your study must make a novel contribution to the literature.

There are actually two steps to coming up with a researchable topic. First, identify the general *area* in which you want to do research (e.g., short-term memory, childhood aggression, social support, or information processing). This is relatively easy and can give you something to say when people ask you what your research is about. The second step involves coming up with a research question and hypotheses. Because these are much more specific, they take more thought, and most students find them more stressful than arriving at a general research area.

Select a General Topic Area First

Let's talk strategy for a minute. Students often ask when the topic selection process should start. We generally answer, "the earlier the better." For some lucky few, it begins during their undergraduate years. They might have taken a particular course that piqued their interest in a research area. They might have worked as research assistants on some faculty member's or graduate student's research project. They might have selected a graduate program because a faculty member was doing research in the same area. For them, the thesis or dissertation will be the logical extension of a program of study that began years earlier.

Most of us haven't had this experience as undergraduates, however. The direct research experience we had, if any, was probably in an area unrepresented by faculty in our current program. If you have not already done so, we advise you to examine descriptions of faculty research interests. Identify several that sound interesting to you. Find out as much as you can about the studies being done. Also, find out as much as possible about the faculty members themselves. Take courses from them. Schedule appointments with them and ask them about their research and whether they have reprints that you could read. Read these reprints and see if they describe research you really want to pursue. If they do, find out ways of getting directly involved, preferably before you start your own research. In research, as in many complex skills, direct experience with the tasks involved serves as a better teacher than simply reading about how to do it.

In the best of cases, students start this process at the beginning of their graduate careers. Then, their graduate program contributes in significant ways to their own research. Each course they take has some relevance. If they start the process early, they will be able to see that relevance more clearly as they advance through the program.

If you are starting early and do not like the experience you have had with a particular professor or research program, try another one. There is nothing wrong with having a deliberate plan to work directly with several faculty in the early stages to find out their styles, the type of work they do, problems and rewards associated with it, and so on. Some of the most productive students we have known have systematically worked with numerous faculty during their graduate years. This helped them gain research experience from a variety of perspectives and led to several viable proposal possibilities when they needed to do their own research. If you choose this route, let the faculty know so they will not be surprised or have their research program disrupted by your "premature" departure.

If you have not had this experience and are further along in graduate school, don't despair. Remember, the first step is only to *identify* a research area, not to plan what you will do for the entire project. The area you pick must meet two key criteria. First, it must interest you enough that you will be willing to spend hours reading about it, writing about it, and analyzing data having to do with it. Second, you must find a faculty member interested in chairing the project.

To identify an area, think about your classes and professional experience. What topics interest you? What do you find yourself stopping to read in the library when you are supposed to be compiling research for a class? What academic topics come up frequently when you are talking shop with other students and faculty? Identifying the things you think, read, and talk about is a good way of clarifying areas that interest you. There will probably be several of these. You can then identify faculty who share these interests and talk with them about the area. If you are planning a thesis, you might ask faculty members if they have projects they would like a student to take on as a master's project. This also provides an opportunity to see what particular faculty members are like, find out what projects might interest them, and make a good impression. In general, it is better to choose a slightly less engrossing area that a faculty member will support than an exotic one that only you find fascinating.

Avoid Going It Alone

Some students, particularly those at the doctoral level, have the impression that their research is supposed to be a solo affair. They spend months developing a research idea and proposal and then approach a faculty member to try to sell it. Yates (1982) described his own experience doing just this and being devastated when his ideal committee chair rejected the idea as infeasible. In situations like this, you are faced with either rejecting the advice of the faculty member and trying to find another who will agree it is a terrific proposal or bagging the idea and starting over. The latter alternative is not high on the hit parade of fun things to do in graduate school.

True, the dissertation is the test of your preparation to conduct independent research. This is not quite so true of master's theses, however, and in neither do you have to generate and develop ideas completely on your own. In fact, solo work at this stage runs the risk of producing unworkable proposals. Another all-too-frequent occurrence is that you cannot find a faculty person with the expertise and interest in your topic to shepherd you through the rest of the process. We have known students who have gone systematically to every single faculty member of a department with an idea only to find no one who would agree to chair their committee. Thesis and dissertation research is challenging enough without making it into a course in salesmanship as well. We strongly recommend that you avoid going it alone. Use the approaches described in this chapter to develop ideas *in conjunction with* a faculty member. If he or she has joint ownership of the idea, there will be a cooperative relationship that will aid enormously in completing the research with minimum hassle.

Develop the Research Question Next

Let's assume that you have successfully identified an area of research (e.g., dental phobia, child sexual abuse, depression, or AIDS prevention), hopefully in collaboration with a respected faculty member. You next have to frame some sort of researchable question within that area. The *form* such questions should take is fairly specific. Form will be addressed later. The *source* of such questions is something we want to take up first.

In general, you want to ask questions that interest the scientific community. It is *not* a good idea to propose a particular study merely because there is a lack of research on a topic. There might be good reasons why no one has published anything on the question. More important, such a rationale does not inform us as to why the question should be asked or answered in the first place.

In coming up with a researchable question, keep in mind that it should have a place in the literature. That is, you should know how it fits, conceptually and methodologically. After all, science is the cumulative process of knowledge generation. What will answering this question tell us? Why is this important? True, it may be useful to know what percentage of students in a given school show particular cognitive deficits associated with learning disabilities. This will have little relevance beyond that particular school, however. Of far more interest would be the correlates of those problems. If you really want to strengthen the study, you will pick variables that have theoretical relevance for particular approaches to learning disabilities, as well. Remember, the purpose of research is to produce generalizable knowledge. It will do this best if it builds on research and theory that has preceded it. We have more to say about this when we talk about hypothesis formulation later in this chapter.

Best Source of Ideas

As you might have guessed from some of our earlier comments, we think that the best source for new research is research that you are already doing. The reasons for this are many. Among the most important is the groundwork you have done or track record you have in the area. You will be familiar with the relevant literature, know the methodology, and have had first-hand exposure to all the ins and outs of obtaining subjects, negotiating with the human subjects committee, and so on. Moreover, if you have been collaborating with a particular faculty member on the research, that person probably has made suggestions that you can develop into a satisfactory proposal. If the research you propose is the logical extension of the faculty member's overall program, that person will want your study to succeed and will provide many of the resources needed for that success. Finally, research often stimulates more questions than it answers, and one of these might easily provide the basis for a thesis or dissertation.

Worst Source of Ideas

A common way to come up with a research idea is from one's own personal experience. The recovering alcoholic decides to study families of alcoholics. The chronically test-anxious student chooses to relate test anxiety and type of question to performance on math exams. The 40-year-old parent decides to study the waning sexual interest of busy executive spouses.

In fact, many of us are in the behavioral sciences, especially psychology, because of an interest in some aspect of our own experience. Don't get us wrong. This is not a bad reason for being in psychology in the first place. But, it is probably not a good idea to plan thesis or dissertation research around something with a high degree of personal emotional relevance. Save these issues for therapy. Research is difficult enough without having it serve as the stimulus for a lot of personal soul searching every time you pick up the pen or run a subject.

Besides interfering with your progress, personally loaded issues are unlikely to be approached from the detached, objective, analytic perspective necessary in science. You are likely to have a "position" on the subject that will interfere with your completing the research satisfactorily on a number of levels. The most important of these is the self-fulfilling prophecy phenomenon (Ambady & Rosenthal, 1992). If you are convinced from your personal experience that test-anxious students do worse on multiple-choice than essay questions, for instance, you may design your study in subtle ways to ensure this outcome. For example, you may inadvertently share your expectation with research assistants who score your essay questions. Research has shown that assistants can be biased to produce data that are consistent with the desired outcomes communicated to them by the experimenter (Kent, O'Leary, Diament, & Dietz, 1974; Shuller & McNamara, 1976). Of course, we do not suggest that you would do this deliberately. Nor is this is a problem only for research in personally relevant areas. It is simply more likely in such research.

Choosing a research topic that evokes strong emotional reactions can interfere with your objectivity in other ways. For example, otherwise helpful suggestions from committee members might be hard to accept if they "don't fit" your personal understanding of the problem. This can result in your appearing rigid, defensive, and inflexible, characteristics faculty do not view positively. In fairness, however, we should note that issues of personal relevance *can* be a good source of research ideas under some circumstances. Your motivation is likely to be higher for such topics, and you might know the area in unique ways that might challenge the conclusions of current investigators. The bottom line is that issues of personal relevance should be considered as a source of research ideas only if you can approach them objectively. If you have resolved the emotional aspects of the issue and can approach it in a detached, relatively disinterested, and unbiased manner, go ahead. You might make a truly useful contribution.

Existing Literature as a Source of Ideas

The simplest and most logical place to come up with researchable questions is from recent literature in an area. Most journal articles end with suggestions for future research. Look for these. If one of them excites you, spend some time thinking about how you might develop the suggestion into a research proposal. Discuss the idea with your respected-faculty-member/possible-chair candidate and get a reaction. If it is generally positive and after you have thoroughly researched the topic, get in touch with the author of the article and find out what he or she is doing currently in the area. Inquire nonchalantly about the specific question you hope to pursue, asking whether the author has already researched it or knows of anyone who has. If the answer to both questions is no, probe a bit and see whether the author knows why. After all, it seemed like such a good idea to you!

This little bit of detective work could be very worthwhile and could save you much wasted time and possible embarrassment. The author might have discarded the suggestion because a colleague pointed out an inherent flaw in its logic. Or, at a presentation at a professional meeting, several people in the audience strongly questioned the ethics of pursuing the research in the manner suggested. Or, you might hear that several people have indeed followed the author's suggestion and will present their results in the very next issue of the *Ratatat Review*. Wouldn't such news be worth the phone call?

Another good approach to developing researchable questions is to apply a paradigm used with one population to another population. For example, Wolfe, Gentile, Michienzi, Sas, and Wolfe (1991) used a scale to assess specific reactions to traumatic events, the Impact of Event Scale, (Horowitz, Wilner, & Alvarez, 1979) as the basis for the development of the Children's Impact of Traumatic Events Scale. Research on the leadership styles of executive women might easily suggest similar studies with executives who are members of a specific ethnic group.

Reviews of the literature in particular areas provide another worthy source of questions. *Psychological Bulletin* contains such reviews in psychology. *Annual Review of Psychology* is another source of such reviews, as are *Clinical Psychology Review* and *Developmental Review*. In addition, many edited books contain literature reviews. The authors of reviews appearing in these sources often point out gaps in the research knowledge and correctable flaws in existing studies. Why not propose research that remedies some flaw that has already been acknowledged as important by the scientific community?

Replications of already published research provide an avenue in some cases. As mentioned earlier, a proposal to replicate a study will be more acceptable for a master's thesis than for a dissertation. There is much to recommend replications. If the original study was done in an exemplary way, you will learn much from modeling. In fact, exemplary studies are the only ones you want to attempt to replicate directly, as there is no virtue in repeating the errors of your predecessors. Check the local norms to see whether replications are acceptable master's thesis possibilities.

You may also find links between literatures that have been relatively unexplored. Many professionals study the same problems psychologists do, including sociologists, scientists in the communication field, physicians, and others. Even within psychology, there are numerous aspects of the discipline that are often not integrated. Pulling together separate but related strands is a challenging and often rewarding way of devising something truly novel.

Other Theses and Dissertations as a Source of Ideas

There is some debate as to the value of other theses and dissertations as a useful source of new research ideas. We know some faculty who deliberately steer students away from consulting previous theses and dissertations. Partly, this is because faculty members sometimes distrust the quality of research supervised by other faculty. Partly, it results from the realization that theses and dissertations have not been subjected to the same peer-review process as most published papers and cannot therefore be as confidently consulted as exemplars of competent research. The faculty argue that if the research is good enough it will be published anyway, and the student will encounter it in the literature.

Our own view is that existing theses and dissertations *can* be a good source of some kinds of information for prospective researchers. When we teach courses in dissertation methodology, we routinely require students to consult one or two carefully selected dissertations or dissertation proposals that have been placed on reserve in the library. This assignment stimulates reality testing as well as pointing to exemplary projects that could serve as models. We also recommend completed theses and dissertations as references if students are proposing a study that extends a program of research taking off from the previous thesis or dissertation.

And, as mentioned in chapter 1, theses and dissertations completed under the direction of a potential chairperson can be an excellent source of concrete information about the finished product that chair is likely to expect. We do not suggest them as sources of ideas, however. Browsing through published literature reviews will probably yield more ideas per hour than examining theses and dissertations on the library shelf or in *Dissertation Abstracts International*.

Still running on empty in spite of these suggestions? Try an idea log. As you read professional materials or attend conferences, keep a notebook and pen by your side. Whenever some interesting question strikes you, write it down. If you write three ideas a week, in a month you will have a dozen! With help from your faculty advisor, you can probably find the germ of a researchable question in that list.

Put the Research Questions in Researchable Form

Once you have decided the area of your topic and the general question to be asked, it is time to word the question so that it can be studied. Well-worded questions share common characteristics (Kerlinger, 1986). The easiest criterion to remember is that the question should be just that. Phrase what you are going to study in the form of a question. For example, within the general area of child sexual abuse, you might have decided to study the adequacy of children's memory for specific events. Your question might be, "Are nonsexually abused children interviewed with sexually anatomically correct (SAC) dolls more likely to describe sexual behavior than such children interviewed with dolls without secondary sexual characteristics?" This question meets the first of our criteria for well-worded research questions in that it is phrased in the form of a question.

A second criterion is that the question should suggest a relationship to be examined. This is a particularly important characteristic, because the purpose of doing research is to advance science. Because science is the study of relationships between variables, no relationship, no science. No science, no thesis or dissertation. It is that simple.

Let us look at whether a relationship is suggested by this example. The children are to be interviewed with dolls that do or do not have complete anatomical features. The independent variable is thus the secondary sexual characteristics of the dolls. The verbal behavior of children exposed to dolls with or without these features will be examined for references to sexual behavior. Such references thus constitute our dependent variable. A relationship between the independent and dependent variables is suggested by the research question. Thus, it meets the second of our criteria.

The third criterion requires that the research question implies the possibility of empirical testing (Kerlinger, 1986). If the question meets the second criterion, namely, suggests a relationship, it is halfway to meeting the requirements of the third criterion. It is not enough to suggest a relationship, however, unless that relationship is empirically testable. The principle ingredient of testability is the specificity of the variables being related in the research question. Can the variables be operationally defined? If the variables cannot be operationalized and measured, the questions pursued in the research cannot be answered. If they can be operationalized, an empirical test of the relationship suggested by the question can be made

Obviously, these criteria are somewhat arbitrary, and good research can be done without following them exactly. For novice researchers, however, we have found these characteristics to be quite helpful in evaluating their research ideas.

You will probably need to spend some time refining and reworking your research question to make it clear and specific enough to guide your research. This process will force you to think through exactly what you want to know. You may start with a vague question such as, "How do parents and teenagers communicate about sex?" This implies no relationship. That is, there are no independent or dependent variables. In discussion with your chairperson, you revise it: "How does parent–adolescent communication about sex relate to impulsive teenage sexual behavior?" You might revise it even further as you decide what specific aspects of communication and sexual behavior you want to study.

Now that you have a question to study, let's talk briefly about the availability of subjects. Subject access is so important that we have known colleagues who advise students to get subjects first and then decide what research they want to do. This falls into the "pragmatic" school of thesis and dissertation advising! If subjects are not available, the greatest idea in the world is not going to make a suitable research topic. Are you working (or doing a practicum or internship) in a setting with a population suitable for your study? Is your mother, father, spouse, or good friend connected with such a setting? Does your potential chairperson have connections that you could tap to gain access to subjects? As a reviewer of this book pointed out, outsiders to a system usually lack the power to collect data within that system in ways orderly enough to make research possible. So, be sure you are sufficiently well-connected to ensure access to the subjects you will need. This is particularly important if your research question requires a select group of individuals (e.g., cancer survivors or displaced executives). It is less important if you could do your study with more readily available populations (e.g., college students).

Develop Scientific Hypotheses

Well-worded research questions that meet these three criteria will help you specify hypotheses. Hypotheses are declarative sentences that conjecture a relationship between two or more variables (Kerlinger, 1986). Well-stated hypotheses are derived directly from the research question. For example, if our question was, "What is the relationship between test anxiety and performance on complex cognitive tasks?" a reasonable hypothesis would be "Performance on complex cognitive tasks will be an inverted U-shaped function of level of anxiety." As another example, consider our previous question, "Are nonabused children interviewed with SAC dolls more likely to describe sexual behavior than such children interviewed with dolls without secondary sexual characteristics?" For this question, we might hypothesize that "nonabused children interviewed with SAC dolls will describe sexual behavior more frequently than nonabused children interviewed with dolls without secondary sexual characteristics." Note that in both examples, our hypotheses start with the basic research question and develop a specific prediction about the nature of the relationship between the variables identified in the question.

It is this specific prediction that leads to the advance of science. Some (e.g., Kerlinger, 1986) argue that hypotheses are required for scientific knowledge to advance. Others (e.g., Skinner, 1950) caution against elaborate theoretical structures that have too few facts to support them. The latter would argue for a more inductive approach to science building, gathering facts carefully and letting general principles be "discovered" therefrom. We believe that both inductive and deductive approaches have merit. Nonetheless, we argue that *some* low level of hypothesis generation is important. Even the straightforward observation of relationships between variables in purely descriptive research should be directed by some previous speculation. For example, suppose our research question was, "What are the differences in interactive patterns between members of abusive and nonabusive families?" Without specific hypotheses predicting certain differences, we could certainly do the research. Our interpretation of the outcome would be somewhat problematic, however. As Kerlinger (1986) has observed, setting up hypotheses in advance is a bit like having rules in games of chance. We cannot first roll the dice and then decide what it takes to win. We cannot wait until the race is over and then place our bets. If we find several differences in the interactive patterns of our abusive and nonabusive families, we do not know whether they are spurious and would have occurred merely by chance. To protect against capitalizing on chance, the statistical tests we can use in such situations (sometimes called *fishing expeditions*) are deliberately less powerful (i.e., more conservative) than the ones we can use in research in which previous hypotheses about relationships (i.e., predictions) are constructed. Chapter 10 says more about these statistics when we discuss the issue of planned comparisons.

One final reason for having hypotheses in scientific research is more a matter of common sense than logic. Research is expensive. It takes a great deal of your time, your committee's time, and, most likely, your subjects' time. In addition, other costs can be substantial, depending on the nature of your project. With such an investment, it makes sense to maximize the potential return. Because science is better served by and more powerful statistical procedures can be used in studies directed by previous formulation of hypotheses, it seems sensible to include them. One response to student proposals without hypotheses is to tell the student to go back to the library and become more familiar with the research area. Surely there are predictions in there somewhere.

At this point, you may be thinking that to come up with some hypotheses you'll just say how you *think* your results will come out. That is easy enough, right? Well, not quite. You need a rationale for making predictions. That rationale can come from two sources: previous empirical research (including applied and program evaluation research) and theory (or both). If a particular research question has been informed by previous research, the nature of hypothesized relationships will have been suggested by that research and the specific hypotheses to examine should then be fairly obvious. Similarly, theory may suggest certain relationships that can be tested.

Having said all this, it is important to acknowledge that some research areas are so new that hypotheses are difficult to develop. Similarly, some fields (e.g., ethology or astronomy) have a stronger descriptive tradition than others. If you are having trouble coming up with hypotheses even though you know your literature and associated theoretical framework, talk with your chairperson. Avoid making something up. Science involves originality, but not creative fiction.

Understanding Different Types of Hypotheses

Now that you are convinced that only the most naive would dare to suggest a predictionless research project, let's talk a bit about *types* of hypothesis. The literature makes several distinctions. Most commonly we read about the *null* and the *research* hypothesis (Ray & Ravizza, 1988). The examples given above were of the research type. They predict a relationship to be confirmed in the study. Null hypotheses, first identified as such by Sir Ronald Fisher, basically state that there is no relationship. Although you are interested in your research hypotheses, statistics cannot confirm them. They can only disconfirm the null hypothesis. That is why null hypotheses are important—they are the only ones you can test directly. With respect to our example involving the SAC dolls, the research hypothesis predicted that such dolls would be associated with more descriptions of sexual behavior than would dolls without secondary sex characteristics. The null version of this hypothesis would be that there is no difference in the frequency of descriptions of sexual behavior by children when they play with SAC dolls or with non-SAC dolls. (Note that both types of hypothesis are phrased in the present tense.) The preferences of thesis and dissertation chairs differ, but we prefer students to include their research hypotheses in their proposal. The null versions can be easily inferred.

Characteristics of Well-Worded Hypotheses

As with research questions, the carefully phrased hypothesis will indicate the specific relationships to be examined. It will also suggest the nature of the relationship. Thus, "There is a relationship between education level and preference for liberal causes" would be less desirable than "There is a positive relationship between education level and preference for liberal causes." Clearly worded hypotheses may also include a third criterion important to some researchers, the nature of the experimental design. In this example, a correlational design is implied. Another recommendation is to include in the hypothesis the population in which the relationship is to be studied. Thus, "There is a positive relationship between education level and preference for liberal causes in executive women" would meet this criterion.

This is probably a good place to stop adding more information to our hypotheses. It is not uncommon for novice researchers to go further, though. A common mistake is to include the specific measures of one's variables in the hypothesis. For example, "There is a positive relationship between education level as assessed by the Horace Mann Scale of Educational Attainment and preference for liberal causes as measured by the ACLU Scale for Consistently Clear Thinking in executive women." It is certainly true that this hypothesis is more specific, although somewhat unwieldy. It misses the point of the research, however. The purpose is to study relationships between variables for the purpose of building a science. Including the specific measures of the variables places undue attention on the methodology of the study. It distracts our attention from the major question at hand. We are interested in these specific measures only as they operationalize the major variables of the research. We could just as well have selected other ways of operationalizing the variables had they been available and previously preferred in the literature. To make this point more strongly, suppose we included even more methodological information in the hypothesis. For example, suppose we said, "There is a positive relationship between education level as assessed by the Horace Mann Scale of Educational Attainment when scored by first-year graduate students in a clinical psychology program using MacIntosh™ computers equipped with Statview 512+™ software and preference for liberal causes as measured by the ACLU Scale for Consistently Clear Thinking in executive women who work at New Organs Biotech." It is easy to see the absurdity of such an approach. In general, phrase your hypotheses at the level at which you want to generalize your findings.

Another common tendency to avoid is including the name of the particular statistical test in the hypothesis. Thus, "It is predicted that a one-way ANOVA will reveal differences between attorneys, psychologists, and accountants in degree of extrinsic religiosity" loses sight of the basic issue. In this case, we are apparently interested in differences among these professional groups in extrinsic religiosity. How we test for differences between them on our measures is methodological detail that does not belong in the hypothesis and can detract from the primary focus.

The basic rule is to avoid cluttering up the hypothesis with methodological detail. The hypothesis should imply relationships between operationally definable variables studied in a particular way. It does not have to include the operational definitions or statistical tests themselves. Leave these details for the method section.

A final word of caution about hypotheses might be helpful. Students often ask, "How many hypotheses should I have?" Our answer is, "not many." We sometimes see proposals with 10 to 20 hypotheses. Often, these involve the administration of some personality inventory, and predictions are developed for each of the subscales of the inventory. These proposals exhibit two mistakes: (a) the "name the specific measure" error and (b) the "I've lost sight of the forest" error. So many hypotheses are a clear sign that one of two things has gone wrong: (a) The candidate has bitten off more than can be chewed, or (b) the candidate has not given the study enough forethought to narrow the specific hypotheses to a manageable number. Remember Occam's razor when doing your dissertation. Keep it parsimonious. There are simply not that many independent behavioral phenomena out there. More than likely, if you have developed hypotheses for 10 to 20 measures, a factor analysis would find the measures to be correlated and reducible to a smaller number of 3 to 4 independent factors. Remember, science advances when the same phenomena are explained with fewer concepts or variables. Ask yourself whether all the hypotheses you are formulating are really tapping different things. If not, combine and reword them to focus on the essence of the problem being studied. If they are tapping too many different things, you have bitten off too much. Go back to the literature or consult with your chair to whittle your project down to a manageable size.

The checklist in Exhibit 3.1 summarizes our recommendations concerning hypotheses. This should help you determine when your hypotheses are adequate.

Exhibit 3.1

Hypothesis Checklist

Yes	No	
☐	☐	1. Do your hypotheses suggest the relationship between two or more variables?
☐	☐	2. Do your hypotheses specify the nature of the relationship?
☐	☐	3. Do your hypotheses imply the research design to be used to study the relationship?
☐	☐	4. Do your hypotheses indicate the population to be studied?
☐	☐	5. Are they free of the mention of specific measures?
☐	☐	6. Are they free of the mention of specific statistical tests?
☐	☐	7. Are they free of other unnecessary methodological detail?
☐	☐	8. Have they been kept to a manageable number (e.g., 5 to 6 or fewer)?

You should now have some idea of the design you will need to use to explore the relationships implied by your hypotheses. Moreover, the nature of your hypotheses will direct the selection of statistical tests. A final issue warrants addressing at this point: Are you adequately prepared to carry out the research as you have now clarified it? If you aren't completely ready, can you realistically prepare yourself within a reasonable amount of time? If not, is consultative help going to be available? Will you still be knowledgeable enough to represent what you and the consultant have done and to defend it on your own to your committee? If the answer to these questions is "no," you better reframe your hypotheses, choose another research question, find another research area, or prepare for a decade-long project!

Perhaps an example will make this clearer—in case it is not painfully obvious already. Novice researchers sometimes launch into an area that does not have adequate (or any) measures for its principal variables or constructs. The first thing the candidate proposes is to develop a measure to use in the research. Our favorite questions of such ambitious persons are (a) What courses have you taken in scale construction and measurement theory? Any course work in factor analysis? Generalizability theory? (b) How many years have you budgeted for the completion of this project? and (c) Are you prepared to do a thesis or dissertation just developing the measures you need? The moral here is to avoid research questions that are too ambitious for your skills or require you to develop or master complex new technical material. Pare down your scope to something manageable.

✔ To Do . . .

Finding and Refining Topics

☐ Select a general topic area

☐ Work with faculty to develop your ideas

☐ Develop the research question

—Consider research in which you have been involved

—Avoid personally loaded topics

—Use recent literature

—Use theses and dissertations cautiously

☐ Put the research question in researchable form

—Phrase the question as a question

—Make sure the question suggests a relationship to be examined

—Make sure the question is empirically testable

☐ Develop scientific hypotheses

☐ Evaluate these hypotheses using the checklist in Exhibit 3.1

4 Time and Trouble Management

Y ou will recall that in chapter 2 we included the Research Readiness Checklist to help you identify overall preparation to do a thesis or dissertation. The checklist could also be used diagnostically, to identify deficiencies to be addressed before embarking on the journey. In discussing the myth of the definitive study and the myth of the methodologically perfect study, we warned that these were based on the irrational assumption that definitive, methodologically perfect studies could be done. Recall our "rule of threes" and warning that the unexpected would occur, so you might as well be ready for it.

This chapter deals with some of those common problems you might encounter in conducting a thesis or dissertation and suggests ways to avoid or overcome them. Our goal is to help you anticipate and plan the many steps involved in successful research.

The first issue will be how effectively you manage your time. Our focus on this important area is the logical outgrowth of Einstein's (1974) definition of time as the occurrence of events in sequence. It follows from this definition that effective use of your time means that you are managing sequenced events in an effective way. But, what do we mean by *effective*? A synonymous phrase might be *gets desired results*. Managing events effectively can be viewed as arranging things to get the results you want. Because most activities in life, especially research projects, involve a sequence of events, managing time effectively means managing these events effectively and accomplishing your goal of a completed thesis or dissertation.

Start With a Goal

Successful completion of a research project starts with a goal. Carefully worded goals contain certain common elements. Most important, they state what you want to accomplish and by when. For maximum effectiveness, the "what" should be stated in terms of measurable behavior or other outcomes. "Complete my dissertation by June 30, ____" would be an example. Another is "Obtain permission for study from schools by March 1, ____."

The most difficult part of such goal setting is deciding the "when" element. Sometimes this is decided for you. You may have a form of financial support that terminates at a specific time, whether you are finished or not. One of us occasionally has a student on a government scholarship from a foreign country. The terms of the scholarship often include a completion date, after which the student must return to the country to perform some type of work for which the student's program has presumably prepared him or her. Obviously, this type of contingency is a bit more exacting than the one that involves simply stopping further monetary support at the end of a specified period. This, in turn, is more exacting than an open-ended completion date, with no contingencies. Careful planning and the effective use of your time become extremely important if you must finish your thesis or dissertation by a specific date.

Estimate Your Time Requirements

Think of your thesis or dissertation as a project. As with any sizable project, there are numerous subprojects or smaller steps that must be identified, sequenced, and then accomplished to complete the larger effort. You can increase the ease and manageability of your research by carefully identifying and sequencing the steps involved. So, how can you identify the steps?

First, sit down and reflect on everything you know about the requirements. Remember to consider both formal and informal rules. If you don't know them, find out now. Make a list of the "facts of the case," as the lawyers would say. Write these in terms of things you have to get done. For ease of later sequencing, it sometimes helps to put these on 3 × 5″ cards, one event per card. For example, subjects have to be recruited. Write this as "Recruit subjects." Work space has to be obtained. Write this as "Find (obtain or acquire) a place to work." Bound copies of the final version of the document might need to be presented to the librarian at your school. Write this as "Turn in __ bound copies to the library." Note that we suggest you start these events with verbs. Much more action is implied this way, and it is pretty clear who is responsible for the action, namely, you. Compare "Recruit subjects" with "Subjects need to be recruited." The first is clearly an instruction to yourself. The second is merely a declarative sentence. So, subjects need to be recruited. Isn't that interesting! Watch the way you talk, and you'll watch the way you behave in other ways. Decisive language is associated with decisiveness in other behavior. Compare the forcefulness of "*Try* to recruit subjects" with "Recruit subjects." Have you ever invited someone to a party and heard "That sounds great! I'll try to be there"? How much money would you bet on their appearance? Get clear on your intentions and then move decisively to accomplish them.

When we teach courses in the methodology of dissertations we routinely require students to develop individual intentions lists with respect to their project. These are merely lists of the sequenced steps necessary to take students from where they are at the beginning of the course to a completed dissertation. We have found this to be a worthwhile exercise, as it concretizes the whole undertaking and helps make it real. We do not restrict the number or sequencing of the steps. Though we generally encourage small, easily accomplished events using the "little steps for little feet" principle, students vary considerably in selecting the number and size of the steps in their intentions lists. Some prefer fairly large chunks, for example, "Write proposal." Others prefer smaller chunks, for example, "Outline proposal," "Write first five pages of proposal," and "Turn in first draft to chairperson."

There are two approaches to sequencing the steps in your list. With backward chaining, you begin with the last step (e.g., "Turn in copies at the library") and work backward to the first step. This is most helpful in the planning stages, especially if you must be finished by a particular date. If an exact completion date does not concern you, you might take the more leisurely forward-chaining approach, starting where you are and listing all the steps between that point and the final one, adding dates for each as you go.

We have gotten as few as six steps in some intentions lists and as many as 46 in others. Some inventive sorts have even put their lists in the form of flowcharts, with alternative courses to pursue depending on outcomes at various decision points. For example, one student had these alternatives following "Defend dissertation successfully." "If 'yes,' leave on much deserved trip to Europe with wife and family. If 'no,' leave immediately for exile in South America with statistical consultant, Roseanne." A little levity can be a great help at all stages in the process!

As you produce your list of things that need to be accomplished to complete your project, think of each item as a goal in itself. Write each step in the form of a goal, including both the behavior to perform and the date by which you will perform it. "Begin recruiting subjects by January 5, ____" and "Hold proposal meeting by November 15, ____" would be good examples. If you have started with the date by which you want to be finished, it is relatively easy to back up from that date and to estimate how long each step should take. It is important to be realistic in estimating your time. Most students grossly underestimate the amount of time it will take to turn a research question into a complete proposal. "Two months should be plenty," they might say. Even if the student is the world's fastest writer and has all his or her literature in hand, what about the time required for the faculty supervisor to read between two and six drafts of the literature review and the method section? How about the time required for committee members to read the proposal? In planning time requirements, first be honest with yourself about what you are likely to accomplish in a given period of time. Second, be sure to consider steps in your time line that rely on others (e.g., your committee chairperson, the committee on human or animal subjects, research assistants). If you are in doubt about time estimates and the sequencing of steps, ask other students what their experience has been. Ask your chairperson if other students' advice is not helpful or reliable.

Schedule the Work

Once you have identified and assigned realistic completion times to each of the steps in the process, it is a good idea to represent these visually. There are numerous approaches you could take, from simple Gantt charts to more complex PERT (Program Evaluation and Review Technique) analyses. Many project scheduling software packages for both MacIntosh and IBM computers could be useful in mapping your task. These vary considerably in complexity and thoroughness, ranging from simple time-line charts to analyses that include cost estimates, conditional completion probabilities, and so on. Unless you are already a project-scheduling whiz kid or have some burning interest in learning such skills, it is probably enough to produce a modest Gantt or time-line chart. (Tablets of blank Gantt charts can be purchased in office supply stores.) An example of a partial Gantt chart for a project is presented in Exhibit 4.1.

As can be seen from the exhibit, each of the identified activities or steps in the project is listed down the left side of the chart. Do this in the

Exhibit 4.1

Milestone Chart for Children's Social Skills Research Project

Activity	Week:	1	2	3	4	5	6	7	8	9
1. Assess children in classes		→								
2. Identify target children and desired playmates (DPs)		→								
3. Randomly assign to groups		X								
4. Interview DPs of target children in template-matching group (TMG)			→							
5. Develop templates				X						
6. Interview choosers of target children				→						
7. Select target behaviors for TMG				X						
8. Design treatment plan				X						
9. Conduct direct observations					→				→	
10. Implement treatment								→		
11. Repeat in-class assessments										→

order they will be accomplished. Across the top of the chart list the time unit (days, weeks, or months) to be used in scheduling the steps. The arrows indicate when an activity or step is to be started and when it is to be completed. Activities that occur at a single point in time are indicated by Xs in the example; sometimes they are indicated by triangles. It can be seen that Activity 1, in-class assessments, is to begin the first day of the first week, continue throughout the week, and conclude at the week's end. Activity 2, identifying target children and their desired playmates, begins in the middle of Week 1 and continues to the end of that week. Activity 3, random assignment to groups, occurs once, at the end of Week 1. Activity 9, conduct direct observations, occurs during all of Weeks 4 and 8. It is obvious from this example that several events must occur before others, that some occur simultaneously, and that some overlap.

A visual representation of the steps and their temporal relationships to one another makes you more aware of the completeness of your planning and the interdependence of the tasks you need to accomplish. The whole job simply becomes clearer. The chart also becomes a tool you can use in communicating with others when describing your project. This is especially useful when meeting with representatives of off-campus agencies from whom you hope to recruit subjects. It also impresses your committee in proposal meetings. Not only does it aid you in explaining just exactly what you plan to do, it also shows your committee that you have thought of everything. Well, almost everything!

The added advantage of even simple computer scheduling software is that you can get immediate feedback on the consequences of changes in your plans. If you are familiar with spread-sheet software, you know the tremendous power afforded by the automatic recalculation of related values when a single value in the data set is changed. Suppose that you decide you want to take a week off in the middle of your project for some R and R that was not planned originally. You know, a great aunt has decided she just has to go to Hawaii and thinks you're the only one who can accompany her (at her expense, of course). What impact will this have on the entire project? Is it a simple matter of moving every time line a week back? Or is it more complex because of the parallel nature of some of the activities and their conditional dependence on one another? Ask at your local software store about project scheduling programs. A popular one for the MacIntosh is MacProject.™ For the MS DOS world, you might look into Super Project.™

When you schedule, remember it is not set in stone. Logistics problems may force you to alter your plans once you actually begin the project. This is to be expected. You may not yet have learned to project reasonable time frames and may need to alter your deadlines as you master this skill. The beauty of computer scheduling software is that the impact of such alterations on the rest of the project can easily be determined.

Plan Your Schedule to Free Yourself

At this point, you may be asking why all this fuss about scheduling, time lines, charts, and so on. You want to get on with your research. Is all this fancy planning just a socially acceptable form of avoidance? It certainly can be, of course. What we want to emphasize, though, is that an ounce of planning can avoid a pound of problems later on. In the Army one of us had a sergeant who used to admonish new recruits daily with the five Ps: Prior Planning Prevents Poor Performance. A little time spent up front identifying, sequencing, and time-lining the steps in your research project will save inordinate time and frustration later.

An interesting story in support of this argument concerns the development of the Polaris missile in the 1950s. The U. S. Navy was involved in the project that involved organizing the work of over 3,000 different companies. The consulting firm of Booz, Allen, and Hamilton developed a project scheduling and management approach, the Program Evaluation and Review Technique, later known as PERT, that resulted in the entire project being completed nearly 2 years ahead of schedule (Radcliff, Kawal, & Stephenson, 1967).

Even more important is the liberating effect of having a schedule and sticking to it. If you have been conscientious in identifying and scheduling all the steps in your project, you have really done the hard part. Now, all you have to do is accomplish each of the steps as it comes up in the schedule. This is why we like to encourage students to make the steps many and small. A good rule of thumb is to make them small enough to be accomplished in a day or at most a week. If you do this, you can enter the steps in your appointment calendar or your personal digital assistant, writing each on the day you have scheduled it to be accomplished. Be sure to specify the outcome you want to produce in behavioral terms or in terms of products having a close relationship to behavior. "Read five articles" is preferable to "Spend two hours reading," and "Read and outline 5 articles" is even better.

Once all the steps are entered into your calendar, you can stop worrying. All you have to do is complete each small task as it comes up on your calendar or daily to-do list. Remember how you eat an elephant? One bite at a time! That is exactly how you complete a major research project. In fact, one of us planned every week to complete five pages of her portion of this book. By sticking to that plan, she produced about one chapter a month and finished her writing on schedule.

We once had a student who sat down at the beginning of each semester and scheduled all his classes and all of his study, paper-writing, and project times for the classes. Each day of the semester was scheduled. When other students asked how he could stand to live under such a confining schedule, he replied that, on the contrary, he found the entire process quite liberating. Now he didn't need to spend any more time figuring out how he was ever going to get all that work done or worrying about whether he would. He could use that time more productively in recreational pursuits, safe in the knowledge that by having a plan and sticking to it all his work would get done.

A final point to keep in mind while making up your initial schedule is to be sure to allow time for supporting your social supports. If your time with significant others is going to be severely limited during particular periods, discuss this with them ahead of time, while you are first making your schedule. They need advance warning and the opportunity to plan alternate activities and supports for themselves during those times. Whenever possible, give them some say in the schedule itself. By being included at this stage, they are less likely to feel excluded and resentful later.

Plan for the Unexpected

No matter how carefully you plan, things will go wrong. The advantage of having a schedule including critical paths, conditional probabilities, and parallel and sequential tasks is that the impact of unexpected events can be evaluated more easily. Even without such high-tech assistance, however, there are certain things that you can do to minimize being derailed by the unexpected.

The most important step is to identify the most probable areas in which unexpected events might occur. In our experience, there are three: subjects, personnel, and equipment. What are the unexpecteds that can be expected in each of these? With respect to subjects, there are two basic considerations: recruitment and appointment keeping. Remember the rule of the threes here. Allow three times as much time as you think it will take to recruit enough subjects.

You might be saying this doesn't apply in your case because you have already obtained the permission of the instructors of three college classes and that will provide more than enough subjects for your administration of the XYZ Scales. Perhaps so, but what happens if the class is cancelled one day because the instructor is ill and the very next class cannot be used because an exam is scheduled? Or, what if a lower percentage of class members volunteers to participate than you expected? Maybe you plan to do your recruiting by calling people on the phone. Do you know how many times on the average you need to call someone to reach them? Do you have any pilot information to indicate what kind of response rate you can expect?

Once you arrange for subjects to appear at the experimental session, do you have some way of ensuring that they do? Do you have any idea what the typical no-show rate is for psychological studies such as yours? What will you do if someone fails to keep an appointment? Will you schedule a makeup or decide not to run the risk of a repeat offense? Take a clue from the way physicians and dentists handle their appointments.

They give you a little card with the exact day and time of your appointment. The more determined ones also call you to remind you of the appointment a day or two before it occurs. Have you made arrangements to do this?

Despite your best efforts at preventing appointment failures, you will get some. How do you plan to use this unexpected period of time? If you are thinking it will be a good time to get caught up on your sleeping or recreational pursuits or to study for a class, consider another possibility. This is time set aside for working on your research. If a subject fails to appear, this is not really "free" time. It only looks that way. You will have to make up this session some time later if you plan to keep the project on schedule. That will take time away from some other research-related activity you had planned. Anticipate the occasional no-show and plan to do some research-related work during that time. Revise the introduction to get it ready for the final version. Write a more detailed method section now that you have had experience actually running the study. Input your latest data into the computer. Chase down that final elusive reference at the library. If you keep to the task this way, the time wasted by no-shows will be minimized, and you will not be derailed from accomplishing your goal.

Another area of potential surprises is that of research assistants or other project-related personnel. Being human, they get sick, fail to keep *their* appointments, forget to collect or enter an important piece of data, and so on. How will you protect yourself from the inconvenience of these little oversights? Standard personnel management practices are the best advice here. Start with the selection of the very best people you can get. Who these are may depend on a number of things. Foremost is the compensation you are willing to exchange for their services. If you can pay them a reasonable amount in money or academic credit, you can select higher caliber people and expect more from them. If you cannot pay, consider nonmonetary rewards. The barter system sometimes works well. You agree to help someone with their data analyses if they will run subjects for you. Or how about a home-cooked meal for every six subjects run?

If you have selected carefully and arranged a satisfactory compensation and benefits package, the next good personnel management practice is to train your assistants thoroughly. In addition, it is a good idea to cross-train them. Make sure each knows at least one other person's job so that substitutions can be arranged when needed. We say more about research assistants in chapter 11. Plan time for frequent monitoring.

Check the data as they come in. Make sure your assistants are following procedures to the letter. Even conscientious assistants make errors, and spot-checking their performance can allow you to catch these before they get out of control.

Finally, you can count on surprises from the equipment in your project. All of these can be anticipated in advance. Some (e.g., projector bulbs burning out) are more likely than others (e.g., someone stealing the polygraph), but it is best to assume that breakdowns can happen and be prepared for them. In case you are thinking that you are doing low- or no-tech research and equipment is not involved, think again. What about the car that gets you back and forth to the research site? What about the computer that you are using for word processing duties? For data analyses?

A very good principle for dealing with all three sources of potential surprises is redundancy. Cross-training of research assistants is an example of this. Have more subjects, personnel, and equipment ready to do the job than you think you will need. Arrange in advance to borrow or rent equipment to use temporarily while yours is being repaired. Have a plan to notify backup or on-call research assistants in case the primary one gets sick. Nowhere is the principle of redundancy more in evidence than on manned flights into outer space conducted by the National Aeronautics and Space Administration. When we hear of failures of one system or another, there is invariably the immediate announcement that its functions have been taken over by a backup system. Run your research this way. In fact, run your life this way and you will suffer fewer unpleasant surprises!

Minimize Procrastination and Avoidance

We alluded earlier to the overuse of scheduling and planning as a way of avoiding getting on with the project. There are many other behaviors that are even more easily seen in this light. There is no cleaner, better organized apartment than that of a dissertation candidate, for example. Procrastination and avoidance (or P and A) should probably be a category in the *Diagnostic and Statistical Manual of Mental Disorders* (*DSM*, of the American Psychiatric Association), it is so common among those doing theses and dissertations. We all do it to some degree or the other.

In the extreme, however, P and A prevent the project from ever being completed. Thus, where dissertations are concerned, the master of

P and A becomes the ABD (All-But-Dissertation, or ABT for master's students). To minimize these behaviors, put this statement on your wall in very large print:

| The Master of P & A Becomes the ABD(T) |

It can then serve as a daily reminder to keep with the program.

You have already undertaken a more complete approach for dealing with P and A if you have followed the suggestions earlier in this chapter. If you have identified small enough steps, sequenced them properly, and written them in your appointment calendar, you have arranged the components of a momentum-gathering machine that will propel you smoothly through the dissertation process. This is because of the energy that is liberated by completions. Ever notice how simply getting something done gives you the motivation to do other things? This is how it works with research projects as well. By getting each day's small step completed, energy seems to be liberated to do more steps. Doing these in turn produces more energy, and so on. The momentum builds and carries the project forward.

With major research projects, the most common time for procrastinating is in the writing stages, namely, producing a proposal and a final version of the thesis or dissertation. Several factors can be operating here. If, despite following our sage advice so far, you still find yourself procrastinating, perhaps you are victimizing yourself with some of the following verbal behavior

1. *"I can't seem to get started. It's so overwhelming."* Feeling overwhelmed is a clue that you have not broken your task into small enough steps. Think about what you can accomplish today toward your goal: Reading five articles? Typing your references? Outlining your method section? Overwhelming tasks can be turned into manageable ones by the simple device of breaking them into small, readily accomplishable steps. If you can't face the one you planned, do something on the project that seems more appealing. Accomplishing that task may give you the energy to tackle the one you originally planned.

2. *"I can't work on my research unless I have huge chunks of time, and I won't have those until next summer."* This is a creative excuse for doing nothing until next summer. The truth is, although you might be more efficient if you had large chunks of time, you can still get something done without them. In addition, can't you find at least one 3-hour block of time each week to work on your research? One of us, for example, has

set aside a morning a week for the past decade to work on scholarly writing. This time is as sacred as classroom teaching (After all, would you cancel a class you were teaching to do school work for another class? To clean your apartment? To go food shopping?). Over the years, many articles and book chapters were written during these periods. As we have pointed out repeatedly, people complete theses and dissertations by steady work—one page at a time.

3. *"I don't know enough (haven't read enough, worked out the problems well enough, or don't have good enough hypotheses) to write anything."* This is a variation on perfectionistic thinking: "I can't do it if it is not perfect." You obsess about doing it, and nothing gets written. No written draft will ever be perfect the first time around. Just write it, knowing and planning for it to be imperfect. Then, build in time for revision, to improve the first draft.

4. *"I can work only with deadlines."* Some people learn to goof off unless a deadline is imminent. Then, they pull all-nighters to produce a paper, study for a final, complete a grant proposal, and so on. These people find themselves in deep trouble when the thesis or dissertation arrives, because these projects involve working toward a long-term goal with many steps and (usually) few immediate deadlines. As you have probably realized, a proposal or final draft is not a project to be pulled off over a single weekend armed with carafes of coffee or bottles of amphetamines.

We suggest two solutions for the deadline worker. First, create a series of real and meaningful deadlines for completing portions of your thesis or dissertation. Perhaps your graduate program has these. Some programs, for example, have a rule that clinical students cannot apply for internships without an approved dissertation proposal. If yours does not, perhaps you and your chairperson can create a similar contingency for you. For example, if you are applying for academic jobs, perhaps you and your chair can agree that letters of recommendation will only be sent after a certain step (e.g., data collection or data analyses) has been completed. Other professional deadlines, such as dates for submitting abstracts to conventions or presenting your results at a job colloquium, may also serve as deadlines for you.

A second strategy involves breaking the deadline habit altogether. If you intend a professional career that involves research and scholarly writing, you will need to reduce your procrastination. So, why not start now? If you create and stick with schedules, as outlined in this chapter, you *will* kick the habit.

One useful approach is to arrange your schedule according to the Premack principle, so named because of the psychologist who popularized it. The simple fact is that behavior of a lower probability can be strengthened by having it precede behavior of a higher probability. This is the behavioral principle behind the old "First you work, then you play" maxim. Do something on your research, then do something you really want or need to do (e.g., shopping or sleeping). Build this "work first, play second" rule into your life-style, and your project will be finished much more painlessly.

It is a good idea to build rewards into the research completion schedule initially. After turning in the final draft of your proposal to your committee members, for example, plan a get-away trip with a loved one. But do not leave unless the draft has been completed. If you make your accomplishments rewarding for significant others, too, they will keep supporting you in the overall effort. If you build the rewards into the schedule in advance, you will have them to look forward to. In this way, you will control a lot more on-task behavior than you would by simply waiting to get the task finished and then deciding what nice thing you can arrange for yourself and others.

Finally, ask members of your social support system to encourage you to make progress. Tell your peers about your accomplishments so they can congratulate you. Some students even band together into dissertation support groups to help keep each other on track. Be careful here, though. These should be groups to reinforce accomplishments, not to commiserate with or get support for "good reasons" for not making progress!

✔   **To Do . . .**

Managing Time and Trouble

☐ Start with a goal

☐ Estimate your time requirements

   —Identify subgoals and activities

   —Break down big tasks into small steps

   —Sequence the subgoals/activities/steps

☐ Schedule the work

☐ Plan for the unexpected

   —Subjects

   —Personnel

   —Equipment

5. Minimize procrastination and avoidance

   —Avoid common thinking patterns

   —Use the Premack principle

5 Selecting a Chairperson and a Committee

One of the most important decisions you will make in the initial stages of thesis or dissertation planning involves selecting a chairperson for your project. A good chairperson will provide expertise in your topic area, specific feedback on your work, and support—as well as an occasional kick in the pants if you need it to keep going. A poor chairperson will provide few of these and may, in fact, make your life miserable as you negotiate the dissertation or thesis process.

Before approaching a faculty member as a potential chairperson, consider the chair's role. Although the specifics of this role vary from school to school and from chairperson to chairperson, some general functions of the chair are reasonably universal. First, the chairperson helps the student develop the research idea and methodology. Second, the chairperson provides the first line of quality assurance for the project. Thus, he or she is expected to read and critique multiple drafts of each section of the thesis or dissertation. Third, the chairperson approves the proposal for and the final version of the project before permitting the student to submit these documents to other committee members.

Although some chairpersons expect students to go it alone and report to them only when the proposal and the final write-up are complete, most chairs work more closely with their students, particularly in guiding master's theses. Thus, you should appraise three major areas in deciding whom to invite to chair your project: (a) how well you could work in collaboration with the faculty member; (b) how much expertise he or she has in your research area; and (c) how skilled the person is at the specific tasks required to guide you smoothly to a completed thesis or dissertation. If you choose well, you will work comfortably with your chairperson and obtain specific, timely, and specialized guidance on your project. Working with a good chairperson is like going to a good dentist: The process may not be enjoyable or painless, but it may not be as bad as you anticipate. And the end product is worth it!

Departments usually have rules about who may or may not serve as dissertation or thesis chairpersons and committee members. Except in rare circumstances, chairs must have earned the doctorate themselves. Some institutions allow only individuals who have adequate, recent publication records or who have been on the faculty for a certain period of time to assume the dissertation chair role. These rules are based on the assumption that inexperienced faculty or those without active programs of scholarship will lack the skills to ensure that the doctoral project has sufficient scope, grounding in the literature, and methodological rigor. Rules regarding who may chair master's theses are often but not always more liberal than those regarding dissertations. Furthermore, some schools require special permission if the student wishes to work with a faculty member outside of the student's specialty area or department. Working with a chairperson who is not a faculty member at all may also be prohibited or allowed only under special circumstances (e.g., when a faculty member is willing to act as a nominal chair or as a cochair). Finding out these rules in advance will help you avoid getting your heart set on working with someone who is not eligible to chair a thesis or dissertation. In addition, find out what forms need to be signed and have those ready for your chairperson and committee members to sign when they agree to assume those roles. This formalizes the agreement and makes it difficult for them to change their minds later on!

Consider the Nature of Chair–Student Collaboration

Working on a dissertation or thesis is a collaborative process between the chairperson and the student. When a final dissertation is archived in *Dissertation Abstracts International*, the chair's and student's names are both listed. Faculty with national and international reputations will be careful about the type of work with which their name is associated. Taking on the responsibility of chairing a dissertation committee is not something most faculty members take lightly.

For your collaboration to succeed, you and your chairperson will need to work reasonably well together. This is especially true if you have little research experience and will need a good deal of guidance (often the case with the master's degree). A first step in assessing how well you might work with a faculty member is to examine the match between what you want from your chairperson and your chairperson's notion of the best way to implement his or her role.

So, what do you want from your chairperson? Do you want someone who will guide you into a topic (which will probably be something interesting to the chairperson), or do you want someone who will be happy for you to follow your own inclinations? Will you work best with a chairperson who is highly structured (e.g., sets deadlines and meets regularly with student) or with one who is more laissez-faire? Do you want to work with someone who is interpersonally warm and supportive, or are other characteristics (e.g., expertise and professional connections) more important? In short, think about and decide what kind of structure, how much input in terms of topic development, and what sort of interpersonal style you prefer. You can then move on to appraise how well the faculty member's style matches the way you prefer to work.

Think About Potential Chairpersons' Expertise

Some students and faculty assert that your chairperson must know a lot more about your topic than you do. Others disagree with this assertion, maintaining that the role of the chair is to critique your methodology and the logic of the your arguments, not to be experts in your topic area. Good methodological and analytic skills should be applicable to any topic area, they say.

We agree with the last statement. We further agree that students sometimes produce excellent research working with chairpersons who know little about the student's area at the outset of the project. We nonetheless believe it is ordinarily in the best interest of both students and the profession for students to find chairs with expertise within the student's topic area. Furthermore, we generally recommend that students develop their topics jointly with a faculty member, working within the faculty member's area of interest. This is particularly important for students conducting research for master's theses, who enter the process with less experience and skill than more advanced graduate students and who generally need more guidance at all stages of the project.

Our recommendation that you work with a chairperson with expertise in your area is based on our opinion that following this advice generally will produce a better product with less time and agony. First, faculty members who have worked in an area for a number of years know the literature well. They know what research has and has not been conducted and what is currently being done. This knowledge can prevent you from spending months designing what you think is the ideal study, only to find that someone published your magnum opus the month before in the *Journal of Personality and Social Psychology*. Furthermore, such faculty members will be likely to guide you into a study that will make a contribution to the literature.

Equally important, knowledgeable faculty members will know the ins and outs of doing research in the area. They will know effective subject recruitment methods, the pitfalls in common designs and procedures, and the methodological norms in the area. Thus, you are unlikely to mistakenly begin a master's thesis that has the scope of a small grant because you are unaware of how time consuming your procedures will be. Nor are you likely to design a study with a "fatal flaw" that is due to ignorance of the topic area (your own *and* your chair's). A chair who knows your literature may be able to point you to relevant articles, chapters, and books. A student of ours, for example, recently announced that she was going to the library to start her literature search. When she discovered that her chair had two file-cabinet drawers full of reprints related to her general topic area, she spent a day with these files and photocopied the articles that she needed, saving many hours in the stacks.

Another reason for working in faculty members' areas is that these chairpersons will have more investment in your project. Faculty members who care deeply about what you are studying are likely to spend more time with you, think about the project more fully, and generally keep a sharper eye on your progress than those who do not. A sense of ownership often promotes accountability among collaborators, and if you share that ownership with your chairperson, you may reap the benefits of more timely and in-depth feedback and support.

Finally, faculty members with active research programs often have laboratory space, equipment, and sometimes even monetary resources (e.g., grant funds to pay subjects). Many will let you use some or all of their facilities if you work in their area.

Of course, working in faculty members' areas is not without its potential drawbacks. Some faculty members may be too controlling, requiring you to do what *they* want, the way *they* want it done, without regard for your ideas or intellectual development. You may find yourself following your chair's instructions rather than developing the skills you need to function autonomously as a researcher. Even at the master's level, which involves considerably less independence than the doctorate, you should be learning new skills rather than functioning as slave labor. Failure to develop research skills at this stage is a particular drawback if you plan a career that involves research. In that kind of career, you will be expected to function well independently and to design your own line of research after completing the doctorate. In addition, faculty members are sometimes more demanding in an area they know than in an area with which they are less familiar. These potential problems are by no means inevitable, however, and we believe that the advantages gained by working in an area the chairperson knows well far outweigh the potential problems for most students.

If working with an expert chairperson is not an option for you, consider recruiting one or more experts in your area to serve on your dissertation or thesis committee. Look for these experts among members of the department, your academic community, other nearby academic institutions, and community sites. Consulting with these individuals on substantive areas can fulfill some of the functions normally served by a knowledgeable chairperson.

Appraise Potential Chairpersons' Skills

Chairing a dissertation or thesis well requires specific skills. Among these are guiding the research process and providing quality control. This means that the chair will read many drafts of your proposal and final write-up, provide feedback on areas that need improvement, and help you solve problems when you are stuck. The chair will also head your committee and ordinarily will oversee the proposal meeting and the oral defense of the project. Good chairpersons will make their expectations clear, provide specific feedback (both positive and negative), read and return drafts to you in reasonable periods of time, meet with you to discuss the project, and manage conflicts among committee members if they arise.

Expectations and Feedback

In most departments, some faculty have very high standards, whereas others are less critical and require fewer rewrites, less extensive methodology, and so on. The implications of working with a "hard" versus an "easy" chair go far beyond how many hours you can expect to put into the project, however.

We must admit our bias: We both are known for our high standards in working with students. These standards, we believe, have several positive consequences for students. First, if you produce a product that satisfies a chair with high standards, you are less likely to encounter serious problems with your committee, because you and the chair will already have considered the major issues involved in your project and have made good decisions. Second, you will be better prepared for your proposal meeting and oral defense, because you and the chair will have discussed many of the major issues your committee members are likely to raise. Finally, a chair you have satisfied is more likely to go to bat for you if a committee member throws you a curve ball.

Beyond considering faculty members' standards, consider whether prospective chairpersons will provide specific feedback and suggestions. Few things are more frustrating than working with someone who tells you to do better but cannot tell you specifically what you need to do to improve. You should not expect faculty members to find specific articles for you, make all your decisions, or rewrite your poor sentences. But you should look for potential chairpersons who can tell you clearly what you need to do to improve the project as you work through the process.

Timeliness and Availability

Most students receive feedback on several drafts of each section of the thesis or dissertation before chairs give the section the final seal of approval. The timeliness of this feedback is important: Potential chairpersons who sit on drafts of your introduction and method section for months may seriously delay your progress. Similarly, chairpersons should be available to meet with you within a reasonable period of time to discuss problems you encounter.

What is a "good" turnaround time? We strive for 2-week turnaround on drafts, recognizing that it will take longer during very busy periods (e.g., final-exam grading periods, weeks when we will be out of town, and right before deadlines when all students want to finish their projects). Similarly, if a student has a problem to discuss or needs an appointment, we ordinarily schedule it within a week to 10 days.

Several things can get in the way of mentors being available and providing timely feedback as soon as you would like. Think about these things as you consider prospective chairpersons. Popular chairs may have many students vying for their time. Some faculty are extremely busy with grant-sponsored research or travel extensively. Others may have active consulting or clinical practices that compete with students' needs for time. No matter how scintillating your prose, it is hard to compete with a paycheck. Also, many faculty are on 9-month contracts with their schools and may not be available during the summer months.

If you have concerns about any of these matters, bring the issue up with prospective chairs: Ask them what their usual turnaround time is, whether their schedules will allow them to meet with you regularly, how often you should plan to meet if you work together, and so on. We will discuss this further in a later section, when we explore how to get information about prospective chairpersons.

Assertiveness Skills

We hope that you will select a chairperson and committee members who work well together. But what if you don't? Is your chair assertive enough to back you up if a committee member makes unreasonable demands? Will the chairperson help you out if something goes wrong in the external agency in which the study is being conducted? Your chairperson's assertiveness skills are particularly important if your study involves procedures that are difficult to implement, and, thus, you require help gaining agency support, meeting with the human subjects research review committee, and so on. Finding an assertive chairperson is also important if your department is a hotbed of interpersonal feuds, and dissertation or thesis meetings become shooting matches between faculty, with students as hapless bystanders.

Finally, remember that your project is both an examination of your competence as a researcher *and* a learning experience. In general, the master's thesis is considered to be more of a learning experience than an examination, whereas the reverse is true for the doctoral project. How well will particular faculty teach you about research as you negotiate the project? Will the person facilitate your growth as a researcher? Will the person do most of the work for you, will you have to find your own way with little guidance, or will you be challenged to learn and grow in your research skills under the tutelage of a skillful mentor?

Investigate Prospective Chairpersons

Three sources provide information about prospective chairpersons. First is your personal experience: You may have taken a class from particular faculty members or talked with them at get-togethers. Better yet, you may have actually worked with the person on research in the past. This is, of course, the best way to get direct information about what it is like to work under the faculty member's guidance.

If you are reading this volume early enough in your graduate career, consider getting experience working with faculty with whom you share common interests, so you can see firsthand how well you work with the person. Working as a paid research assistant or as an unpaid volunteer (e.g., taking a secondary role as part of the faculty member's research) can provide this information. If you volunteer, make sure that you assess the requirements and degree of contact you will have with the faculty member before you agree to participate. If you are getting involved to see how well you like working with a particular faculty member, you want to have contact with that faculty member—not be shuttled off to be an unpaid research assistant for the postdoctoral student who is working in the person's lab. Doing a master's thesis with someone is another way of gaining information about a prospective dissertation chairperson.

As you think about what you did and did not like about your experiences with prospective chairpersons in your previous interactions, remember the differences between the requirements of the chair role and the requirements of other faculty roles. For example, you may have loved Dr. Smith's lecture style. But Dr. Smith will not be lecturing in your dissertation meetings! Think instead about whether Dr. Smith gave you specific, helpful feedback on your paper and returned exams to you promptly. Of course, Dr. Smith may not be cross-situationally consistent, so you need to look at other kinds of data to supplement your own experience.

A second source of information comes from classmates who have worked with the faculty member. We are not talking about the proverbial grapevine, however. The grapevine, like grocery store tabloids, is generally a source of *entertaining* information. Unfortunately, it is not always a source of *accurate* information, largely because the grapevine is created and fed almost entirely by students and therefore tends to be one sided. In faculty—student matters, as in most of life, there are two sides to every problem, and the truth ordinarily lies somewhere between them. Faculty members who appropriately refrain from gossiping with students never see their points of view reflected in the contents of the rumor mill.

Sure, some faculty reputations are well deserved. The problem, however, is that without credible data it is hard to know whether the reputation—good or bad—is based on fact or on fiction. Rumors do not provide this credible data.

To get more reliable information, talk with students who have worked under the guidance of prospective chairs. They, after all, have firsthand experience with these individuals in chair–student relationships. Get other students to describe their experiences. Talk to more than one to get a decent sample. Ask questions about areas that concern you: How many drafts did they write of each section? How fast did the faculty member return them? What kind of feedback did the faculty member give? What kinds of problems did the committee raise, and how did the chair respond? Note that these questions ask about specific faculty behavior rather than student subjective impressions. Although knowing whether the student liked or hated the chair may be interesting, more important is how the chair interacted with the student. Knowing that information, you can decide whether *you* would profit from working with a prospective chairperson, regardless of whether your informant did.

In addition, in evaluating students' reports, be sure to consider the source. Weak students may find intellectually rigorous professors "too picky," whereas strong students think they are stimulating and helpful. It is hard for any faculty member to be supportive enough for extremely needy students. Remember, chairs are not randomly assigned to students: Selection biases operate. In our experience, strong students often select demanding but fair chairs, weak or lazy students often choose faculty members who will allow them to cut corners, and no one (if he or she can help it) works with irresponsible or autocratic individuals who change their demands from week to week.

A final source of information comes from interviews with faculty members themselves. At some point you will have a "short list" of possible chairs and questions to ask them. How a faculty member answers your questions provides another valuable source of information. Approaching the faculty member is part of "dissertation and thesis etiquette," a topic to which we now turn.

Approach Prospective Chairpersons: Dissertation and Thesis Etiquette I

You've thought about what you want from a chairperson. You've talked with other students. You have one or more possible topic areas. It's time to select a chairperson.

As you sally forth, remember that faculty members have choices about the projects they will and will not chair. Most have explicit or implicit guidelines that they follow in making these choices. For example, one of our colleagues once proposed the following criteria to screen prospective dissertation students:

1. The design must involve comparisons.
2. These comparisons must involve hypotheses generated from relevant literature.
3. Some of the measures must use a method other than self-report.
4. The student must have taken at least one course from the faculty member.
5. The student must have the necessary methodological preparation to complete the particular project.
6. The student must have adequate time to (a) work on the dissertation continuously and (b) meet to discuss progress during the faculty member's normal office schedule.

Even if you have worked in someone's lab, you cannot assume that this faculty member will automatically assume the chair role or that you know the individual's expectations. You need to ask.

How you approach prospective chairs depends on whether you are still shopping and want more information or whether you have narrowed the list to a specific faculty member with whom you wish to work. In either case, a first step is to make an appointment to discuss chairing your project. In doing this, be direct about your agenda. If you are still shopping around, you might say to the faculty member,

> I'm thinking about my thesis (dissertation), and one of the areas I'm considering is _____. I'd like to talk with you about whether you might be interested in chairing something in this area, if I decide on this topic, and about how you go about chairing theses (dissertations). Do you have time to discuss this with me?

If you know that you want the faculty member to chair the project, you might say,

> I'm interested in doing my thesis (dissertation) in the _____ area. I'd like to discuss my specific ideas with you and see whether you might be interested in chairing my project.

Be prepared for the faculty member to ask you some questions on the spot or to give you a quick decision. For example, we routinely ask students we do not know well about their prospective topic and why they are interested in us (rather than someone else). This allows us to refer students with topics in which we have no expertise to other faculty members and saves us (and the student) wasted appointment time. Similarly, we will agree immediately if the topic interests us and we know the student and are willing to work with him or her. We will immediately turn away students if we are overcommitted, not interested in the topic, or not willing to work with the person.

If the faculty member agrees to meet with you, go to your meeting with an agenda you wish to discuss. If you are shopping, ask questions that will help you decide whether this would be a good chairperson for you. Start by mentioning briefly your general area of interest, if you have one. Find out faculty members' explicit and implicit rules: how they generally work with students, how much input they generally have in topic development, what kinds of students they work best with, and whether they have any openings currently. Do not necessarily expect a faculty member to agree to chair your project, however, until you have a specific research question: Many are not willing to invest the time and energy involved in chairing a project if they believe the research is trivial or uninteresting. If you lack ideas, ask the faculty member for suggestions or for readings that will assist in formulating a research question. If the faculty member agrees to meet with you further to discuss or develop topics, this is a good first step. It does not necessarily mean the person will chair the project, however.

If the faculty member indicates potential or definite interest in chairing your project and you are still interested, end the meeting by asking, "What should I do next?" This gives the faculty member a chance to make expectations explicit about what you need to do to keep the process rolling. If you are still chair-shopping, you may want to tell the faculty member that you are talking with several individuals and will get back to each if you want to discuss the process further, thanking the faculty member for the appointment time.

We cannot emphasize enough the importance of establishing clear, direct communication with a chairperson regarding expectations and roles. Knowing what is expected makes the process less ambiguous for all concerned. Faculty members may or may not provide this explicit information, so students should think about how they can tactfully and directly communicate about issues involved in planning the project. Direct communication early on both sets the stage for a good working relationship and helps prevent later problems that are due to mistaken assumptions on the part of either chair or student.

Consider the Nature and Function of the Committee

Dissertation and thesis committees vary in size, composition, and specific duties, depending on the institution and the degree. Committee members' general roles are reasonably consistent, however: (a) They provide suggestions for improving the proposed study and, later, the final written project; (b) they serve as additional checks on the quality of the proposal and final document; and (c) they take the lead in examining the student during the oral defense. In the thesis defense, the committee ordinarily wishes to ensure that the student understands and can talk intelligently about the research. In the dissertation defense, the committee also assesses the student's competence to function as an independent researcher. Thus, committee members serve partially as consultants and partially as examiners—two vastly different roles. The balance between assistance and inquisition varies from school to school and committee to committee, and also depends on whether the project is a thesis or a dissertation.

Ideally, committee members should provide expertise that supplements the chair's and contributes new insights and ideas that will enhance the research. One of us, for example, will only agree to serve on a committee if she has some expertise regarding the population, the independent variable, or the major dependent variables of the proposed investigation. At the same time, committee members' theoretical perspectives and points of view should be reasonably compatible with the student's, and members should have some interest in the topic. Students working closely with an outside agency should consider inviting a doctoral-level person in the agency to serve on the committee. This person typically becomes the student's advocate and liaison within the agency and also provides valuable information about agency regulations as well as feedback about what requests for agency resources are reasonable. Adding a statistics expert to the committee may be useful if you will be using complex statistical procedures and will need more than occasional consultation with this individual.

Committee members should also get along reasonably well interpersonally with the chair. And, obviously, committee members should be fair, direct, and trustworthy. Although committee members who praise the student privately and then torpedo the project in oral defense are rare, the experience is traumatic enough that you should gather enough information about prospective committee members to ensure that this will not happen.

Before considering specifics about selecting committee members, find out the written and unwritten rules about committee members' involvement in preparing the proposal and the final written document. Many departments follow the "strong-chairperson" model in which committee members read the proposal and full write-up only after the chair has approved these documents. This approval follows extensive work between student and chair to fashion the document into acceptable form. Although members of the committee are expected to be available for consultation regarding specific aspects of the project that fall within their areas of expertise (e.g., specific measurement issues or statistical treatment of the data), they usually do not serve as substitute chairs (the exception to this is when a committee member knows more than the chairperson about the topic area under study and assumes more extensive responsibility than usual for some aspect of the project). The chair, not the committee, consults with the student on the hypotheses, design, measure selection, and other details. Committee members voice their opinions after the chair is satisfied with the proposal, unless they are invited earlier to help solve a problem for which their skills are well suited.

The strong-chairperson model is not the only one, of course. In some schools, committee members assume roles much closer to that of the chair, sometimes reading drafts of the proposal and final project as the student prepares them. Our experience in these situations is that often members' roles are ambiguously defined, leaving the student to figure out when and how committee members should be involved. When this process is the norm, students can clarify the process by asking the chairperson to specify what role the chairperson wants committee members to serve. Getting chairs to be specific is important. When and what should committee members agree to read? How many drafts? Will there be a formal proposal meeting? The student should then communicate these expectations to prospective committee members.

Another risk when roles are ambiguous is that the student will get caught between different members' ideas about how particular research issues should be handled. This can result in students running from chair to committee member and back again, sometimes misquoting or forgetting what each person has told them about the issue. In these cases, we believe family therapists' approach provides the best solution: Arrange a meeting among all involved parties and hash out the issues face-to-face.

Investigate Prospective Committee Members

Many suggestions we gave about finding a chair apply equally to committee members: Find out the formal rules about the composition of the committee and who can and cannot serve as a committee member; talk to students about their experiences with different faculty as committee members; and take information from the rumor mill with a large grain of salt. In addition, ask your chairperson about prospective committee members. Your mentor may have worked with them and know what their points of view and expertise will contribute to your particular project. It is imperative to discuss prospective committee members with your chairperson *before* issuing invitations, because your chair may have specific recommendations and may work better with certain colleagues than with others.

Your chairperson will also guide you regarding *when* to approach committee members. In general, we advise students not to form a committee until they have decided on a research question, developed their methodology, and have a reasonable timetable for completing the proposal and conducting the study. Knowing the specific topic is important for obvious reasons. Knowing the time frame of the project is important because faculty members go on leaves of absence and sabbaticals, do not want to be on a dozen committees that all will be meeting during the same week, and so on. Many who are not paid by the school during the summer do not meet with students or participate in proposal meetings or oral defenses during this period. Replacing a committee member can be difficult. Form a committee of individuals who plan to be available during the time frame you propose.

Approach Prospective Committee Members: Dissertation and Thesis Etiquette II

As with chairpersons, invite committee members by telling them first that you would like them to serve on your committee. Provide a brief overview of your topic, your proposed method, and your timetable for completing the proposal and the final write-up. You may also want to tell prospective committee members what you believe they could contribute to the project. If you wish potential committee members to be available for specific tasks (e.g., to consult on statistics or to assist with your methodology), tell them about these requirements. As committee members agree to serve, ask about any special requirements they might have about your project. A committee member who is a statistician, for example, may wish to discuss your statistics with you only *after* you have discussed them with your chairperson.

Anticipate Trouble Spots

Several issues can be troublesome when seeking a chairperson and committee members. Below, we list some common concerns students have, along with our ideas for how to cope with each.

1. *"I worked in Dr. McGee's lab and did my master's thesis with Dr. McGee, but I want to work with Dr. Jones on my dissertation. Is there any way to do this without alienating Dr. McGee?"* Many students fear that leaving someone's lab means that they forego the goodwill and letters of recommendation from that faculty member. This is not necessarily so. In many schools, students are allowed (in some cases, encouraged) to shift mentors if their interests change or if they wish to get exposure to another research area. Most faculty understand this, although they may be sorry to lose a student they have invested years in training.

In these situations, we recommend discussing the issue with the faculty member you wish to leave, saying something to the effect of

> I'm thinking about my dissertation topic. Although I've learned a lot from working with you, my interests are really in the area of _____. I'd like to talk to Dr. Jones about possibly working together on this, but I wanted to talk with you first to get your reaction.

The gracious faculty member will say, "I'd love to have you, but it's your choice," and there will be no negative repercussions. In fact, faculty members may appreciate your consulting them before approaching someone else. Less gracious but equally direct faculty members may tell you that they put a lot of time into your training and that your "payback" is to do your thesis or dissertation on a topic that interests them. Then, you can decide whether maintaining the faculty member's good will is worth altering your topic and your plans.

2. *"I want to study the influence of sunlamps on worms' turning behavior. This is in Dr. Barton's area, but I don't want to work with Dr. Barton."* This is a problem for at least two reasons. First, unless someone else shares Dr. Barton's expertise, you may not find a faculty member qualified to chair your project. Second, Dr. Barton will likely find out about your topic and figure out that you chose another chairperson for a reason. Dr. Barton may or may not make an issue of this. Moreover, colleagues who are close to Dr. Barton may not be willing to serve as a chairperson or as committee members.

We suggest that you consider two questions in thinking through this issue. First, determine your reasons for not selecting Dr. Barton. Is there any way you could arrange the process so that the problems you anticipate are minimized? Small problems can even be discussed with the faculty member when you shop for a chair: "I'd love to work in your area, but you seem very busy and I know I'll need a fair amount of guidance. If we decide to work together, would it be possible to schedule regular meetings?" Logistic problems can often be solved by open discussion in advance; problems involving irresponsible behavior and a negative interpersonal style are not so easily broached and prevented through advance problem solving, however.

A second question revolves around a realistic appraisal of the consequences of choosing someone other than Dr. Barton. Will Dr. Barton really care? Will Barton do anything? Will Dr. Barton's feelings or opinion have any impact on your life after you complete your degree? Many students catastrophize about the impact of not choosing Dr. Barton, when Dr. Barton may be happy not to have another student or may dislike the student as much as the student dislikes Dr. Barton! At the same time, if you intend to pursue an academic career in Dr. Barton's area and Dr. Barton is a national expert, it may be wise to put up with Dr. Barton's idiosyncrasies in exchange for his or her expertise.

Alternatively, you could do your research on another topic. Surely you can find another idea that interests you and that would allow you and Dr. Barton to save face when you select another chair. You can always change your research interests after you complete the thesis or the doctorate.

3. *"I can't find anyone to chair my project."* If this is your problem, it is important to consider the cause. The most common reason for this problem, in our experience, lies in the student's choice of topic. Faculty members may turn you down because they think your topic is trivial, poorly thought out, or outside their areas of expertise. Students who get their hearts set on a particular research question, develop it without faculty guidance, and present it to faculty members as a fait accompli are particularly likely to be turned down on topical grounds. The solution, of course, is to approach faculty members earlier in the process, talk with them about topics that fit their interest areas as well as your own, and let the faculty member know you are flexible and open to feedback about what is important and what is not.

Another reason for failure to find a chair lies in the student's failure to investigate fully: You get your heart set on a particular faculty member and then discover that faculty member cannot take on another student, is going on sabbatical, or for some other reason is unavailable. You then conclude that you "can't find a chair." As disappointing as it may be, you may need to explore other topic areas that would increase other faculty members' interest in your research.

Finally, some students cannot find mentors because their academic or personal problems drive prospective chairs away. Students who have had repeated difficulty in their training program may find that few faculty members are willing to undergo the projected agony of working with them. If this is your difficulty, you should honestly appraise the situation. Ask yourself whether, in light of your past problems, you need high-quality professional help to assist you. First, you will need to identify your contribution to these problems. Have you been unreliable, antagonistic, abrasive, or inflexible? Do you lack basic graduate-level academic skills and need extensive remediation? Second, you will need to decide whether a change in your skills, behavior, or attitude can be achieved in a relatively short period of time. If you are able to achieve these two goals, communicate this good-faith effort to a faculty member, show them at least one demonstrable change you have made, and ask for another chance. It is very difficult to shift a negative reputation, and you may need to work harder and make more compromises than other students in order to talk a faculty member into taking you on as a student and to overcome their negative expectations of you.

If you cannot change, perhaps now is the time to exit gracefully and find a career that suits your personality or skills better. Repeated problems in graduate school are likely to predict similar problems in job situations that have comparable requirements.

4. *"How can I put together a committee? Everyone in my department hates everyone else!"* The key to dealing with this issue is to evaluate its accuracy. The grapevine, hungry for juicy tidbits, often creates conflict where none exists. How often we have been told that we do not get along with some of our favorite colleagues, on the basis of misinterpretation and speculation! Check out better sources of data (e.g., chairpersons' opinions about how well they work with prospective committee members and good students' experiences with different committees). In addition, recall that hot academic disputes do not necessarily mean that faculty hate one another personally or cannot reach compromises. Finally, many professionals have the maturity not to let personal or collegial disagreements interfere with their fairness on committees. Mature faculty who do not feel that they can work with other faculty will not agree to serve with that person. Again, obtaining observations from reliable sources regarding faculty members' interactions in committee meetings is the best way of finding out who works well with whom.

Summary

A compatible chairperson and helpful committee members will contribute greatly to your project and the research process. Collecting reliable information about prospective faculty chairpersons can help you select a mentor wisely. Even if compromises are necessary (how many perfect chairpersons exist, after all?), you are likely to make better choices if you think through the chairperson's role and find out the person's style than if you select someone without this information.

✔ To Do . . .

Selecting a Chairperson and a Committee

☐ Identify formal rules about chairpersons and committee members

☐ Identify informal norms about chairpersons' and committee members' roles

☐ Identify what you want from the chair–student collaboration

☐ Identify potential chairpersons' expertise in areas that interest you

☐ Appraise potential chairpersons' skills

   —Expectations

   —Feedback

   —Timeliness and availability

   —Assertiveness

☐ Investigate prospective chairpersons

   —Consider past experiences with these individuals

   —Talk with classmates

   —Talk with faculty members

☐ Approach prospective chairpersons

   —Identify important issues to discuss with them

   —Communicate clearly

   —Obtain commitment from chairperson

☐ Investigate prospective committee members

   —Talk with chairperson

   —Talk with classmates

☐ Approach prospective committee members

   —Provide overview of your study and timetable

   —Obtain commitment from committee members

☐ Anticipate and prevent trouble spots

6

Formulating and Communicating Your Plans: An Overview of the Proposal

At this point, you know what you want to do and have chosen people to guide and assist you in doing it. Next, you need to formalize your plans. In this chapter, we talk about the content and structure of the proposal. Chapter 14 discusses how you present and defend this proposal at a meeting of your committee.

Understand the Functions and Importance of the Dissertation or Thesis Proposal

Your proposal specifies what you expect to do and how you will do it. It is important from several perspectives. First, the proposal is the first significant piece of writing you will do on your thesis or dissertation. In a sense, it serves as the training ground and testing period of the research. Producing the proposal will give you firsthand insights into the complexity of the investigatory process and the particular research area you have chosen. Your proposal also provides your chair and committee members evidence of your preparation to carry out the research and of how you operate as a scholar. Because it sets the tone in this fashion, you should approach the process in ways that communicate how you wish to be perceived by your committee members. Do you want to be seen as a helpless, dependent person who needs guidance and reassurance at every turn? Are you more interested in being seen as self-reliant and independent, with good judgment about when and when not to seek consultation?

Another reason the proposal is so important is that, once accepted by your committee, it serves as a blueprint for what you intend to do. Your proposal specifies exactly how you plan to complete your research.

By approving your proposal, your committee says that if you do exactly as you specified in the proposal, you will have carried out a project that meets their specifications.

In some schools, the proposal is considered an informal contract: If you follow your procedures to the letter, your committee cannot, after the fact, ask you to run more subjects, follow an adapted procedure, or run another control condition. Some schools actually have committee members sign an approval (following the addition of changes suggested in the proposal meeting) that is then filed with the amended proposal in the dean's or some other administrative office. Years later, when the weary doctoral candidate returns from Fiji with her completed dissertation and none of her original committee members are still on the faculty, there is some proof that the university really did consent to a study on the underwater aerobic exercise of South Sea island octogenarians. Sternberg (1981) provides a more complete discussion of the proposal as a formal contract.

Not all faculty and departments hold the "contract" view, however. Even those who do are quick to point out that approving the proposal does not mean the final project will also be approved: You must also conduct the study well, analyze the data appropriately, produce an acceptable final version of the study, and so on. Furthermore, most researchers need to change something that they proposed once they actually implement the study. Nonetheless, it will behoove you to assess local norms about how binding the proposal is, both to students and to faculty.

The proposal seems a formidable obstacle for many students. But, believe it or not, you have probably done a great deal of the work for it already. What you need to do now is organize all those slips of paper, all those references, and all those measures you've been collecting as you researched your topic and turn them into a single document. In the next section, we give you an overview of what to put into the proposal.

Your written product is your opportunity to show what you can do as a scholar. Be aware, however, that while creativity and originality are valued characteristics in conceptualizing and conducting research, they are *not* popular when writing about it. The proposal is no place for you to challenge the rules and come up with your own "improved" way of doing things. Find out the proposal requirements of your department or school. Do it their way and save your creativity for more important challenges.

Know the Elements of the Dissertation or Thesis Proposal

So what goes into a proposal? A good rule of thumb is "everything that you can find that will go into the complete dissertation (thesis) eventually." Don't hold back at this point. Your ideas, references, and insights are relatively fresh and available now, not lost in the synaptic jungle of your brain or the disorganization of your writing space. Put them into the proposal, and you won't have to worry about losing them. In addition, remember that the proposal allows your committee members to give you feedback on your ideas and plans. The more complete you are now, the less room there is for a committee member to say at your oral defense, "Oh—I *assumed* that of course you would do this my way. You didn't. You really need to run all those subjects again to correct that egregious error."

Although formal rules as well as chairpersons' and committee members' preferences can vary, a good way to organize a proposal is in terms of three major sections: Introduction (Literature Review), Method, and Results. Of course, some material will go before (e.g., title page and table of contents) and after (e.g., references and appendixes) these major sections. Nonetheless, these three sections constitute the heart of the proposal. The material that follows provides an overview of each section. Subsequent chapters go into much greater detail.

Introduction (Literature Review)

Here, you will talk generally about the area of your research and include your review of relevant literature. Two general variations of the dissertation literature review predominate. The first is the two-chapter model. This consists of a relatively short chapter (usually the first chapter of the document) that introduces the topic, provides a brief overview, and then states the research problem and sometimes the hypotheses. A longer second chapter provides a critical, integrative review of the literature. The challenge of this model is to present sufficient information in the first chapter for the reader to understand why the research question is important without being redundant with the longer chapter.

The more streamlined one-chapter model combines the material of the two-chapter version into one. It ordinarily begins with a brief introduction to the topic, then launches into a focused literature review that concludes with a statement of the problem and hypotheses. A rarer version of this model is the length of the introductory section of a journal article (4–8 pages), sometimes accompanied by a lengthier, more comprehensive review in an appendix.

Your proposal should contain a complete review of literature relevant to your specific topic. In other words, write the literature review that you will include in the final version of your project (the final write-up will also include the few new studies that get published while you are conducting yours). Although some schools accept abbreviated reviews for the proposal, we strongly recommend writing a complete review at the proposal stage. What is our logic? You will need to do all the work required for a complete review in order to write your proposal, anyway. Otherwise, you won't know whether someone has beaten you to the punch and already explored your idea. A thorough review of the literature also acquaints you with all the nitty-gritty procedural and design details of research in your area, thereby helping you to avoid the mistakes others have made. The precision required to write a review will force you to think through these details in much more depth than if you just read the literature and gave a brief overview in the proposal. In addition, if you write a thorough literature review and methodology section, your final project is halfway written! If you leave the review for later, you'll have a demanding writing task left to do at the end of the project. You are not likely to be highly motivated to reread all those articles that you've forgotten while you were collecting your data.

In the literature review, you should use the "funnel" approach: Start with the general literature in your topic area and gradually narrow your focus to the specific area of research and precise research question you are going to explore. After introducing the subject and reviewing relevant literature, you will lead the reader skillfully to the point at which the rationale for your specific study should seem readily apparent to any reader who stayed awake for the previous material. In the one-chapter literature review, you will place your statement of the problem, research questions, and hypotheses at the close of this chapter.

Method

Using a cookbook analogy, if your introduction has been carefully composed, the reader now knows *why* you have decided on chocolate mousse cake. Your logic and organization have been so compelling that no one would dream of selecting any other dessert. Now for the recipe! The method section can be thought of as the "how it is going be done" section of the proposal. The rule of thumb here is replicability. Your method section should provide sufficient details so that anyone reading them would be able to replicate your study in all essential aspects. In other words, the cake should come out exactly the same each time.

There are a number of fairly standard subsections that are included in the method section. The first subsection will almost always be labeled *subjects*. Subsequent sections will cover design, independent variables, measures (dependent and other), apparatus, setting, and procedures. Exactly what content you cover, and in what order, will depend on your study.

A key thing to keep in mind in writing the method section is your reader. *You* may be very clear on exactly what you are doing and how, but your reader is not. Remember, you are presenting your methodology to a reader who knows next to nothing about what you intend to do. Make sure you organize and present the material so that your reader can follow your prose clearly. It makes little sense, for example, to begin talking about your independent variables if the reader has no idea of the general design of the study.

Results

Here is the place where, ultimately, you will present the fruits of your data collection for the world to see. Start this section with an analysis subsection detailing the statistical procedures you will apply to your dependent measures. You will make statements such as "A 2 x 2 ANCOVA will be used to analyze the effects of anxiety and task complexity on errors, with GPA serving as the covariate." Indicate that you will provide appropriate tables of means and standard deviations for each of your groups on each dependent variable. If you use analyses of variance (ANOVAs) or analyses of covariance (ANCOVAs), include a summary (source) table indicating the main effects, interactions, error terms, and degrees of freedom you will use. You might present figures to show graphically the main effects and interactions that you expect to find if the study turns out exactly as you predict. Figuring this out ahead of time will help you get clear about what you are really doing and will permit you to check computer printouts later for errors. Make sure you indicate what statistical test you will use for every score you plan to analyze. Your reader should also know exactly how each variable will be scored.

A good place to look for suggestions about the type of analyses you will do is those studies closely related to the research question you are pursuing. In fact, if you have chosen wisely, you will be doing a variant of some research already in the literature and for which the analyses have been stated by others. Chapter 10 provides guidelines for matching statistics to research questions.

One way to clarify your results section for yourself and your committee is to create a full-scale mock results section. Thus, you would provide appropriate tables of means and standard deviations for each of your groups on each dependent measure. If you use multiple regression analyses, present tables showing R^2 values, beta weights, and so on. Present figures to show, graphically, the effects you might find. Show your results in the ideal form. That is, show how they will look if the study turns out exactly as your hypotheses predict. Then, show how they will look if the study is a total bust. Finally, show the most likely case, namely, a mixture of positive, negative, and confusing results. If your design calls for repeated measures on single cases or groups of participants, you should provide figures and tables appropriate to these data. If your study is descriptive and includes correlations among a number of measures, show the correlation matrixes you are likely to obtain.

You may wonder why we would include a results section in our suggestions for your thesis or dissertation proposal. After all, almost no one requires this, so why do something you don't have to do? In addition, after all, you are *proposing* to do the research. You haven't done it yet, so where are the results to include in this section?

It might help you appreciate our suggestions if you consider this section as a "mock results," or "anticipated results," or "hoped for results" section. Although not everyone would agree with the need for a results section in a proposal, we agree with Sternberg (1981) that there are very good reasons for including one. Most important, such a section forces you to think about exactly how you are going to analyze and present your data. By developing a mock results section, you will be forced to identify in advance the statistical procedures you will use. This will help you discover whether your data are likely to meet the assumptions of the various statistics, whether your data can even be analyzed to answer the questions you have posed, and what type of consultative or other resources you will need at this point in the process.

Doing this should also help you learn more about your statistics in advance of running the study. For example, if your study will require relatively complex path analyses, LISREL, or confirmatory factor analysis, you may need to prepare yourself by learning more about these procedures. You might also want to seek out software packages that will assist in, or actually do, all of the data analyses. And, you might want to find experts you could call on for occasional consultation when the data are actually available to analyze. If you have put together a mock results section early in the process, you will be aware of just what you will need, and any shortfall in resources can be overcome during the data collection phase. This will save you lots of time later on. When your data are collected, you can begin your analyses immediately and will not have to stop and decide just what you are going to do and how. Keeping the momentum going on complex, drawn-out research projects is extremely important.

Another reason for assembling a mock results section in advance of your proposal meeting is that it gives your committee a chance to see that you have planned your research thoroughly and attempted to think of every detail. It also gives them the opportunity to point out problems you might encounter. Often, mock results provide just the level of detail needed for busy committee members to understand fully exactly what you are planning to do. With this additional detail, they can identify potential snags and help you steer around them before you run into problems.

References

Include a list of the references cited in your proposal. Prepare this list using the format suggested in the APA *Publication Manual* (APA, 1994), unless your school specifies otherwise. Be sure to include only those references you actually cited. Some novice writers prepare a reference list that reflects every article they read. Although this may impress your committee and stand as a memorial to your extensive time in the library, such a list is overly inclusive. References you read but wind up not using should be deleted from the list. Once you prepare your references, you can update the list quite easily when you complete your study and you are preparing the final version of your project.

Appendixes

This is the repository of all that extra detail that might be useful to someone attempting to replicate your study in the future or that might be important to committee members to assure them that you approached your task in a competent way. Copies of instructions to subjects, consent forms, debriefing scripts, data collection instruments that are not copyrighted, construction blueprints, wiring diagrams for apparatus, and treatment manuals are examples of the kinds of entries one might expect to find in appendixes that accompany the proposal. Ordinarily, instruments copyrighted by others are not included in an appendix; if you wish to include them, you must obtain written permission to do so from the copyright holder.

Place items in appendixes in the order that the reader encounters them in the proposal. Thus, appendix A would contain a copy of the advertisement placed in the local newspaper for subject recruitment, if this is the first time the reader is referred to material in an appendix. Appendix B would contain the next such material, and so on.

Table of Contents

Once the rest of the proposal has been completed, you can produce the table of contents, right? Actually, it can be a good idea to prepare it ahead of time in the form of an outline. This can help you organize your literature review and method sections, for example. It will also help you identify and avoid problems in conceptualizing your material. Preparing the table of contents ahead of time also provides a task analysis or checklist of what needs to be done to complete the dissertation. A carefully prepared, three-level (I, II . . . , A, B . . . , 1, 2 . . .) outline or table of contents shows quite clearly just what needs to be done. As you complete the different sections, you can obtain immense satisfaction from checking off your accomplishments.

Of course, the table of contents would not have page numbers until the entire proposal is complete. In fact, the table should be regarded as a tentative outline, which can be revised as your writing proceeds. When you are ready to insert page numbers (i.e., just before submitting your proposal to your committee), be sure to assign titles to the appendixes as well. Thus, "Appendix A: Instructions to subjects . . . . p. 86" tells exactly where to go to find what the subjects are told. (Some dissertations merely indicate that appendix A begins on p. 86 without indicating what the appendix contains. This is unnecessarily shabby.) Another nice touch is to give the actual page numbers of the appendixes when referring to them in the text. Thus, ". . . were told they would receive relaxation training for 10 minutes at the start of each session (see appendix A, p. 86)" is much more helpful to the reader than ". . . (see appendix A)."

Exhibit 6.1 presents a copy of the table of contents for the final version of a dissertation one of us chaired. By studying it carefully, you will know the components of a good dissertation proposal (and a good

Exhibit 6.1

Sample Dissertation Table of Contents

Acknowledgments ii
Table of Contents iv
List of Tables vii
Dedication ix

1. Introduction and literature review 1
   1.1 Father involvement in parent training 2
   1.2 Father–child interaction 7
       a. Interaction patterns 7
       b. Father involvement in child management 9
   1.3 Influence of father–mother relationship on child behavior 11
       a. Role of social support 12
       b. Role of marital conflict: Overview 15
       c. Role of marital conflict: Poor problem solving 18
       d. Role of marital conflict: Poor modeling 22
       e. Role of marital conflict: Disruption of child management 23
   1.4 Summary and conclusions 26
   1.5 Statement of purpose 28

2. Method 33
   2.1 Subjects 33
       a. Criteria for inclusion in study 33
       b. Recruitment of subjects 35
       c. Characteristics of subject population 38
   2.2 Procedures and measures 44
       a. Referral process 44
       b. Phase 1 – Questionnaire measures 45
       c. Phase 2 – Direct observation procedures and family interaction
          patterns 48
       d. Observational coding systems 53
       e. Phase 3 – Daily home recordings 70

3. Results 75
   3.1 Parent–child interaction data 75
   3.2 Daily shared activity records 79
   3.3 Parent problem-solving interactions 81
   3.4 Mother–father interactions during triadic play situations 84

4. Discussion 88
   4.1 Quality of father–child interactions 88
   4.2 Quantity of father–child interactions 95
   4.3 Interparental discussion of child behavior problems 98
   4.4 Mother–father interactions during play situation 103
   4.5 Methodological issues 105
   4.6 Summary 108

5. References 112

continued

Exhibit 6.1, continued

6. Appendixes 121
   6.1 Appendix A: Parent consent forms. 121
   6.2 Appendix B: Child assent form and child assent statement. 130
   6.3 Appendix C: Demographic information form 133
   6.4 Appendix D: Behavior categories and definitions for the modified   137
       Behavioral Coding System . . . .
   6.5 Appendix E: List and definitions for the Marital Interaction   143
       Coding System . . . .
   6.6 Appendix F: Modified Marital Interaction Coding System 146
   6.7 Appendix G: Daily Shared Activity Record 151

7. Abstract 155

8. Vita 157

Note. From *Paternal and Marital Factors Related to Child Conduct Problems* by V. V. Wolfe, 1986, Doctoral dissertation, West Virginia University. Reprinted by permission of the author.

dissertation, generally). Studying the tables of contents of theses and dissertations your chairperson recommends as models will show you alternate ways of organizing a proposal. Note that acknowledgement and dedication sections are usually added to the document after the committee has approved the final write-up.

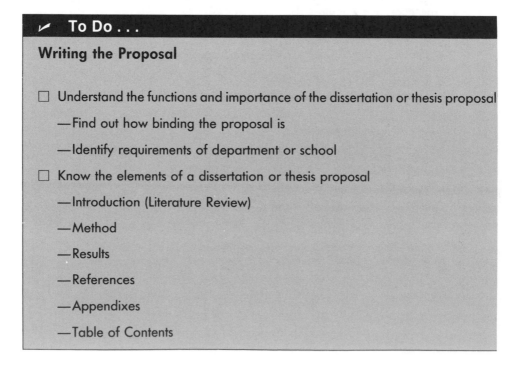

To Do . . .

Writing the Proposal

☐ Understand the functions and importance of the dissertation or thesis proposal

   —Find out how binding the proposal is

   —Identify requirements of department or school

☐ Know the elements of a dissertation or thesis proposal

   —Introduction (Literature Review)

   —Method

   —Results

   —References

   —Appendixes

   —Table of Contents

7

Reviewing the Literature

After you find a topic, you must learn more about it. This involves finding, reading, and summarizing (in written form) the relevant professional literature on your topic. Reading and thinking about what others have done and said will teach you about key conceptual and methodological issues in the field. This process will also allow you to see whether another enterprising individual has already done your study. A related benefit is that you can spend hours avoiding writing anything at all by sitting in an armchair and reading.

Locate Relevant Literature

Literature relevant to your research comes in three major forms: books, book chapters, and published journal articles. Conference papers and unpublished theses and doctoral dissertations may also be relevant to examine. Several old-fashioned and some more technologically sophisticated methods provide vehicles for locating relevant literature. Although none of these is perfect, using *all* of them together will ensure a reasonably comprehensive literature search.

Identify Key Authors and Journals

A good initial step in compiling relevant literature is to locate key players in your research area and their favorite publication outlets. Who are the Big Names? What journals regularly publish their work? Others who know the area better than you are good sources of this information (e.g., your chairperson and committee members).

A second excellent source is the bibliography of a recent book or chapter on your topic. Scan the references to locate relevant articles and to find out who's working in your area. Read the book or chapter to orient yourself to key issues and concepts in the field.

As we scan bibliographies for relevant articles, we like to copy complete references (in APA style) onto index cards (one reference per card) or into a computer file. These can be used to locate the actual articles or books in the library. Cards can be inserted into journals or books to mark pages for photocopying and taking notes. Later on, they can be put in alphabetical order and typed (or printed out) to form your bibliography, saving trips back to the library to relocate page numbers, author initials, and the like. Whatever your referencing system, be sure to check the accuracy of each entry as you look up the article—not all citations in published articles and chapters are accurate.

Use Bibliographic Reference Sources

Various reference sources can assist you with your literature search. *Psychological Abstracts*, for example, contains abbreviated abstracts from psychological journals and indexes these abstracts by topic and author. *Dissertation Abstracts International* is a similar reference source for dissertations, as is *PsycBOOKS* for books and chapters in books. The Educational Resources Information Center (ERIC) is a major clearinghouse for information related to education. *Current Contents* is a periodical that lists tables of contents of recent journals and indicates to whom one can write for reprints. Finally, the American Psychological Association publishes a series of topical *PsycSCANS*, each of which provides abstracts of journal publications in related fields. For example, *Developmental PsycSCAN* covers journals related to child development. Although *Current Contents* and *PsycSCAN* are not always found in libraries, faculty may subscribe to them and let you borrow their copies. Cooper (1989) describes many of these in more detail and provides an overview of how to use several of these reference sources.

One underutilized reference source bears special mention. The *Social Sciences Citation Index* (*SSCI*) allows you to look up who has cited a particular article since its publication. To use it, you must know the citation for the original article. *SSCI* is very useful when you wish to ascertain what has been done since a seminal piece of work was published: You can track the influence of an article through time and will often find references that computerized literature searches may not locate. *SSCI* is also helpful for locating research containing information about the psychometric properties of measurement devices you might decide to use: Most users of a device cite the original or seminal article on the measurement tool. Read the instructions carefully and ask a reference librarian to help you the first time you use this source; most people find it hard to master *SSCI* without instructions.

Published bibliographies of references in specific areas within or outside psychology may also prove useful. Librarians in major university libraries should be able to help you locate pertinent bibliographies.

Use Computerized Literature Searches

Computers provide valuable ways of searching literature quickly. To use these resources well, you will have to learn how to execute searches. Although search programs differ in their mechanics, most have similar characteristics. First, you must locate *keywords* or *search terms*: words or phrases that you think describe the contents of the papers. You then tell the computer what these are and where to look for them, whether in the abstract, title, or body of the paper, or in the descriptors that the author or indexer applied to the paper (where the computer looks for the key words depends on the particular computer program). Authors' names and journal names can also be used as keywords. In addition, you can tell the computer to search for abstracts that contain more than one keyword (usually you list the ones you want, connected by the word *and*. The computer then lists abstracts that contain all the words you have listed). Alternatively, you can use *or* to instruct the computer to pick out papers that contain any one (not all) of the keywords connected by *or*. You can scan results of searches on the computer screen, print them, and (sometimes) download them to hard or floppy disk.

Finding the right keywords is the key to a successful computer search. This is by no means easy; not all investigators use the same jargon to describe their studies. In addition, some programs have professional indexers select the terms by which the article will be indexed. One excellent way to locate good keywords is to find some articles in your area and look in their abstracts. Words that show up frequently are good candidates as keywords. In addition, some journals list descriptors by which the study will be indexed.

A trap with computerized searches is to believe you have done an exhaustive literature search this way. The problem is that the search is only as good as (a) your keywords; (b) the extent to which writers (and indexers) in the field use the same words in their titles, abstracts, and so on; (c) the range of journals the database contains; and (d) the number of years covered by the database. These limitations lead us to recommend that computer searches be supplemented with other methods described in this chapter.

Probably the most useful widely available computerized databases in psychology are *PsycLIT* and *PsycINFO*. Both are versions of *Psychological Abstracts* (*PsycLIT* is a compact disc version of the *PsycINFO* on-line database), and both incorporate information from *PsycBOOKS*. A user-friendly tutorial guides the unfamiliar user of *PsycLIT* through the options the program provides for searching the literature. One especially useful feature is a thesaurus of terms, which allows you to look at terms related to the keywords you select and may give you ideas about topics that relate to your project but that had not occurred to you. You can also consult the thesaurus for more inclusive or more specific categories associated with your keywords. Appendix B provides a list of some additional widely used computerized literature databases, as does an informative volume on library use in psychology by Reed and Baxter (1992).

Before moving on, we should mention a service that is rapidly becoming one of the most useful computerized bibliographic databases in the world. This service, known as *UnCover* is available through the Colorado Alliance of Research Libraries (CARL Systems Inc.; see appendix B) and contains records describing the content of over 10,000 journals. Nearly 2,000,000 articles are included, and more than 600,000 are added annually. *UnCover 2* now permits users to order copies of complete articles and charge them to major credit cards. Articles can be transmitted through your fax machine within 24 hours.

Write for Reprints and Preprints

Once you have identified key contributors in your area, write or telephone them and request reprints. Authors ordinarily provide copies of journal articles for the asking, although some will ask that you pay for photocopying and postage. Also ask for chapters, which you may not find as readily as journal articles, for preprints (articles that are submitted or accepted for publication), and for conference presentations. Although not everyone will send reprints of chapters, preprints, and presentations, if you get them, you'll find out what's about to published. Check the author's current address in the directories of the American Psychological Association or the American Psychological Society (available in many school or departmental libraries, or in psychology department chairpersons' offices) or in the most recent directory of a professional organization to which the person belongs (e.g., Society for Research in Child Development). A telephone call may be more effective than a letter at prompting a quick response: It's harder to forget or ignore a request from a person with whom you have spoken than from a letter in a low-priority stack of correspondence.

As Yates (1982) points out, you can also look in convention programs to find titles of papers that were presented in your area. Many of these studies will be published over the next few years, and locating these studies will help you find out what is in the publication pipeline.

Look At Literature From Other Disciplines

Psychological Abstracts, PsycLIT, and other resources are limited by the journals they include. Your research area may overlap with other disciplines. Medicine, communications, education, and sociology all have journals that publish articles relevant to some areas of psychology. Many disciplines have printed abstract services like *Psychological Abstracts* and should be consulted if your research area is addressed by more than one discipline. They also have computerized databases you can access.

Scan the Tables of Contents of Key Journals

As you become familiar with your topic area, identify the journals in which most articles in your area have been published. Then, look at their tables of contents (usually listed by author at the end of the last issue of each volume) for the last 10 years. This will help you find articles that may be too recent to be in reference and bibliographic materials, and it will serve as a double check on the yields provided by your other methods.

Use Reference Lists

As you scan relevant articles, look at their bibliographies and note relevant references. This is an invaluable source of references your other sources may not have turned up.

Cooper (1989) points out a trap with using both the key journals and the reference scanning approaches. Most researchers in a particular area, Cooper says, have informal interpersonal and journal networks. Thus, they tend to publish in and cite articles from their journal network, leading to overrepresentation of articles in journals inside the network and undercitation of articles in journals outside the network. This is yet another reason for using multiple methods to conduct a comprehensive literature search in your area.

Use Primary Sources

Do not rely on others' descriptions of studies and their findings, often referred to as *secondary sources*. Look up the original articles and read them yourself. Reviewers too often cite studies erroneously, indicating the authors said something they did not say or did something they did not do. We know—our own work has actually been cited to support points that opposed the very stand we were taking in the article being cited! In addition, you may not agree with others' conclusions about the paper. Now is the time to stand on your own intellectual feet and draw your own conclusions.

If you cannot find the original article because it is in an out-of-the-way journal or was presented at a conference but not published, do not cite the article as though you actually read it. Instead, follow APA guidelines to indicate citation of a secondary source (e.g., "Foster, 1985, cited in Cone, 1989").

Avoid the Popular Press

Although *Time* magazine, the *New York Times*, *Glamour*, and similar sources may be excellent ways of gaining daily knowledge of what is happening in the world, they are no substitute for scholarly articles in peer-reviewed journals. Although the information in popular periodicals may be accurate, you cannot evaluate it as you can a journal article in which the methodology used to collect and analyze the data is delineated clearly, for all to critique.

Your search is over when you have done all of the above and keep turning up the same articles, over and over, as you look at others' reference lists and bibliographic sources. This may not mean you have collected everything ever written on a topic, but you have probably found the major articles produced in the area.

Critically Read What You Found

As you are collecting your literature, read it critically. Remember, you are going to synthesize this information into a coherent review that highlights the main themes, strengths, and weaknesses of the work. To do that, you need to get a sense of the forest as well as the trees. Start thinking about how you will organize this literature in a literature review: Look for themes and commonalities in the methodologies and conceptual frameworks authors use. In addition, you probably will not cite every article you read. Which material is most relevant to your study, and which is more tangential? Which topics will you really need to cover, and which can you skip?

Pay attention to unanswered questions and methodological strengths and weakness of studies you peruse, and keep notes on these. These will come in handy as you write the review. Exhibit 7.1 provides a list of questions you can use to evaluate empirical studies.

With empirical articles, read the rationale for the study, the method, and the results sections most carefully—*not* the conclusions. You should be able to figure out the conclusions for yourself; you can then check whether you agree with the authors about what they said they found. Don't be surprised if you think the findings have implications the authors do not discuss or if you think the authors overplay some of their findings. Write down your observations to keep a record of them. If these observations characterize much of the literature, they may lead you to some major insights about your topic.

You will end this process with pages and pages of photocopied articles and chapters or—if you can't afford to make copies—with pages and pages of notes taken from articles and chapters. We recommend the former, despite the expense, mainly because you never know when you'll have to go back to an article to seek a detail you failed to write down in your notes. And, if you plan to continue research in the area, photocopies provide a good beginning library you will use again and again.

If you go the note route, be sure to include complete details on the methodology in your notes: Details that do not seem important now may become important later as you try to reconcile discrepant findings and search out potential confounds in others' procedures. One idea is to develop a list of information that you will note about every article you read (e.g., number and characteristics of subjects, independent variables, etc.). You can even systematize this into a prepared "control sheet" on which to record specific details from each study. For example, one of us once reviewed the behavioral parent-training literature using the form in Exhibit 7.2. This kind of systematic approach makes it less likely that you will forget to record certain details of a particular paper that you

Exhibit 7.1

Guidelines for Evaluating Empirical Studies

Introduction

1. Does the introduction provide a strong rationale for why the study is needed?
2. Are research questions and hypotheses clearly articulated? (Note that research questions are often presented implicitly within a description of the purpose of the study.)

Method

1. Is the method described so that replication is possible without further information?
2. Subjects
    (a) Are subject recruitment and selection methods described?
    (b) Were subjects randomly selected? Are there any probable biases in sampling?
    (c) Is the sample appropriate in terms of the population to which the researcher wished to generalize?
    (d) Are characteristics of the sample described adequately?
    (e) If two or more groups are being compared, are they shown to be comparable on potentially confounding variables (e.g., demographics)? If they are not comparable, is this handled appropriately?
    (f) Was informed consent obtained?
    (g) Was the size of the sample large enough for the number of measures and for the effect being sought?
3. Design
    (a) If appropriate, was a control group used?
    (b) Was the control appropriate?
    (c) What was being controlled for?
    (d) If an experimental study, were subjects randomly assigned to groups?
4. Measures
    (a) For all measures (measures used to classify subjects, dependent variables, etc.), did the authors provide evidence of reliability and validity, either by summarizing data or by referring the reader to an available source that provides the information?
    (b) Do the reliability and validity data justify the use of the measure? Specific evidence is particularly important if a measure is created just for this study.
    (c) Do the measures match the research questions and hypotheses being addressed?
    (d) If different tasks or measures are used, was their order counterbalanced? Do the authors analyze for potential order effects?

continued

Exhibit 7.1, continued

(e) Are multiple measures used, particularly those that sample the same domains or constructs but with different methods (e.g., self-report, ratings by others, self-monitoring, or direct observation)?

(f) If human observers, judges, or raters were involved, was interobserver or interrater agreement (reliability) assessed? Was it obtained for a representative sample of the data? Did the two raters do their ratings independently? Was their reliability satisfactory?

5. Bias and Artifacts

(a) Was administration and scoring of the measures done blindly (i.e., by someone who was unaware of experimental hypotheses)?

(b) If a quasi-experimental study, do the authors include appropriate steps to rule out competing explanations of the findings?

(c) Were procedures constant across subjects in all groups? Were any confounds introduced through use of different procedures? How troublesome are these?

6. Independent variables

(a) If an experimental study, was there a check that the independent variable was manipulated as described?

(b) If an intervention study, did a sufficient sample of therapists or change agents implement the intervention (i.e., to enhance generalizability)?

(c) If more than one treatment or condition are being compared, did the authors document that these conditions differ in ways they are supposed to differ? Are they the same in every other way (e.g., length, qualifications of therapists or change agents)? If not, is this confound likely to influence the conclusions seriously?

(d) What aspects of the procedures and independent variables limit the external validity of the study?

Results

1. Do the data fulfill the assumptions and requirements of the statistics (e.g., homogeneity of variance for repeated-measures analyses of variance)?

2. Were tests of significance used and reported appropriately (i.e., with sufficient detail to understand what analysis was being conducted)?

3. In correlational studies, did the authors interpret low but significant correlations as though they indicated a great deal of shared variance between the measures? Are the correlations limited by restricted ranges on one or more measures? Do the authors provide means and standard deviations so that you can determine this?

4. If there were a large number of statistical tests performed, do the authors adjust the alpha level or use appropriate multivariate techniques to reduce the probability of Type I error that could be due to the large number of tests performed?

continued

Exhibit 7.1, continued

5. Do the authors report means and standard deviations (if relevant) so that the reader can examine whether statistically significant differences are large enough to be meaningful?
6. For multivariate statistics, is there an appropriately large ratio of subjects to variables (at least 7 for every dependent variable used in an analysis)?

Discussion

1. Do the authors discuss marginally significant or nonsignificant results as though they were significant?
2. Do the authors overinterpret the data (e.g., use causal language to integrate correlational findings or interpret self-report of behavior as equivalent to direct observation)?
3. Do the authors consider alternative explanations for the findings?
4. Do the authors have a "humility" section that mentions the limitations of the research (including methodological problems)? Do the authors point out aspects of subject selection, procedures, and dependent variables that limit the generalizability of the findings?
5. Do the authors "accept" the null hypothesis?

Note. From "A Reader's, Writer's, and Reviewer's Guide to Assessing Research Reports in Clinical Psychology" by B. A. Maher, 1978, *Journal of Consulting and Clinical Psychology, 46,* pp. 835–838. Copyright 1987 by the American Psychological Association. Adapted by permission.

need later (Cooper, 1989, provides an extended discussion of control ["coding"] sheets).

If you copy someone's words into your notes, *put them in quotation marks.* It is easy to forget later which notes you wrote in your own words and which were quotes or close paraphrases. Even if you do it by accident, using others' words without appropriate citation is plagiarism. We discuss this topic again at the end of this chapter.

Finally, avoid the trap of overreading, a popular procrastination strategy. Memorizing or taking copious notes on every article published in your area is not necessary before starting to write your review. Experience suggests that you may need to read the literature at least twice, but in different ways. You will review it the first time to learn about the key issues in the field and to decide what material is relevant and how to organize it. You will consult selected articles and chapters again as you write the review and realize that you need to know more about what particular authors did and found. Expect this focused rereading once you begin to put your ideas on paper.

Exhibit 7.2

Sample Control Sheet for Recording Information from Research Article

Author(s): _____

Title: _____

Source: _____

Availability: _____ on file _____ requested _____ unavailable

Type of Study: _____ single family _____ multiple family

Problem Behavior(s): _____

_____

Number of children directly involved: _____

Type of dependent measure and on whom taken: _____

_____

Observation of behavior by Experimenter (E): _____ yes _____ no

Locus of Observation by Experimenter (E): _____ home _____ clinic

_____ lab _____ residential facility _____ school

Number of therapy (training) sessions: _____

Design: _____ case study, no measurement

_____ case study with measurement: _____ pre _____ during

_____ post

_____ time series (O O O X O O O)

_____ equivalent time samples: _____ A-B _____ A-B-A

_____ A-B-A-B _____ $A-B_1-A-B_2$ _____ $A-B_1-B_2$

_____ B-A-B _____ other: _____

_____ multiple baseline (sequential) design

_____ single group, no measurement

_____ single group with measurement: _____ pre _____ during

_____ post

_____ single group time series (O O O X O O O)

_____ single group, equivalent time samples: _____ A-B _____ A-B-A

_____ A-B-A-B _____ $A-B_1-A-B_2$ _____ B-A-B

_____ other: _____

_____ two-group classic (experimental vs. control)

_____ more than two groups: control, treatment, and other treatment comparisons

_____ two or more groups: other treatment comparisons, no untreated controls

_____ factorial design

_____ other: _____

Follow-up: _____ yes _____ no _____ unclear _____

amount of time since termination mode _____

Comments:

Get Ready to Write

Before you start to write, get one feature of your written thesis or dissertation clearly in mind. *You are not writing for yourself.* You are writing for an audience. *You* know what you know, but your committee members cannot see directly into your brain. Nor do most of them know the literature as well as you do; some may be completely unfamiliar with the topic. Thus, your job in writing the literature review is to educate your committee about the topic. In so doing, you can also convince them that you are a competent researcher: Show them that you have integrated the material you read and that you have evaluated the quality of the information. After finishing your literature review, committee members should understand the research questions, procedures, and findings that characterize the field. They should also know the weaknesses of past studies and what needs to be done to move the field forward. By the time they read your final sections, the rationale for your research question should be obvious, as should ways you are attempting to improve on past methods, designs, and procedures. If you have organized the review skillfully, you will have led the reader to the conclusion that the absolutely best next study to be done in the area is the one you are proposing.

Investigate Length and Format Parameters

Before you put pen to paper or fingers to keyboard, find out the local norms for reviews of the literature in projects like yours. These vary widely across schools, and it is important to know the parameters of what you are writing before you begin. Chapter 6 described differences between the one- and two-chapter models for presenting this material—important format distinctions that will influence how you organize your material.

Literature reviews vary considerably in length as well as format. Ask your chairperson how long and how comprehensive the literature review is expected to be: This determines how you define the scope of what you cover. Note that we tell you to *ask your chairperson* rather than looking at others' literature reviews. This is because, as paradoxical as it may seem, it is easier to write excessively long reviews than to limit their scope and be concise. Thus, faculty often complain in private about 40- to 50-page (and longer!) literature reviews but let students keep producing them, when 20 to 25 pages would suffice to demonstrate the student's skill at synthesizing a body of literature. Personally, we prefer briefer, more focused reviews to lengthy treatises that try to cover everything and do so poorly. An added advantage of shorter reviews lies in their potential for publication: Many journals will not accept over 25 to 30 pages of text, so you might as well get used to being succinct.

Make a Preliminary Outline

To get an idea of what you want to cover and how, make an outline of the major headings you plan to use in your literature review. Next to each, indicate the approximate number of pages you plan to allocate to each section. Exhibit 7.3 shows one student's working outline for a literature review for a dissertation studying the relationship between ethnicity, gender, and types of strategies older elementary school children use to manage conflicts with their peers. This outline is fairly typical in terms of the section page allocations we recommend for a one-chapter literature review of about 25 pages. But because norms and preferences can vary so widely, be sure to ask your chairperson for feedback about your organization and page allocations.

Note that the outline in Exhibit 7.3 follows the funnel approach we described in chapter 6. It begins with the general context and becomes more and more specific, ultimately focusing on specific criticisms of existing studies and leading to the specific rationale for the study being proposed.

A preliminary outline will let you see how long your chapter will be if you write it as planned and whether you need to limit or expand your scope. In addition, making an outline often reduces the anxiety and procrastination associated with the seemingly amorphous and enormous task of writing a literature review. Look at your page allocations and remember that all you are really doing is writing a series of 5- to 10-page papers (the subsections of your review) with a lot of transitions to connect them. How many 5- to 10-page papers have you knocked off in graduate school? These are just more of the same.

Don't be surprised if your outline changes as you write the review. The author of the outline just presented, for example, had to cut one section ("toddlers") because she had a great deal more than two pages of material about ethnicity. Think of your outline as a way of helping you get started and organize your material, but be flexible about altering it as you begin to write.

Limit the Scope of Your Review

After putting page numbers on your outline you may wonder, "How can I get all that information into only 25 pages?" If this is your problem,

---

Exhibit 7.3

Literature Review Outline and Page Allocations

Dissertation topic: Relationship of ethnicity and gender to type of conflict resolution strategy and peer conflict outcome in 9- to 12-year-old children

Outline
  I. Introduction (2–3 pages)
     A. Historical context of peer conflict research
     B. Importance of conflict in development
     C. Definition of conflict

  II. Toddlers (ages 6 months–3 years; 2 pages)
     A. Issues of conflict
     B. Resolution strategies

  III. Preschoolers (ages 3–5 years; 5 pages)
     A. Incidence and duration of conflicts
     B. Issues of conflict
     C. Resolution strategies
     D. Outcome
     E. Gender differences

  IV. Early childhood (ages 5–9 years; 5 pages)
     A. Incidence and duration of conflicts
     B. Issues of conflict
     C. Resolution strategies
     D. Outcome
     E. Gender differences

  V. Late childhood (ages 9–12 years; 2 pages)
     A. Goals
     B. Strategies

  VI. Ethnicity (2 pages)
     A. Cooperation/competition research
     B. Conflict resolution styles

  VII. Summary and critique (3–5 pages)
  VIII. Statement of the problem and hypotheses

Note. Outline prepared by Avid Khorram, California School of Professional Psychology, San Diego, December 1991. Reproduced by permission of the author.

chances are you are making two mistakes. First, you may think you must cite everything you read and cover everything related to the topic: history, theory, old research, new research, speculations, anecdotal evidence, and so on. Wrong! You need to *know* all that information and be able to answer questions about it, but you do not need to demonstrate that knowledge in writing for the committee. An evaluation of the current state of the field should suffice.

A second, related mistake lies in not limiting explicitly the scope of what you will write about. Although you do not need to cite every article you read, you *do* need decision rules for what you include and what you leave out. "I like this study" and "I didn't understand the statistics in this one" are not good reasons. Limiting the literature to a particular group of subjects (e.g., by age, race, gender, or other characteristic relevant to the study you are proposing), by type or quality of design (e.g., only controlled studies), or by independent or dependent variables may be appropriate, depending on the literature you are reviewing. State your criteria for inclusion very specifically and as far in advance of writing as you can, to avoid allowing personal biases (e.g., "I just didn't like this one") to sneak into your selections (Cooper, 1989). Be sure to write these criteria into the introduction to your literature review, too.

As an example, Julie planned a study to evaluate a program to teach children to deal effectively with peer provocation. She amassed huge literatures on peer rejection and its correlates, social-skills training programs, and generalization of behavior change from skill-training programs to the natural environment. After some thought and discussion, she realized that very few social skills studies addressed peer provocation problems directly, that much of the literature on correlates of rejection was tangential to her project, and that the conclusions of the literature on generalization should be incorporated into her review of why certain studies failed, rather than being reviewed study by study. Most of her 25 pages would be devoted to reviewing studies that attempted to teach social skills to intellectually normal children with identified excesses in negative behavior. The rest of the literature would be mentioned in passing, if at all. By limiting the populations and the topics she would cover, writing the review became far more manageable.

Lisa, another student, encountered a different problem. She was interested in the effects of therapist self-disclosure on adolescent involvement in therapy. She found large literatures on self-disclosure in therapy with adults, on self-disclosure in personal relationships (adults and adolescents), on the effects of different kinds of therapy for adolescents, and theoretical writings on the effects of self-disclosure in personal relationships. She found very little, however, that was specific to her topic. What should she include in her literature review? Lisa decided that she needed to review the literature on self-disclosure in adult therapy to justify her independent variable and highlight the innovations in her methodology. She also needed to review the role of self-disclosure in adolescents' personal relationships to make a case for why self-disclosure might play a useful role in therapy. She did not need to review the theoretical literature, adolescent treatment outcome studies, or the adult interpersonal relationships literature, although she might integrate key points from these literatures as they contributed to her analysis of the two areas of research she would cover in depth.

Organize the Literature

Making an outline requires that you organize and synthesize material from all those articles, chapters, and books—something you should also have been thinking about as you read those materials. You can group the literature into manageable, coherent subgroupings in several ways. Below we list some of the most common.

1. Cover studies that examine *related independent variables* together. If, for example, you are reviewing different strategies for enhancing organizational effectiveness, grouping them by types of strategies may provide a good, easy-to-follow framework.

2. Organize your studies by examining *related dependent variables* together. If you are looking at the characteristics of adult children of alcoholics, for example, you could review studies examining personality, then those examining drinking patterns, then those examining relationship skills, and so on. Alternatively, you could group findings on this population by *assessment method*: self-report, ratings by others, direct observation, and so on.

3. Organize by *type of design*. Ordinarily, this kind of coverage begins with weaker and then progresses to stronger designs. Thus, present uncontrolled case studies before controlled designs, correlational studies before experimental, and cross-sectional before longitudinal. Paul's (1969) classic chapter describing research on systematic desensitization exemplifies this organizational strategy.

4. Organize around *theoretical premises*. This method is useful if your study tests competing explanations of a phenomenon or if different theoretical threads all lead to the formulation of your research question. For example, Wolfe (1986) studied fathers' interactions in families with conduct-disordered and non-conduct-disordered children. She organized her literature review around the ways in which fathers could influence the etiology and maintenance of children's disruptive behavior, from a social learning perspective (see Exhibit 6.1 [p. 89] for the major sections of her literature review).

These strategies describe only a few of the many ways of organizing literature. Select an organizational framework that highlights important aspects of the literature, particularly ones you wish to address or improve on in your study. For example, suppose your study improves over past research by using direct observation instead of self-report methods. By presenting findings and studies according to the methods used to assess the dependent variables, you may clearly show the reader the absence of research using direct observation. Remember the funnel: Work from the general to the specific.

Start Writing

You are now ready to put pen to paper or fingers to keyboard. Organize your notes or photocopies, pull out your outline, and write individual sections of the review.

Beware of writer's block at this point. This malady affects many students, even those who regularly produce literature reviews with little difficulty for class assignments. Sometimes this block results from the mistaken assumption that your review must be perfect. All relevant studies must be cited and all insights must be brilliant before you dare hand a draft of your review to your chairperson, says this unrealistic self-talk.

Not so. Most students hand in and revise several drafts of their literature reviews before they are finished. No matter how polished your prose, your chairperson will have suggestions and expects that the first draft will need work. Everyone's first draft needs work. Because it is impossible for your draft to be perfect, give yourself permission for your work to be improvable. Remember, this is a learning experience. If your manuscript were without flaw on the first try, there would be nothing left for you to learn.

A second difficulty students sometimes encounter when they begin to write results from their mistaken assumption that they must start at the beginning, write the introduction, and then proceed sequentially. They then sit before the page or the computer for hours as the words to begin the document elude them.

If you find it hard to start with the introduction, start with a section that comes more easily. If paragraphs don't come easily, write the ideas you want to cover first and then build paragraphs around them. If you can't figure out good transitions between studies, describe the studies first and write the transitions later. The key is to write whatever you can, because tasks that seem impossible one day may be much easier at a later point. Getting started is more important than completing sections one by one in a specified order. And remember, revising your words is easier than writing the words in the first place. Write something, anything—then polish it later.

In addition, several of the ideas we mentioned in chapter 4 may be useful here. If you encounter problems getting started, set very small goals. Set *product* rather than *process* goals. A product goal indicates what you must accomplish: "Write one page." A process goal indicates what you must do, but not the end product: "Work on dissertation for 2 hours." To accomplish the latter goal, all you have to do is stare at your computer, not actually produce anything! Small product goals help you see progress and work more efficiently.

You can also reward accomplishing small product goals with small rewards. Remember the Premack principle: Any behavior that is higher in probability than writing your dissertation or thesis can serve as a reward. For many writers, that's almost anything! In writing this book, for example, we often said to ourselves, "I'll get a cup of coffee after I finish three pages," "I'll read that magazine after I type this table," or "I'll call my friend after I edit this chapter." These examples show that rewards need not be expensive or time consuming to be motivating.

Write the Introduction

Begin your literature review with a brief introduction. The introduction should do just that—introduce and make a brief pitch for the topic, introduce key concepts and terms, and describe the scope and organization of the review. A brief introduction occupies about 3 pages in a 25-page literature review.

A good way to end the introduction is with a paragraph that lays out the scope of the literature review. Sometimes referred to as an *advance organizer*, this material should describe both the literature you will cover and the sequence the reader can expect to follow. In addition, if you omit studies to keep the length of your review manageable, let the reader know your criteria for inclusion or exclusion and why you selected them. For example, suppose a whole group of studies on your topic area was later found to have a particular methodological problem, and you do not think you have the space to cover these studies. The final paragraph of your introduction could say,

> The remainder of the chapter that follows critically reviews contemporary literature regarding _____ . Early studies in the area (e.g., _____) generally concluded that _____ . As _____

and _____ (1989) pointed out, however, these studies all failed to distinguish between _____ and _____, and thus, their conclusions are suspect. Later studies have corrected this flaw, and will be the focus of the review that follows. Initial sections discuss _____, _____, and _____. The review concludes with a summary and critique of existing literature, followed by a discussion of the specific research question and hypotheses suggested by the review and examined in this thesis (dissertation).

Write the Subsections of Your Literature Review

After the introduction will come subsections that review and synthesize the literature. These subsections can follow various formats. Perhaps the easiest is to provide an introduction to the section, then to describe relevant studies one by one, grouping related studies together. Provide comparable information for each study: subjects, independent variables, dependent variables, design, findings, and noteworthy details (e.g., methodological problems). Then go on to the next. Pull the material together with a summary and overall critique at the end of the subsection.

This one-by-one method requires considerable skill to keep it from being incredibly boring and reading like a series of index cards typed up one after the other. Liberal use of transitions helps. In addition, brief comparisons of methods and findings help link studies together and highlight their progression as well as similarities and differences among them. A study-by-study literature review by Inderbitzen-Pisaruk and Foster (1990) illustrates the use of these kinds of phrases. Here, we remove the content of the paragraphs, reprinting only transitional and integrative phrasing from a brief portion of the review (note, however, that despite our best efforts, one reviewer who examined this paper when it was first submitted criticized it for being too much like an annotated bibliography!):

> Kuhlen and Bretsch . . . [description of study]. . . .
> In a study that more clearly specified behaviors necessary for. . . .
> Unfortunately, these two studies are dated, and therefore. . . .
> In addition, both. . . . This leads to uncertainty about whether. . . .
> This [uncertainty] has been addressed in more recent studies. Interestingly, despite changes in adolescent culture over the past four decades, [results] have supported those of [study just described]. For example, ... (Inderbitzen-Pisaruk & Foster, 1990, pp. 426–427)

A second method of organizing subsections of a literature review groups weaker studies or studies that share similar methods, reviews them only briefly, and devotes greater attention to seminal, prototypical, or stronger studies. With this method, a section might begin with a few paragraphs overviewing a large number of studies, their findings, and the strengths and weaknesses they share as a group. Later paragraphs devote greater individual attention to more important studies.

A third way of reviewing the literature organizes studies by their findings. This type of review contains less description of individual studies than those presented previously. Instead, the writer uses findings to support the logical series of points developed in the review. This is the most difficult type of review to write, because you must develop your points logically and use literature in an even-handed way to consider the support (pro and con) for your ideas. This multifaceted consideration of the literature may be most appropriate when your study will pit different theoretical explanations against one another or when your selection of variables is guided more by theory than by atheoretical empirical findings.

The three methods of writing a literature review just described all involve qualitative synthesis of the literature. A fourth alternative is more quantitative and involves systematically scoring particular studies for particular characteristics and/or conducting a meta-analysis. With a meta-analysis, results of studies that investigated the same issue are grouped statistically to evaluate the characteristics of the group of studies as a whole. Although meta-analyses appear frequently in review journals, they are unusual in thesis and dissertation literature reviews, and thus we do not cover them here other than to mention the approach. Cooper (1989) and Hunter and Schmidt (1990) describe meta-analytic procedures concisely but in good detail.

Synthesize and Critically Analyze the Literature

Novice literature reviewers often provide excessive description coupled with inadequate critical analysis. Do not simply describe what you read. Instead, synthesize the literature. What patterns do you see in investigators' findings? Are findings consistent? If not, why not? Consider potential explanations, including methodological, design, and population differences among studies, and assumptions that may be erroneous about how the independent variables operate or relate to the dependent variables. By the end of your literature review, your reader should have a good idea of the patterns of findings and methods that characterize your area.

In addition, you should evaluate the literature critically. Which studies are best, and why? Which studies are worst, and why? Consider methodological as well as conceptual strengths and weaknesses. Remember the checklist in Exhibit 7.1. Just because something gets published does not mean it is free of methodological problems. Help the reader see the methodological issues that future studies in your area should address. Highlight topics that merit further study. If you kept a record of problems and issues as you read the literature, consult it for ideas about what to say.

Use a professional tone in criticizing others' work. Obviously, you will not want to trash your chairperson's work. Less obvious is the fact that you should not overstate your criticisms of others who think differently than you. Ad hominem criticisms (criticizing the *person* rather than the *work*) are never appropriate. Be evenhanded, and remember that all research has strengths as well as weaknesses.

Your synthesis and analysis of the literature should pave the way for your study. By the time your reader finishes the bulk of the literature review, the rationale for what you propose (your questions) and why you propose to do it a certain way (your method) should be obvious. Thus, your synthesis should highlight important unanswered questions (i.e., the ones you are proposing to examine). Similarly, your critique should emphasize methodological problems with past studies you plan to correct with your study.

You can integrate statements that synthesize and evaluate the literature into the review in several ways. First, use integrative transition sentences and phrases to help readers see patterns as they read the document. For example, note how the following paragraph introduction ties a group of studies together and highlights major similarities and differences with the study about to be discussed:

> Although most studies described thus far used correlational designs, Smith and Jones (1988) explored the issue of _____ with an experimental design. Their findings were remarkably similar to those of previous correlational studies.

Second, use comparative and evaluative phrases. Some evaluative comments are unique to a particular study. These fit best when you describe the study:

> The authors failed to replicate others' findings. Unfortunately, the small n in some of their groups (as low as 8) may have seriously limited their power to detect significant effects.

Other comments pertain to a whole group of studies but not to the area as a whole, and they can be covered as you end a particular section of the review:

Most of these studies share similar strengths and weaknesses. (Elaborate these.) Despite their methodological problems, most tentatively point to similar conclusions. (Tell what they are.)

In addition to integrating and analyzing the literature throughout the review, you may wish to include a final "summary and critique" subsection. This subsection can specify unexplored topics worthy of future study as well as strengths and weaknesses of past literature. Go beyond a summary of what you have already said. Instead, weave together the threads you have been developing in the rest of the review. Most important, use this section as a logical precursor to your statement of the problem and hypotheses sections.

If you need examples, peruse journals that publish literature reviews, such as *Psychological Bulletin*, *Clinical Psychology Review*, and *Developmental Review*. Some edited books contain chapters that provide integrative overviews of the literature. Examine the structure and organization of different reviews, and see how different writers integrate and analyze the literature. Studying others' writing may give you ideas for how to write your own review.

Introduce Your Study and Hypotheses

If you write a one-chapter literature review, subsections such as Statement of the Problem and Research Questions and Hypotheses will follow your Summary and Critique subsection. If you write a two-chapter version, these subsections will usually follow a general introduction to the problem area and to your specific topic. In the two-chapter version, the introduction to your specific topic will *precede* your literature review and should therefore summarize the material you plan to cover in your literature review. The introductory material in a two-chapter version should also provide a rationale for your topic, indicating why your study will make a novel contribution to the field. Remember in writing this section that your readers will read this material *before* the literature review, so make it clear enough to stand by itself.

Regardless of whether you use a one- or two-chapter format, your Statement of the Problem subsection should introduce the rationale for your study. You should also provide a brief overview of your population, design, independent variables, and dependent variables. This will help the reader understand the specific research questions and hypotheses to follow.

Chapter 3 described how to state hypotheses and research questions, and your written presentation of these should reflect these suggestions. In addition, if the rationale for a particular hypothesis is not obvious, briefly give the reason for your prediction, saying something such as, "This hypothesis is based on so-and-so's findings that _____."

As chapter 3 suggested, you should be able to make predictions regarding your major research questions. You may, however, have certain secondary comparisons for which deriving hypotheses may be very difficult (e.g., if the area is very new or if previous findings conflict). If you truly have no basis in research or in theory for making a prediction, you have several options. First, you can simply state that this is the case and offer no directional hypotheses. As an alternative, you could subdivide your research questions into those that address the primary purposes of your study (for which you offer hypotheses) and those that are secondary (for which you offer no hypotheses). Finally, you could drop the particular question as part of the formal study. We prefer the first or second of these, provided, of course, that the question is worth asking in the first place.

Write Additional Subsections

Most schools require that dissertations include the subsections we have just covered. In addition, some require additional material such as definitions of terms, descriptions of limitations of the study you propose, and discussion of the theoretical orientation underlying the study. Check your local requirements for any additional material that must be covered as you prepare your literature review.

Be Careful Not to Plagiarize

Earlier we mentioned plagiarism in passing. Its definition bears repeating here. To plagiarize, according to *Webster's New World Dictionary of the American Language* (1970), is "to take (ideas, writings, etc.) from (another) and pass them off as one's own" (p. 1987). Lifting someone's words without quotation marks is obviously plagiarism. So, however, is closely paraphrasing another's sentences. So is presenting another's *ideas* as though they were original to you. Copying paragraph organization—or a general way of organizing a topic—is also plagiarism. Find your own way of organizing ideas in your own words. Limit direct quotes, and acknowledge others' ideas and organizational frameworks when you cite or borrow them. If you are in doubt, ask a colleague or your chairperson for feedback.

Summary

This chapter reviewed various strategies for conducting the literature search you probably began as you developed and refined your topic. Pulling together the information you found into a coherent, focused review does more than just help you get a major writing task out of the way. It also should sharpen your thinking about your topic and help you see conceptual and methodological themes in the literature. In addition, the process should lead you to identify methodological issues and possible procedures for your study. Your method section will describe the choices you make about how to conduct your research. Chapters 8 and 9 assist you in articulating those choices on paper as you prepare that part of your proposal.

✓ To Do . . .

Reviewing the Literature

☐ Locate relevant literature

—Identify key authors and journals

—Use bibliographic reference sources

—Use computerized literature searches

—Obtain reprints and preprints

—Look at literature from other disciplines

—Scan tables of contents of key journals

—Use reference lists from articles, chapters, and books

—Use primary sources

—Avoid the popular press

☐ Critically read the literature

—Identify themes

—Identify strengths and weaknesses of individual articles

—Identify strengths and weaknesses of field as a whole

—Collect photocopies or notes

☐ Prepare to write

—Investigate length and format parameters

—Make a preliminary outline

   • Include page allocations

   • Limit the scope of your review

   • Organize the literature you will cover

☐ Write the review

—Write the introduction

—Write subsections

   • Use transitions and integrative phrasing

   • Synthesize and critically analyze the literature

☐ Introduce your study and hypotheses

☐ Be careful not to plagiarize

8

Methodology (or, How You're Gonna Do What You're Gonna Do!)

In this chapter, we elaborate the elements of the method section that we introduced in chapter 6. Then, we discuss ethical principles governing research in psychology and examine the process involved in designing and conducting studies in accord with these principles. This section covers negotiating requirements of institutional review boards (IRBs) for the protection of human and animal subjects, obtaining informed consent, protecting confidentiality of data, and debriefing subjects.

Be aware that this chapter is not an instruction book on research design and procedures. It will not tell you, for example, whether it is better to use a correlational or a group design for your research or whether you have thought of all the appropriate controls. If your background in research methodology is rusty, scanty, or otherwise lacking, take a look at appendix D. This bibliography will point you toward information that will help you bone up on material you never learned or cannot remember.

Know the Elements of a Method Section

The *Publication Manual of the American Psychological Association* (1994) describes three basic subsections of a method section: participants, apparatus (or materials), and procedure. Although this organization works for some studies, most need additional elements. Below, we describe different aspects of methodology that should be included in a complete method section. Not all are relevant to all studies, of course. Similarly, although the order we suggest works for many method sections, it does not work for all of them. Before dealing specifically with the components of method sections, let's say a few words about designs.

Design

This is *not* one of the subsections explicitly identified for the method section by APA's *Publication Manual.* That is because it is probably better to place any specific reference to design elements in a paragraph or two just *before* the method section. Be flexible about placement, however, and put it where it seems to make most sense for your particular project. We prefer to describe the design before the method section because all of the method section elements will be greatly influenced by the nature of the design you are using.

In describing your design, the initial point to make clear is whether it is of the within- or between-subjects variety. If the variation needed for studying the relationships involved in your study is obtained from changes in the same subjects over time or across situations, you are using a within-subjects approach. If the variation comes from differences between subjects at a single point in time, you are using a between-subjects approach. If you are fuzzy about these distinctions, see Cook and Campbell (1979), who provide the classic treatment of the differences between these major design approaches.

Once you have clarified the basic nature of your approach, you are ready to present the details of your particular design. In describing your design it is useful to provide both labels (e.g., a two-group, true experimental design; A-B-A-B withdrawal design; Solomon four-group design; correlational design; survey research) and descriptions of what you plan to do. Avoid confusing design and statistics in this subsection. "A one-way ANOVA will test the differences between the groups. . ." is a statement of the statistical test to be used, not the design. This statement should be placed in the analyses portion (in the results section) of the proposal, described in chapter 6. "A multiple-baseline design will be used, in which wives will be instructed to compliment their husbands at breakfast initially, then later during the period just after returning from work, and finally at dinner" is an example of the type of description to include in the design subsection. Another example would be "Subjects will be assigned randomly to high- and low-expectancy conditions and tasks of high and low complexity in a 2 × 2 factorial design." If multiple measures are to be administered, be sure to counterbalance their order and describe this here. If groups will be matched for certain subject characteristics (e.g., gender, IQ, or problem severity), describe how this will be accomplished. If you have forgotten why counterbalancing and matching may be important, dust off your old research design text and get reacquainted with these concepts.

A diagram or chart showing the design can help describe those that are complex or hard to follow. Good examples for designs involving between-subjects comparisons can be found in Cook and Campbell (1979). Examples for designs involving within-subjects comparisons can be found in Barlow, Hayes, and Nelson (1984). Figure 8.1 provides a rather complex but very informative diagram of a study by Sobell, Bogardis, Schuller, Leo, and Sobell (1989).

Subjects

In the subjects subsection, you should answer three questions: (a) Who will participate? (b) how many will participate? and (c) how will they be selected? If they will be sorted into groups on the basis of some subject

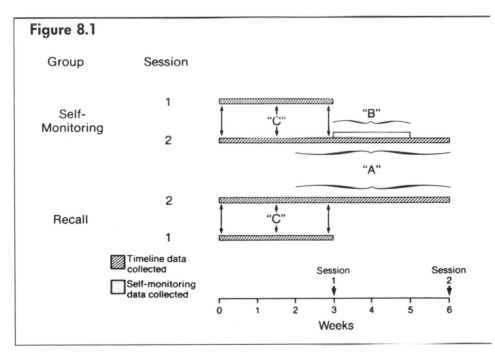

Figure 8.1

Diagram of experimental design indicating when time-line and self-monitoring drinking data were gathered from both groups of subjects, the temporal placement of sessions, and the data sets used in the major statistical analyses (designated by letter in the figure). Contrast A was a between-subjects analysis that used Session 2 time-line data to test for reactivity of self-monitoring. Contrast B was a within-subjects analysis performed using Session 2 self-monitoring and time-line data from subjects in the Self-Monitoring group; it compared data gathered from the same subjects for the same time period using the time-line versus self-monitoring method. Contrast C compared each subject's Session 2 time-line data with data given by that subject for the same time interval in Session 1 (usually 21 days). From "Is Self-Monitoring of Alcohol Consumption Reactive?" by M. B. Sobell, J. Bogardis, R. Schuller, G. I. Leo, and L. C. Sobell, 1989, *Behavioral Assessment, 11*, 451. Copyright 1989 by Pergamon Press. Reprinted by permission.

characteristic and not randomly assigned (as, for example, when a subject variable such as age, diagnostic classification, or performance on a specific task is used to classify subjects, and that classification is an independent variable), indicate how this classification will be made.

Studies vary considerably in the amount of detail they include about subjects, but, assuming they are human, it is a good idea to provide information on gender, age (mean and range), geographic area represented, socioeconomic status, source (e.g., university undergraduate classes or mental health clinics), and basis for participation (e.g., voluntary, paid, or course credit). Depending on the nature of your study, you will want to include other information, such as intellectual functioning (mean and range on a standard IQ measure), scores on any selection variable (e.g., depression, anxiety, or percent overweight), and DSM grouping. Also indicate any exclusion criteria, describing subject characteristics that will disqualify them from participating.

The novice researcher sometimes gets confused about just who the subjects are in the study. The distinction can become difficult when different groups of people are used at different times in the research. For example, in constructing a scale to assess problem spending, one of our students used consumer-credit experts to judge the adequacy of various responses to specified problem situations involving how people handle money. She used these judgments to weight the responses of persons taking the instrument, in order to establish preliminary norms. Because the primary thrust of the research was to develop a reliable and valid instrument for identifying problem spending, the persons who provided the data relevant to reliability and validity were considered the subjects. The persons providing the adequacy ratings were referred to as *judges*. Of course, she needed to describe the characteristics of the judges in detail somewhere in the method section as well. Generally speaking, the persons described in the subjects subsection are those who provide the data to answer the specific hypotheses of the study. Persons involved in producing instruments or collecting data (e.g., raters or observers) are not considered subjects.

Describe your sampling strategy and how you plan to recruit participants. Will you advertise in the local paper? Put up notices around campus? Sample birth registers? Describe exactly what you will do. Put copies of your proposed wording for inviting subjects to participate in an appendix.

If nonhuman subjects are involved, similar issues need to be addressed. State the number of animals you will use, their genus, species, and strain number, if available. Information on the source of animals is also useful. Finally, indicate their gender, age, and weight, and describe their general condition. A description of any essential details of their history, care, and handling should also be included (APA, 1983).

Be sure to design a method to keep track of the number of potential subjects contacted as well as the number who actually participated, including the number who were screened out because they met your exclusion criteria. The representativeness of your subjects is crucial to the external validity of the study. Therefore, in the final document report not only these figures but also any information you can obtain related to the differences between volunteering and nonvolunteering persons. If subjects drop out prematurely, you will want to cite the percentage and say why they dropped out.

When deciding whom to select as subjects and how to select them, a good rule of thumb is the "representativeness" rule. That is, consider the larger population of persons you want your subjects to represent. To whom do you wish to generalize? Design procedures to attract those people and gather supplemental information to see whether your subjects match the characteristics of that population. To whom do you *not* wish to generalize? Include procedures and measures that will allow you to screen out these individuals.

Your design will also have implications for decisions about whom to include and exclude. In general, more homogeneous populations are likely as a group to have less variable scores on your measures than heterogeneous populations. This is because extraneous subject characteristics that are related to scores on your measures are more likely to occur in the heterogeneous population. On the one hand, such variability is generally prized in purely correlational designs in which r and its variants (e.g., multiple regression statistics and factor analysis) will be used. This is because restricted ranges on variables being correlated limit the values correlations can obtain (McNemar, 1962).

Another possibility is that you may be comparing discrete groups in your study, using ANOVA and related approaches. In this case, extraneous and variable subject characteristics, unless they are controlled, will contribute to your error variance. This will require you to have a more potent independent variable to detect significant findings than if your extraneous variance is more limited. In these cases, it makes sense to limit your population, thinking especially about characteristics that are not particularly important to your generalizability but have been shown to correlate with your major dependent variables. Subjects can then be restricted to a certain subpopulation, on the basis of these characteristics.

Variability in subject characteristics can also be handled in two other ways in group designs. Some can be controlled by adding one or more subject characteristics as independent variables in your design. For example, if you are concerned about socioeconomic status (SES) in your study of the effects of watching "Sesame Street" on preschool reading-test scores, you could add SES as an independent variable. Of course, this would add to the total number of subjects you would need. A second way to handle this problem is statistical: measure SES and see if it correlates with your dependent variable after your data are collected. If it does, use SES as a covariate in subsequent analyses.

From this material, it should be obvious that you will need to collect information on your subjects, in part to exclude ones you decide not to study and in part to know what the subjects were like. Particularly important information has to do with subject characteristics that could provide alternative explanations for your anticipated results or be inadvertently confounded with your independent variables. Pick potential confounds by looking in the literature: What subject variables correlate with your dependent variables? These are good nominees as potential confounding variables that you should measure and later analyze to see whether they can be ruled out as explanations for your findings.

You will also need to indicate how you will measure the subject characteristics you plan to assess. If you will include a demographic data sheet and two questionnaires to gather subject information, indicate this and refer the reader to an appendix for copies of instruments that are not copyrighted. You will also describe the psychometric properties of these instruments, either here in the subjects subsection or later in a measures subsection. Last, we turn to the question virtually every student asks: How many subjects do I have to have? There are two ways to figure this out. The first is to look at the literature and see what the norm is. This is the easy way, and unfortunately, except for individual organism designs, it is not a good one. Repeated reviews of even the most prestigious professional journals indicate that most group-design studies use too few subjects to have sufficient statistical power to detect all but the most powerful effects (Rossi, 1990).

What is the preferred way to figure out how many subjects you really need? There are two things to consider when answering this question. The first involves the statistics you plan to use. Multivariate analyses require certain subjects-to-variables ratios to yield stable findings. If you are using multiple regression, factor analysis, multivariate analyses of variance (MANOVA), discriminant function analysis, or related statistics, here's one way to figure out what you need to meet the minimum requirements from a statistical standpoint. Count up the number of scores your dependent variables will generate. Sort these into subsets. Each subset should contain the names of the scores you will need in a particular analysis. For example, you may plan one MANOVA involving three different dependent variables assessing aggression. This is your first subset. A second subset contains five demographic variables to be used in a second MANOVA, and so on. Count the number of dependent variables in each subset. Select the number that represents the largest number of scores in any subset (in the example just given, this would be five). Then, multiply this number by some number between 7 and 20 that you select in concert with your chairperson (really conservative statisticians will require even more than 20 subjects per variable, whereas very liberal ones will go as low as 7) . This is how many subjects your statistics require.

What your statistics require is not related to their power, however. *Power* refers to the extent to which the statistics you use can detect the effects of the independent variable. Power is a function of your sample size, the magnitude of the effects of your independent variables (i.e., how much of a difference your independent variable makes in relation to the dependent variable in question), and the alpha level you select. Thus, a second step in figuring out how many subjects you should recruit is to calculate a power analysis. Power analyses allow you to estimate how many subjects you will need to detect small effects, medium effects, and large effects. Given a fixed number of subjects and alpha level (ordinarily $p <$ .05), the larger the effect, the less the power needed to detect it.

To calculate power analyses for group designs, you first need to figure out how small an effect you wish to be able to detect. You will learn quickly that detecting tiny effects can mean that you will need thousands of subjects (see Keppel, 1991; Kraemer & Thiemann, 1987). A good rule of thumb is to ask yourself, "What is the minimum effect that would be meaningful in this area?" In the clinical arena, this is often a moderate effect: Smaller than moderate effects may be too small to be of any meaningful practical significance. Whether this is the case, however, will depend on your field of study. In fields in which a great deal is known about factors that affect the dependent variable, such as some aspects of medicine, documenting a small effect can be very important.

To do your power analysis, you will have to have various pieces of information. First, you will need to select the level of power you wish to have in your study; .80 is a reasonable value. Second, power calculations require estimates of actual numbers that are based on your anticipated data. Depending on the formula you will use, you may need to come up with means, standard deviations, and omega squared (i.e., effect size values, the calculation of which requires sums of squares and mean squared error values, based on ANOVA calculations) for group designs using parametric statistics. For correlational statistics, you may need to provide values of the correlations you anticipate.

How, you may ask, can I get these numbers without doing the research? Answer: you can't, not precisely. But you can estimate what these might be, on the basis of pilot data or of published studies that used the same dependent variable and related independent variables. You then use these in formulas that allow you to calculate the number of subjects you will need. Cohen (1988), Keppel (1991), and Kraemer and Thiemann (1987) all explain how to calculate power analyses. Goldstein (1989) reviews a number of statistical programs for DOS-based microcomputers that will compute power.

If you have not done power calculations before and your study does not map readily onto one of these authors' or the programming examples, get someone knowledgeable to check your calculations or to help you. Cohen (1992) provides a brief, very readable discussion of power analysis as well as tables you can use to estimate the number of subjects you will need to detect small, medium, or large effect sizes at the $p < .01$, .05, and .10 levels. The tables cover t tests, correlations, tests of proportions, chi-square, ANOVA, and multiple regression statistics.

Setting and Apparatus

Describe the general context in which the research will take place. If these characteristics are fairly standard, they need not be specified in detail. It is a good idea to give the general dimensions and furnishings of any experimental room and indicate the position of the experimenter and the subject (e.g., "The study took place in a 9 ft. x 12 ft. experimental room with the subject and experimenter seated and facing each other across a 4 ft. wide table"). Such details would generally not be necessary for studies involving data collected from groups of subjects in college or elementary school classrooms, however. If a particular piece of apparatus is used to present stimuli or afford subjects a way of responding and it is unique to this study, describe it in detail and include construction plans (either in the text or an appendix). If the apparatus is commercially available, include the brand and model number.

Independent Variables

Indicate how you will operationalize your independent variables, and place this information either in the design subsection, the procedures subsection, or in a subsection of its own. Where you put this depends on the complexity of your independent variables: More complex ones, such as an intervention project or exposure to a specific set of stimuli, may require a separate subsection.

Regardless of where you place this information, certain details are essential. How will you operationalize your independent variables? Also include the ways you will assure the integrity of these variables, namely, that they were manipulated consistently and as planned (cf. Billingsley, White, & Munson, 1980; Peterson, Homer, & Wonderlich, 1982). This may involve manipulation checks by judges (e.g., ratings of therapist or experimenter behavior to ensure that they did what they were supposed to do) and precautions taken by the experimenter (e.g., observing sessions through a one-way mirror). If your study involves instructional manipulations (e.g., to make your subjects think they are winning a game played single handedly against a two-person team in another room), include some way of assessing whether they really believed these manipulations.

Sometimes manipulation checks can be quite complex. One of our students, for example, was interested in whether fourth grade girls would be rated as more socially competent by peers if they engaged in higher frequencies of certain behaviors thought important to the peers (Hoier, 1984; see Hoier & Cone, 1987, for published version). Increases in these social behaviors served as the independent variable, and ratings of competence as the dependent variable. To make sure the social behaviors actually were increased, Hoier made videotapes of the experimental sessions. Trained observers scored these later. It was important to describe the reliability of this scoring system in the method section of the proposal. Whether information about manipulation checks such as this one would be placed in the independent variables subsection or a measurement subsection would depend on where the material will be clearest for the reader.

Be sure to explain who will serve as the experimenter. An abundance of literature shows that any experimenter or data gatherer who will interact with subjects should be "blind" to the experimental hypotheses, so this person should not be you unless you can use creative methods to keep yourself blind concerning who is in which condition. One of our less affluent students, for example, managed to do this cleverly. She was evaluating the discriminative validity of a new questionnaire assessing beliefs associated with personality disorders. She classified subjects into diagnostic groups using a standardized structured interview. This interview took about an hour to administer and required extensive training. She did not want to pay someone to conduct these interviews. At the same time, she needed to make sure that if she served as the interviewer, she would not know the subjects' probable diagnoses. She therefore arranged that clinicians would refer potential subjects to her but not inform her of their probable diagnoses. That way she could conduct the interviews herself and remain blind to such knowledge about the subjects.

If you cannot keep yourself blind to factors that might bias your interactions with subjects, and you cannot afford to hire someone to act as your experimenter, several options are available to you. If you are in a university setting, perhaps you can give independent study credit to an undergraduate for acting as your experimenter. Or, perhaps you and an equally poor colleague can trade services: Your friend will be your experimenter, and you will be his or hers (be aware, however, that you cannot then discuss your project in detail with this person for social support!). A final and least preferred option is to act as the experimenter yourself and include some procedure to ensure that you do not treat subjects in different conditions differently. This might include administering a questionnaire that all subjects complete about the experimenter or audiotaping experimental sessions and having raters blind to the hypotheses evaluate them.

If implementing the independent variable requires skill or elaborate procedures, indicate how you will train your experimenters and assure their competence before and during the study. This is particularly important with studies that involve interventions, animal surgery, and use of experimental confederates.

Finally, include information on control procedures you have instituted to prevent confounds. For example, if subjects will view a series of videotaped stimuli, indicate how you will control for possible order effects. If different experimenters implement different levels of the independent variable, how will you ensure that levels of this variable, and not experimenter differences, influenced the results? Provide the information to convince your reader that your conditions will differ on only the independent variable and nothing else. To do this will, of course, require that you figure out potential confounds and eliminate them or assess the effects of their presence.

Measures (Dependent Variables)

The measures or dependent variables subsection provides details about the data collection devices you will use. Chapter 9 describes what to look for in decent instrumentation. Here, we mention the information to provide about these devices once you have selected them.

Instruments generally available should be described by name, author, and date of publication (if published). Include a copy of unpublished measures in one or more appendixes to the proposal. In addition to where the measure has appeared in the literature, describe what it looks like. That is, paraphrase or quote the instructions to the subject, describe representative test stimuli or items, and state the response alternatives provided (e.g., yes–no or 1- to 4-point ratings). It may be useful to include representative items in a table or in the text of the main body of the proposal to make them readily available to the reader, even if the entire instrument is reproduced in an appendix. Of course, if you are using a well-known instrument such as the Minnesota Multiphasic Personality Inventory (MMPI), it is generally not necessary to go into detail because most readers will be familiar with it. Items from some tests (e.g., Wechsler Adult Intelligence Scale–Revised) cannot be reproduced in publicly available documents for test security reasons. Ask your chair for advice if you are unsure how well known your measures are. Finally, be sure to describe how the measure will be scored. If it yields more than one score, indicate each score you intend to use.

In addition to describing the topographic characteristics of your measures, include information about their psychometric adequacy. It is generally not enough to state that the instrument has been found to be reliable and valid. Reliability and validity are relative. Show that you have selected instrumentation that is appropriate for answering the specific questions of interest in your particular project. A measure shown to be reliable by someone else might not be adequately reliable for your anticipated use. The general term *reliability* is too general to be very informative, anyway. There are different types of reliability or generalizability (Cone, 1977; Cronbach, Gleser, Nanda, & Rajaratnam, 1972) that will be more or less important for your particular study. For example, if your research calls for pre- and post-measures of subject behavior, the temporal stability (e.g., test–retest reliability) of your instruments will be an important characteristic. Their internal consistency may be of less concern. Moreover, if mean changes in groups of subjects from pre to post are at issue, you will want to know something about the stability of mean scores, not just that an instrument has been shown to be stable over time. Similarly, a retest interval of 2 weeks might give you some information about the temporal stability of your measure, but if your intervention is going to take considerably longer, you might need to look further to find literature showing your instrument's performance over periods longer than 2 weeks.

In addition to examining different types of reliability, you will want to present some data on the different sorts of validity evidence relevant to your measures. Examine the extent to which the measure has been shown to have discriminant validity (Campbell, 1960), especially for self-report instruments. Convergent validity information should also be mentioned. Other types of validity (e.g., criterion related, construct, treatment, and discriminative) will be more or less important depending on your particular research. We say more about these in chapter 9.

These suggestions deal with measures of your dependent variables, of course. What about your independent variable? As mentioned earlier, you should take steps to ensure that your independent variable does indeed occur at the level you intended, and one place to indicate the steps you took is the measures subsection (the independent variable or procedures subsections are alternatives). Similarly, measures you gather to describe your subjects can be described either here or in the subjects subsection. In deciding where to put this information, ask yourself, "What will be easiest for the reader to follow?"

In addition, if you are using humans as observers or judges, indicate who they will be (e.g., undergraduates); how they will be recruited, selected, and trained; and how you will know that they are ready to be let loose on the real data (see Foster, Bell-Dolan, & Burge, 1988, for practical guidelines for direct observation, most of which can be extrapolated to other uses of human judges). Indicate, furthermore, what percentage of data will be checked for interobserver or interjudge agreement (at least 20%, selected randomly from each condition or subject, is our minimum) and how agreement will be calculated. Foster and Cone (1986) and Hartmann (1982) provide reviews of the myriad of different statistics that can be used to calculate interjudge agreement and present some formulas (see also House, House, & Campbell, 1981, for a discussion of others). Finally, indicate the procedures you will use in assessing interrater or interobserver agreement. Try to make sure observers or raters do not know when and by whom agreement will be checked, if possible, as this knowledge leads to inflated agreement estimates (Romanczyk, Kent, Diament, & O'Leary, 1973).

A final piece of information to include when using observations or judges' ratings is a complete description of the category system (including definitions) and procedures (including data-collection sheets) they will follow. Ordinarily, you should summarize these in the method section and provide a copy of the coding manual or guidelines and scoring sheets in an appendix.

If you develop the instrumentation de novo in your study, you may not have information on the psychometric properties of its scores. In this case, if you cannot collect pilot data before your proposal meeting, be sure to include information in the proposal about how you plan to obtain reliability and validity information during the course of your research. In most cases, this should be done before collecting the data needed to answer the main research questions. The reason for this is that if you collect generalizability data at the same time you are collecting data to answer the main research questions, you run the risk that your data will show that your measure is poor. This throws the interpretation of your data into question, because your instrumentation is not sufficiently reliable or valid in ways needed for your particular research. Cone (1992) provides a more detailed discussion of this issue.

Procedure

In this subsection, describe the actual steps you will take to obtain data from your subjects. Walk the reader through the process just as a subject will experience it (Yates, 1982). Start at the beginning. If a research assistant will telephone or screen subjects from a list of volunteers, indicate this and state exactly what subjects will be told on the phone. If your study involves mailing questionnaires or other information to the subjects, state how this will be done. Describe the procedures to be followed when subjects arrive at the data collection site, including who will be responsible for each of the procedures. For example, if subjects will be randomly assigned to an experimental or control group, state how randomization will occur. Be particularly alert to protecting against subject reactivity to experimental conditions and other forms of subject bias, such as the infamous Hawthorne effect (cf. Ray & Ravizza, 1988). Tell subjects only what they need for informed participation. Be aware of the double-blind approach to minimizing experimenter bias and use it if possible.

Exhibit 8.1

Checklist of Elements to Include in a Method Section

Subjects

_____ How many
_____ Criteria for inclusion
          _____ How each will be determined
_____ Criteria for exclusion
          _____ How each will be determined
_____ Other characteristics of subjects
          _____ How each will be determined
_____ Sampling and recruitment procedures
_____ How informed consent will be obtained

Design

_____ Name of design
_____ Independent variables and levels
_____ Dependent variables
_____ Way of assigning subjects to groups

Setting and apparatus

Setting
          _____ Where study will be conducted
          _____ Important features of setting

Equipment described
          _____ Make and model
          _____ Construction details for apparatus unique to study

Independent variables

_____ How operationalized
_____ Potential confounds and how avoided and assessed
_____ Who serves as experimenter (E)
_____ How E will be kept blind to hypotheses
_____ Training E will receive
_____ How integrity of independent variables will be assessed
          _____ Manipulation checks
          _____ Instruments and methods

continued

Exhibit 8.1, continued

Measures

Measures of subject characteristics
_____ Description
_____ Scoring
_____ What scores you will use
_____ Psychometric data from literature
_____ Psychometric data you will collect

Measures of dependent variables
_____ Description
_____ Scoring
_____ What scores you will use
_____ Psychometric data from literature
_____ Psychometric data you will collect

Measures of independent variables
_____ Description
_____ Scoring
_____ What scores you will use
_____ Psychometric data from literature
_____ Psychometric data you will collect

Measures involving human judges, raters, and observers
_____ How many judges
_____ Who will serve as judges
_____ Training judges will receive
_____ Criteria for judge competence
_____ How interjudge agreement will be assessed on actual data
_____ % of data checked for agreement
_____ Statistic used to calculate agreement

Procedure

_____ Instructions to subjects
_____ How and when informed consent will be obtained
_____ Who has contact with subjects
_____ Sequence and timing of tasks
_____ Steps to prevent subject reactivity
_____ Debriefing

Describe your procedures for ensuring informed consent. Include the human subjects review process you will follow, and place a copy of the informed consent form you will use in an appendix. Describe the process you will use to debrief subjects after they have participated. Compose a script for this, and place it in an appendix. Don't forget to offer the subjects a chance to obtain a summary of the research findings. A good way to do this is to provide a box for them to check on the consent form if they are interested in receiving such a summary (include a place for their address as well).

Provide the word-for-word instructions you will be using with each subject. If different groups will receive different instructions, indicate how instructions will differ, and put copies of all instructions in an appendix. Tape recording instructions and playing these for subjects assures standardization and helps avoid experimenter burnout, communication of boredom or impatience, or any of a number of normal (but idiosyncratic) experimenter reactions that might inadvertently affect the outcome of the study. If subjects are told as part of the independent variable manipulation that they are to get a treatment that has been shown to be successful with many other people, include a description of your plans to assess their expectations or belief in this.

Finally, if your design calls for posttest assessment or follow up, be sure to describe how these will be accomplished. When will they occur? Will subjects be brought back? Will they be telephoned, contacted only by mail, and so on?

If you have followed all of these suggestions, you will have a complete, clear method section. To help you assess whether your method section covers all relevant bases, you can use the checklist in Exhibit 8.1. Realize, of course, that not all items may be relevant to your study.

Be Familiar With Research Ethics in Psychology

This section treats research ethics in some detail to assist you in conducting your own research in as ethically sensitive a manner as possible. We have divided the discussion into two major sections to help you understand what your responsibilities are and how you might discharge them effectively. The first section outlines the ethical principles governing the conduct of research in psychology. The second offers practical suggestions for implementing the principles.

Ethical Standards Governing Research by Psychologists

The professional conduct of psychologists, whether practitioner or researcher, whether student or seasoned veteran, is governed by the ethical principles and standards promulgated by the American Psychological Association (APA, 1992). Appendix A reproduces Standards 6.06–6.26 (among others), those most directly relevant for research. Their essence is summarized in the requirement that "psychologists conduct research competently and with due concern for the dignity and welfare of participants" (Standard 6.07[a]).

In discharging the responsibility to respect the dignity and welfare of subjects, you must

(a) evaluate the ethical acceptability of the research
(b) assess the degree of risk involved for participants
(c) ensure the ethical conduct of the research by you and others involved in it
(d) obtain a clear and fair, informed, and voluntary agreement by subjects to participate
(e) avoid deception and concealment unless absolutely necessary and justifiable
(f) protect the subject's right to decline or withdraw from participation at any time
(g) protect the subject from any physical harm, danger, or discomfort possibly associated with the research procedures
(h) protect the subject from any emotional harm, danger, or discomfort possibly associated with the research procedures
(i) debrief the subject after data collection has been completed
(j) correct any undesirable consequences to individual subjects that result from participating in the study
(k) maintain strict confidentiality of any information collected about a subject during the research in accord with agreements reached with the subject while obtaining informed consent.

If your research involves the use of nonhuman animals, the most important of the ethical principles is Standard 6.20, "Care and Use of Animals in Research." In conducting such research in the ethically most acceptable way you must

(a) conform with all laws pertaining to caring for and handling the animals
(b) ensure that a psychologist trained and experienced in animal care supervises the use of the animals and is ultimately responsible for their humane treatment
(c) ensure that all persons involved in the research have been specifically trained to handle the particular animals being used

(d) minimize any physical harm, danger, or discomfort possibly associated with the research procedures

(e) use procedures involving stress, pain, or privation only if alternatives are unavailable and the research goal is justified by the practical, educational, or scientific value expected

(f) perform any surgery under appropriate anesthesia and use procedures to prevent infection and minimize pain both during and after surgery

(g) use humane, painless, rapid life-terminating procedures when it is appropriate to sacrifice the animal.

Implementing the Standards

If your behavior as a researcher follows these standards, you will be acting in an ethically responsible way. This section gives you some suggestions in this regard. More detailed coverage can be found in *Ethical Principles in the Conduct of Research with Human Participants* (APA, 1982).

The first requirement is that your research be ethically acceptable. How do you find out if it is? A simple test is to examine the principles just listed. Can your research be done if you adhere to each of them? If it can, it is probably ethically acceptable. If it cannot, it still may be ethically acceptable, but you will have to take some extra steps to determine this and to assure yourself and others that it is.

One common problem concerns deception and concealment. For example, a study might involve a task in which the subject competes against other persons. To exercise precise control over the other "persons'" performance, the experimenter might actually program a computer to compete against the real subject. Subjects are told the persons against whom they are competing are in other experimental rooms. They will be communicating with each other but will not be able to see one another. Unbeknownst to the subject, the persons in the other rooms are really a computer. It is quite clear that you are deceiving the subject in this experiment. On its face, this is inconsistent with the prohibition against deception. You are protected against a charge of acting unethically, however, if you can establish that the research is important and that it cannot be done without the deception.

Unfortunately, doing a thorough job of ensuring the ethicality of research can be time consuming and is often beyond the resources of the fledgling researcher. In the example just given, it is possible the research could be done without the deception. Conceivably, subjects would behave the same in a competitive task whether they were working against a real person or a computer. A study would be needed to establish this, however. In other words, you would need to do a preliminary study before doing your main study. This is generally not realistic if you ever want to finish your project and receive your degree while you are still able to walk across the stage at graduation.

Ensuring that your research is ethical is another reason to plan a study within the context of a research area that is currently viable in the literature. If there is a body of research to draw on, chances are it has been done in ways consistent with the APA ethical principles. You can refer to precedents in the established literature to assure yourself, committee members, and others that you are conducting your own research ethically. Of course, it is not enough simply to refer to existing literature to prove that yours is ethical. You will need to address each of the principles and be able to assure your committee and your institution's human subjects review panel that you are proceeding ethically.

In doing so, the issue of risk to your subjects will be paramount. The extent of any risk posed to participants, whether physical, emotional, or other, must be assessed. This can generally be ascertained from existing literature if researchers have used procedures comparable with those in the anticipated study. In some cases, the potential harmful nature of research procedures has actually been studied directly (cf. Bell-Dolan, Foster, & Sikora, 1989). You can refer to the results of such studies in designing your voluntary consent form. In most cases, however, potential risks have not been studied directly and must be inferred from the literature. In this event, you should refer to the body of literature and indicate that there have (or have not) been any reported instances of physical, emotional, or other harm to subjects in the "dozens of studies reported in the literature using these procedures," or words to that effect.

With respect to making sure that you and anyone assisting you with your research behaves in an ethically acceptable fashion at all times, you should start first with a thorough understanding of the APA principles pertaining to research. Once you know these principles and their implications for your specific study, you can instruct your research assistants and others accordingly. Designing procedures that are consistent with the principles is a second way of ensuring ethically responsible research. For example, having a way of informing potential subjects thoroughly, including about the risks involved, their right to refuse to participate, and their right to withdraw at any time, will ensure their participation is informed. You can also establish procedurally that your subjects are participating voluntarily. This can be done by using a carefully designed consent form (described below), together with noncoercive consent procedures. Constructing a research apparatus that is safe (e.g., contains no electrical wiring that might short out and shock the subject) is another procedural way of ensuring ethical compliance. Having ways of debriefing subjects appropriately and storing and handling their data to maintain confidentiality are additional procedures that assist in conducting research ethically.

Instructing yourself and others and having procedures that ensure ethical conduct are only part of this process, however. It is just as important to monitor the way you carry out the research. If you are using assistants, this can take the form of sitting in on or listening to tape recordings of their interviews with subjects to check that informed consent is really being obtained and that all subjects' rights are being explained to them. You should also file consent forms in an organized way and check periodically to make sure you have forms on file for all subjects. The same is true for data forms themselves. Make sure that subjects' names are not on the forms and that the key that codes their names with identifying numbers is up-to-date. Furthermore, keep the data in a secure, locked place. Sit in on or listen to tapes of debriefing sessions to make sure your assistants tell participants the essential details of the experiment they have just participated in. If you are using clinical samples, be especially sensitive to the possibility of changes for the worse in subjects' clinical picture. Frequent phone calls to check on this will permit you to make an appropriate referral if they do get worse (Yates, 1982).

Subjects' informed consent is a key element in ethically conducted research. The exact contents that must be included in consent forms will vary from place to place, in keeping with institutional variations in human subjects review procedures. The minimum essential elements of any consent form include:

(a) a description of the study and its purpose
(b) the information the subject will be asked to provide, if any
(c) a description of what the subject will be asked to do
(d) a description of potential risks and benefits to individual subjects
(e) a statement that participation is voluntary and that the subject can withdraw at any time without penalty
(f) reassurance that all data will be kept confidential
(g) the name and phone number of a person the subject may call to get further information about the research

(h) the name and phone number of a person (other than the researcher) the subject may call if he or she has any complaints as a result of participating in the study

(i) places for the subject and researcher to sign the form.

Exhibits 8.2 through 8.5 provide samples of fairly typical consent

---

Exhibit 8.2

Adult Consent for Own Participation

We would like you to participate in a research study titled "A Functional Assessment of Heterosocial Initiation Behaviors in Adults." The purpose of this study is to gain a better understanding of what types of conversations college students like to engage in. If you decide to participate in the study, your involvement will take no more than 1 hour of your time. We will ask you to listen to a series of audiotapes in which one man and one woman are talking. Then, we will ask you to make some ratings concerning what the man said. For example, you will be asked to rate how much you like this man based on what he said to the woman. There are no foreseeable risks or benefits from your participation, because this is simply an assessment study and not a treatment study.

Your particpation is completely voluntary and you will be free to refuse or stop at any time without penalty. Your grades or class standing will not be affected in any way if you decide to stop. All information will be number coded and strictly confidential. Your identity will not be revealed without your written consent.

Do you have any questions?

If you have any questions later, please feel free to contact us.

Bill Carr, MA
Psychology Department
West Virginia University
Phone: 292-8690

Barry A. Edelstein, PhD
Psychology Department
West Virginia University
Phone: 293-2511

Please read the following paragraph, and, if you agree to participate, please sign below.

I understand that any information about me obtained from this research will be kept strictly confidential. I do understand that my research records may be subpoenaed by court order or may be inspected by federal regulatory authorities.

Signature _____ Date _____

Investigator _____ Date _____

Please place your initials here acknowledging receipt of a copy of this consent form. _____

Note. From *A Functional Assessment of Heterosocial Initiation Behaviors in Adults* by T. M. DiLorenzo, 1984. Unpublished doctoral dissertation, West Virginia University. Adapted by permission of the author.

Exhibit 8.3

Parent Consent for Son or Daughter to Participate

Dear Parent or Guardian:

We would like to ask your permission for your son or daughter to help us develop a questionnaire that will ask about the ways teenagers act with their classmates. This research project, called "Development of a Social Skills Questionnaire," will help us see whether teenagers see themselves the same way from week to week. We will also be looking at whether teenagers see the behaviors in the questionnaire as positive or negative.

What is involved? Teenagers who participate will be asked to spend a total of about 30 minutes completing three questionnaires. On the first, your son or daughter would indicate how often they engage in certain actions. Examples of the kinds of actions on the questionnaire are helping someone with homework, sharing lunch with others, arguing with teachers, and keeping secrets private. On the second, your son or daughter would indicate how good or bad he or she thought these same actions were. The third questionnaire would be the same questionnaire as the first one and would be completed 2 weeks after the first one in order to determine whether or not one's answers stay the same over time.

Potential Benefits and Concerns. Although we will schedule completing the questionnaires so that your son or daughter does not miss important lessons, he or she may have to make up missed work. One possible benefit of being in the project may be that the questionnaires encourage teenagers to think about how what they do affects the way they get along with others.

Participation is voluntary. Your son's or daughter's participation in this study is completely voluntary. There will be no penalty if you do not wish your son or daughter to be in this study, and he or she may withdraw at any time during the study and refuse to answer any of the questions. This project has been approved by the Board of Education and your son's or daughter's school.

Information is confidential. All information will be held as confidential as is legally possible. Only the researchers will see the questionnaires. Once the questionnaires have been collected, your teenager's name will be removed and replaced with a number so that he or she can no longer be connected to any specific answers.

Questions? We would appreciate it if you would return the form on the back of this page whether or not you would like your teenager to participate, so that we know that this information has reached you. You may keep the attached copy of this letter for your records. If you have any questions, please feel free to call Ms. Heidi Inderbitzen-Pisaruk (293-2001) or Dr. Sharon Foster (293-2511 or 293-2360). Either of us can arrange for you to see the questionnaires in advance if you wish. The Institutional Review Board at West Virginia University (293-7073) can also answer questions about the rights of participants in research.

Thank you for your consideration.

continued

Exhibit 8.3, continued

Sincerely,

Heidi Inderbitzen-Pisaruk, MA Sharon L. Foster, PhD
Graduate Student   Associate Professor
Department of Psychology   Department of Psychology

 Please check the appropriate boxes and send this form back to school with your son or daughter:
 ☐ I have read and I understand the permission letter. I give consent for my teenager to participate in this study.
 ☐ I have received a copy of Ms. Inderbitzen-Pisaruk and Dr. Foster's letter for my records.
 ☐ I would like more information before giving consent for my teenager to participate in this study. Call me at _____ .
 ☐ I do not wish my teenager to participate in this study.

Parent's Signature/Date _____

Teenager's name _____

Please send this form back to school with your son or daughter. Thanks!!!

---

forms for different situations involving human subjects. The first consent form (Exhibit 8.2) is for a study in which adult subjects consent for their own participation. With the second (Exhibit 8.3), a parent consents for his or her teenage son or daughter to participate. Because the research is conducted in a school setting, the form is sent home for the parents to sign. The third form (Exhibit 8.4) is an assent form for the teenage subjects in the same study to sign. The final example (Exhibit 8.5) is an assent form for a different study that was developed for much younger children (from Grades 2 and 5) and illustrates appropriate language modification for younger children.

 In the event you are working with children or other persons who are not considered legally able to give informed consent, the consent must be signed by a parent or legal guardian. It is also a good idea to give the person an opportunity to assent or refuse by describing the study in simple terms and asking them directly. Children can also be asked to sign an assent form (see Exhibit 8.2), similar to a consent form but in simpler

---

Exhibit 8.4

Assent Form Used With Teenagers

Subject Assent Form

Study Title: Development of a Social Skills Questionnaire
Investigators: Heidi Inderbitzen-Pisaruk, MA (293-2001)
                     Sharon L. Foster, PhD (293-2511)

I am being asked to help Ms. Inderbitzen-Pisaruk and Dr. Foster in a project. The goal of this project is to make a questionnaire about the things teenagers do that cause their classmates to like them better or worse.

If I decide to participate, my part in the project will take about 30 minutes total: 20 minutes the first day and 10 minutes the second day. The first time I would fill out two questionnaires that ask about how much I do certain things (e.g., share my lunch with other people, help other people with their homework, or argue with teachers) and whether I think these things are good or bad. The second time I would fill out one of the questionnaires again.

If I miss part of a class, I may have to make up the work I miss. I also understand that thinking about what my classmates do that I like and don't like may help me better understand my relationships with other students.

This project has been explained to me and I have been allowed to ask questions about it. I understand that I do not have to fill out the questionnaire if I don't want to and no one will treat me badly. I can stop part way through if I want to and skip questions I don't want to answer. I have read this form, understand the project, and agree to participate.

Student _____   Date _____
Investigator _____   Date _____

---

language. If *either* the legal guardian *or* the potential subject declines, the individual must not be included in the study.

As a procedural matter, signing the informed consent form usually occurs as the first order of business when the subject appears for the initial experimental session. If school children are participating, the form will commonly be sent home with the child to be returned with a parent's signature. Ask the parent to return the form after assenting *or* declining. This way you can be sure the parent at least received the form. Some researchers (e.g., Clarke, Lewinsohn, Hops, & Seeley, 1992; Roberts, Lewinsohn, & Seeley, 1991) have successfully used passive consent procedures in recent years. In the Clarke et al. study, for example, parents of potential participating children were given the opportunity to refuse their child's participation by returning a "decline" card to the researchers. Children

---

Exhibit 8.5

Assent Form Used With Elementary School Children

I understand that I have been asked to be in a project looking at things that make children mad or hurt their feelings. If I agree to be in this project, I will be interviewed alone and asked about things that happened that I saw that hurt children's feelings or make them mad. This will take about 20 minutes.

I understand that I don't have to answer any questions I don't want to and I can go back to my class early if I want. I can stop being in this project any time that I want and no one will get mad at me. It won't make any difference in my grades if I don't want to be in the project. If I feel bad about any of the questions I answer, I can talk to my teacher or Dr. Foster about it.

I understand that my name won't be used and the interviewer will not tell anyone what I said because it's private. I will keep my answers private, too.

If I have any questions, I can ask my parents or teacher or have them call Dr. Foster at 452-1664.

I have had a chance to ask questions. I volunteer to be in this project.

Child Signature _____   Date _____
Interviewer Signature _____   Date _____

---

were enrolled in the study if their parents did not return the card. Of course, the children were also given the opportunity to decline participation themselves after the procedures were explained to them. Such procedures might lead to higher levels of participation than more active approaches. If you are considering the passive tactic, however, be sure you have the approval of your IRB for the protection of human subjects first, and discuss the potential ramifications with your chairperson. Be aware that passive consent procedures can be controversial. One researcher, a story goes, used them for a study involving controversial procedures with school children. A parent complained after data were collected, and ultimately the researcher had to destroy data from hundreds of subjects.

Include additional items on consent forms depending on the preferences of the IRB at your particular school. Let's talk about IRBs for a moment. As a condition of receiving federal monies, the U.S. Department of Health and Human Services requires agencies to have formal procedures in place to ensure the humane treatment of persons receiving services from the agency, whether it be a college, university, hospital, clinic, or public residential facility. Each agency that permits research must have a committee or group of people serving as guardians of individual rights. The procedures followed by the IRB in overseeing research will typically be published. You should get a copy of these and read them. They will include the steps you must follow in having your research approved *before* beginning to collect data. Because IRB procedures usually cover pilot testing as well, it is important to examine them early in your planning. Pay particular attention to the dates of IRB meetings and the deadlines and rules for submitting proposals. If the meetings occur only monthly, missing one could mean a delay of as much as a month in getting started. Look also at the different categories of research to make sure exactly what the requirements are in your particular case. Perhaps the research you plan is actually exempt from IRB review or can be subjected to an expedited review. When data are being obtained only from archival sources or when you are using relatively benign surveys, it is usually the case that full IRB review will not be necessary. If the research you are planning is the least bit controversial, plan for a difficult steerage through the IRB process. Rely on the experience of your chair or other committee members. They will, no doubt, be knowledgeable concerning the politics of the local IRB and will have sage advice for navigating successfully.

An interesting example relevant to this discussion comes from some research in the area of children's social skills that Sharon Foster attempted to conduct several years ago. The procedure involved having children nominate their three most- and three least-liked peers. One of the members of the IRB was especially insistent that such a procedure was potentially harmful, arguing that the process would call attention to disliked children and that peers might respond to these children even more negatively than usual as a result of the nominations. Foster decided to recruit the concerned IRB member's assistance in designing a study to test this very concern. She argued that no data showed the procedure to be harmful. To reassure the IRB, however, a study could be designed that would examine whether children were negatively impacted by the nomination procedure. Surely, the IRB member would have to give permission for such a test, at least. He did, and a student conducted the study as a master's thesis. Incidentally, no negative effects emerged (Bell-Dolan et al., 1989).

✔ **To Do . . .**

Writing the Method Section

☐ Write the different subsections of the method section

— Design

— Subjects

— Setting and apparatus

— Independent variables

— Measures (dependent variables)

— Procedure

☐ Use Exhibit 8.1 to check that you've included relevant information

☐ Follow research ethics in psychology

— Read ethical guidelines

— Write consent and assent forms

— Obtain approval from relevant research review boards

9

Measurement

In this chapter, we deal with operationalizing your dependent and independent variables. These operationalizations are the measures of your study. We suggest places to look for measures and information about them. We discuss the characteristics of good measures and what to do when the psychometric adequacy of your measure has not already been established.

Operationalize Your Variables

If you are at the point of considering a thesis or dissertation, you probably know what operational definitions are. If not, avail yourself of a good text in research design (e.g., McBurney, 1990; Ray & Ravizza, 1988; see appendix D for additional suggestions) and review the relevant sections.

Your method section will cover just how you plan to objectify all of your variables, both dependent and independent. For example, suppose you plan to examine the differences between high, middle, and low SES families on cohesiveness. How will SES be established? How will cohesiveness be measured? Or, suppose you want to look at differences in nursing care provided to children with acquired immune deficiency syndrome (AIDS) versus similar children with other or non-AIDS diagnoses. How will you determine the AIDS or non-AIDS status of your subjects? If you predict nursing care will vary depending on the nurses' previous experience with or knowledge about AIDS, how will you assess experience or knowledge? Imagine you are interested in whether adults molested as children are more likely to have psychological problems than similar adults not so molested. How will you define and assess molestation? Will you lump different forms of it into a single category? Will you distinguish between abuse and molestation? If so, how? If you are studying racial or ethnic differences on some variable, how are you defining race or ethnicity? What about mixed race persons? Will degree of acculturation into the dominant culture be an issue? If so, how will this be assessed? If you are going to expose subjects high and low in "appraisal anxiety" to high-, medium-, and low-stress public speaking situations, how will stress be manipulated? Just as important, how will you determine that your manipulation was successful? If you are going to describe how obese and nonobese patrons eat in fast food restaurants, how will you make your observations?

The answer to most of these questions is that you will use an objective instrument of some type. The instrument may be a short, rather gross categorization of subjects into SES levels or racial groups. Or, it may be a lengthy, rather specific index of "appraisal anxiety" or some other personality characteristic. Whatever its nature, your operational index will need to have certain qualities to be acceptable to the scientific community. Let's look at these for a moment.

Know Important Characteristics of Potential Instruments

The major requirements of any measure used in scientific research are that it (a) be chosen wisely, (b) show appropriate forms of generalizability (i.e., reliability and validity), and (c) be adequately direct. With respect to choice, we refer to whether the measure fits the variables that interest you. If you are concerned with conflict in marital relationships, for example, your measure should reflect this. Thus, before selecting measures you will need to define your variables precisely. *Conflict* is a rather general term and could refer to a number of behaviors. These might involve interaction with one's spouse or they might not. A person might be having many conflicting thoughts about staying in the relationship, for example. If the construct as you view it concerns interaction between the spouses, is this verbal conflict, physical conflict, or both?

It will be easier to choose the right measure if you know precisely what it is you want to assess than if you don't. This is true of any of the constructs you plan to study, whether they are independent or dependent variables. Anxiety is not anxiety is not anxiety. There are many different ways of viewing it. Ethnicity is not ethnicity is not ethnicity, either. Furthermore, you cannot rely merely on the name a measure has been given by its developer. You must examine its content to determine whether it assesses the construct in ways consistent with the definition you will use in your study.

You should also think about whether you are interested in behavior (including motor actions, the experience of thoughts and feelings, and physiological reactions) in its own right or as an index of an hypothetical construct. This distinction has important implications for how you evaluate the data on the characteristics of a particular measure. If behavior is your interest, it will be important that your measure reflect the subjects' actions in the real world. If constructs are your interest, whether your measure directly reflects "reality" will be less important than that it correlates appropriately with other measures in the same nomological net as your constructs.

Let's assume behavior is your interest. In this case, a good measure will be one that is adequately direct. A direct measure assesses *the* behavior of interest, at the *time* and *place* the behavior occurs naturally (Cone, 1978). In the marital conflict example discussed earlier, you might have chosen to focus on verbal forms of conflict. One way to assess verbal conflict would be to ask your subjects about it in an interview. Other forms of assessment include administering an appropriate self-report measure, having others who know the couple well rate each member on verbal conflict, having the couple self-monitor (i.e., observe and record their conflict at home), or having trained observers watch the couple and record all instances of verbal conflict.

These alternative types of assessment can be arrayed along a continuum representing the degree of topographic, temporal, and spatial similarity between the behavior that interests you and the behavior the particular assessment method reflects. Normally, you will be interested in subject responses that are as close as possible to those that occur naturally. This is because you want your data to have "real world" implications. You will want your study to have as much external validity as possible. Direct measures enhance external validity. It does not take a rocket scientist to appreciate that asking someone to tell you about something they did at some other time and some other place is likely to produce poorer data than you would get from actually observing their performance.

Unfortunately, directness relates in an inverse fashion to cost. Having trained observers watch people in their natural environments is difficult. Direct observation involves spending hours developing and standardizing an observation code, finding and training observers, gaining access to the subjects' natural settings, observing them unobtrusively in those settings, and reducing the observers' data to usable form. Compare this with a few hours to develop a structured interview and meeting with and administering it to someone. Even if you train interviewers, tape record the interviews, and produce transcripts from the tapes, you will still invest much less than if you had chosen the direct observation approach.

Even less cost would be involved if you used self-report measures. Instead of training interviewers, transcribing tape recordings, and scoring the transcriptions, why not merely ask your subjects to respond to a limited set of descriptive statements describing their behavior? Why not, indeed, has been the answer of many a researcher, novice and otherwise. In fact, self-report measures are so common that they are generally the first form of assessment we think of when launching the search for objective measures. In the example above, we could ask our couple to respond "true" or "false" to statements asking whether they "argue about money," "raise their voices in front of others," and so on. When we do this, we make the important assumption that what the couple says corresponds to some degree with what they really do. Unfortunately, research attempting to show correspondence between reports of what people say they do and what they actually do indicates this assumption is often false (Bellack & Hersen, 1977; Mischel, 1968).

That is not to say that self-report measures do not relate to other measures. They often do, especially to reports on other self-report measures. We are merely pointing out that the common practice of using self-reports as substitutes for more direct forms of assessment has not received much support in the research literature. Indeed, many researchers openly acknowledge that self-report may not mirror behavior, but then they do not take the next step to determine whether it does.

We encourage you to consider alternatives to sole reliance on self-report measures. Ratings by others offer an improvement in objectivity, for example, because the data are provided by individuals with less personal investment in how their ratings are to be used. They are still indirect, however, as they rely on reports of others about behavior that has occurred at other times and places. The alert investigator will become informed of the many well-documented difficulties with such data (e.g., Cairns & Green, 1979) before using this assessment approach.

Self-observations provide yet another alternative. These are more direct than interviews, self-reports, and ratings by others because they require the subject to observe and record the occurrence of *the* behavior of interest and to do so at the *time* and *place* of its occurrence. Although self-observation lacks the objectivity afforded by the independence of the assessor and the assessed, you can mitigate this problem by having the subject focus on very well-defined, specific responses. You can determine the accuracy of self-observation just as you can determine the accuracy of observation by others. (See Johnston & Pennypacker, 1980, for descriptions of how.)

Finally, direct observation should be considered as a way of assessing your variables. True, it is a costly procedure, as we have already mentioned. There are ways of using direct observations that are less costly than others, however (Foster et al., 1988; Foster & Cone, 1986). For example, rather than having trained observers travel to natural contexts and station themselves unobtrusively to collect data, you could record (using video- or audiotapes) the behavior for later analysis. Or, observers could watch subjects in research rooms from behind one-way mirrors. Although such an approach removes the behavior from its natural context, it is still likely to yield higher quality data about actual performance than some of the less direct methods just described. Video- or audiotaping the behavior at the same time will provide a relatively permanent record that can be reviewed frequently to produce highly objective data.

As this discussion has indicated, the variables in your study can be operationalized in several alternative ways. In the next section, we describe several sources to consult to find existing measures. If you are lucky enough to find an existing measure of your variables in the literature, you will be able to avoid the work of developing one and establishing its psychometric adequacy. This assumes, of course, the measure you locate is psychometrically sound.

We said earlier that good measures are ones that are chosen wisely, are adequately direct, and demonstrate appropriate forms of generalizability (i.e., reliability and validity). In the next section, we review important psychometric characteristics and offer some suggestions and minimal criteria for evaluating measures. Space does not permit us to present an entire course in test construction or measurement theory. Most of these concepts should be familiar to you, although you might not have thought about them in the context of your own particular research project. The literature provides many excellent treatments of these issues (Anastasi, 1988; Cronbach, 1990; Cronbach et al., 1972; Guilford, 1956; Kaplan & Saccuzzo, 1989; Nunnally, 1967).

Evaluate the Reliability of Prospective Instruments

The essential criterion for any instrument, whether it be in the physical or behavioral sciences, is that it produces data that are reliable. Over the years, measurement scholars have defined different forms of reliability (Wiggins, 1973). You have heard of these before: test–retest or temporal reliability, alternate form reliability, internal consistency, and so on. In 1972, Cronbach and colleagues proposed consolidating various forms of reliability under the general rubric of generalizability theory. Essentially, what they noted was that the different types of reliability all had to do with different ways in which the data from measuring devices could be generalized.

At the very least, an instrument has to be scored reliably. This means simply that independent persons scoring responses to the instrument will come up with the same score. Cronbach et al. (1972) observed that if they did, we could say the scores obtained by a particular subject or subjects do not depend on the person doing the scoring. This is obviously a desirable state of affairs because we are interested in assessing characteristics of the subject, not those of the scorer! So, the first thing you will want to ask in selecting an operational index of a variable is whether it is reliably scorable. If it is not, it is very unlikely to have any other form of reliability or validity either. The authors of a given instrument will generally present information concerning scorer generalizability or reliability. This is especially true for the more direct forms of assessment referred to earlier, such as direct observation. Users of self-report measures do not often address scorer reliability, as most such instruments are scored by keys or computers, and users *assume* these procedures are reliable. This is not necessarily a safe assumption, however. If you use such measures in your own research, it is a good idea to test the reliability of your scoring procedures from time to time just to make sure.

If your instrument involves ratings by others, there should be published information concerning the agreement between independent raters when using the measure on the same subjects. These interrater reliability data represent scorer generalizability for rating-scale data. Similarly, if you are using direct observation, good systems will always contain some information concerning agreement between observers. Interobserver agreement constitutes scorer generalizability for direct observation measures.

If the instrument you are considering has been shown to have scorer generalizability, you can then examine other forms of generalizability. If it has not, you must establish this important characteristic when using the measure in your own research. Even if there are published data concerning scorer generalizability, it will be important for you to provide checks on this in your own study. Just because Max Efficient found that judges' scores correlated when rating managers' social skills in a study conducted in Cutbank, Montana, in 1953 does not mean the same will hold true for your study. Although such data offer *promise* that the instrument is reliable in the scorer sense, it does not follow that it *will* be so in your particular circumstances. In other words, generalizability data arc not always generalizable themselves! Meehl referred to this in discussing context dependent stochastologicals (Meehl, 1978), a problem plaguing psychology, generally. Thus, when evaluating published data on interrater or interobserver agreement, remember that *your* raters or observers may not agree as well as those working with other researchers. Whenever you use human judges to evaluate data, you must establish satisfactory agreement for the data *in that particular study*. To do so will require that you obtain information on both the coding scheme and the training procedures you decide to use with observers, raters, and judges.

The next most frequently examined type of generalizability concerns stability over time. If you obtain data from your subjects today, will these data be representative of those you might have collected at some other time? Traditionally referred to as test–retest reliability or temporal stability, this form of generalizability is fundamental to a subject matter dealing with psychological constructs or individual difference variables that are thought to be the result of early childhood experience and to be stable over time. If you conceptualize your variables as stable ones, you will need to show that scores on the measures of these variables are stable also. This is logically required, because without stability, your device cannot be adequately assessing your variables.

How much stability your measures must show will depend on the nature of the variables you are measuring and how you plan to use them in your particular research. For example, if you are selecting subjects on the basis of some characteristic, such as altruism, you will look for evidence that your measure is stable over at least a 1- or 2-week period. Thus, a reasonably high ($r > .80$) correlation might satisfy you that altruism as assessed in this way is adequately consistent. At the same time, if altruism is something you plan to change in your study, you will want more specific information concerning its stability over time. Let's say you are going to expose participants to a program designed to increase altruistic behavior. Your design calls for pretesting after random assignment to groups, the application of a 4-week altruism-building program, and posttesting at the end of the 4th week. It would be useful to know something about the stability of scores on your altruism measure over an interval (i.e., 4 weeks) as long as the time between pre- and posttestings.

This would allow you to estimate whether pre–post differences are more than would normally attend the passage of time given this particular measure. Including an assessment-only control group would provide similar information, of course.

If you are using a pre–post design such as this, you will want to examine not only the correlation representing temporal generalizability, but the means of the two assessments as well. Recall from your statistics classes that most correlation coefficients tell you only the extent to which scores on two different variables occupy the same ordinal positions relative to one another. (The exception is the intraclass correlation coefficient that takes into account differences in actual scores as well as differences in rank ordering of scores.) It is not uncommon for high test–retest correlations to occur concurrently with significant changes in mean scores. Suppose this were true of your altruism measure. If it were, the altruism score could change as much as the change you observed pre- to posttest merely because of the passage of time. Knowing the mean differences normally expected over assessment intervals comparable with the ones you are planning would be as important as knowing the correlations representing temporal stability.

Another type of generalizability relevant to our altruism example has traditionally been referred to as alternate form reliability. If you give the same measure to your subjects before and after exposing them to some form of treatment, you will want the measure to pick up any differences produced by the treatment. Other things being equal, people will generally strive to be consistent in what they say about themselves. If you use the same instrument before and after your treatment, you run the risk of this consistency working against you. That is, subjects may try to appear the same, when the treatment has actually had some impact. Your experiment will not be as sensitive to real changes as it might be. If you administered different forms of the same measure before and after your treatment, you might be more apt to detect real changes in your subjects. Of course, the two forms of this measure would need to have shown a high degree of comparability. That is, a high correlation should exist between them, and their means should be the same. In terms of generalizability theory, such comparability would mean that both forms of the test are sampling from the same universe of altruistic content. It would not matter which you used; you would arrive at the same conclusion concerning your subjects. If alternate forms of the measure you select are not available, all is not lost. You might be able to create one yourself, or you might be able to design your study to protect against the potentially conservative effects of pretreatment assessment.

Alternate forms of tests can sometimes be produced fairly easily when the original measure is long. If, for instance, your test has 50 items, it might be possible to split it into two 25-item forms. To find out whether this would be possible would not be difficult. If you know the reliability of the test, you can use the Spearman–Brown prophecy formula (Kaplan & Saccuzzo, 1989) to estimate the effects on that reliability of reducing its length by half. If the original instrument is highly reliable, cutting it in half might produce alternate forms that themselves are reliable. If the original instrument is not highly reliable or is too short to make splitting feasible, your task will be more difficult. Rather than set about to create more items and go through the lengthy process of establishing their measurement characteristics, you might be wise to choose a design solution to your problem. For example, a Solomon four-group design could be selected. Such a research design specifically allows you to estimate pretest effects.

As mentioned previously, an important characteristic of measuring instruments is that they adequately represent the domain of interest. To do this well, they should be focused measures of the construct you are studying. That simply means that each score on the device should represent a single phenomenon. For this to occur, the instrument (or the relevant subscale) has to be assessing the same thing at all points within it. Said another way, it has to be internally consistent. To the extent that all items in an assessment device are tapping the same thing, they will be correlated with one another. In generalizability theory terms, it is as though all items were drawn from the same universe of content. It does not matter which items are involved to produce a score of 10 on a particular 30-item test. The same score could have resulted from responses to the first, middle, or last 10, or to any combination of items. Assessment devices with a high degree of internal consistency are said to be homogeneous. The correlation is the basic statistical tool for demonstrating such homogeneity, with split-half, Kuder-Richardson, and coefficient alpha procedures all being variations appropriate under different circumstances (Cronbach, 1990; Kaplan & Saccuzzo, 1989).

We have talked about a number of ways in which scores on measuring instruments may or may not be generalizable. Obviously, these are not all the same, conceptually or practically. As a result, it is not very informative to say in your method section that you chose your particular instrument because it is reliable. The really important statement is that it has the types of generalizability necessary for your own research. To make this assessment is not easy, if it is done correctly. It requires a clear understanding of your subject matter and just how you plan to study it. For example, if you are studying a psychological construct, different generalizability issues will come up than if you are studying behavior from a natural science perspective. (For an important discussion of the measurement differences for these two subject matters, see Johnston & Pennypacker, 1980.) Assuming you are studying a psychological construct, what are your assumptions about it? Is it supposed to be relatively consistent across time? Across situations? Is it a relatively unitary construct or one made up of multiple dimensions? Is it best revealed in the verbal behavior of the subject or in motor or physiological responding?

Your answers to these and other questions will bear on the types of generalizability information to examine when selecting among possible measures. Ideally, you will be able to identify the information you need in advance, select a measure that has it, and present the information to support your choice in your method section. At the very least, you should say more than that the measure has adequate evidence supporting its reliability and validity. It is a good idea to say that, for your purposes, "the following types of reliability data are needed." Then state what they are. Cite evidence that they have been shown for your measure. Finally, repeat the process for validity, a subject to which we now turn.

Evaluate the Validity of Prospective Instruments

In addition to producing scores on your variables in consistent ways, you will want your measures to mean something. Whether they do turns on the evidence for their validity. An instrument may produce highly generalizable data in the reliability sense, and these data may not relate to anything. In other words, you may have a reliable measure that is not valid. Incidentally, contrary to what you might occasionally see in textbooks, the reverse is not possible within the context of classical measurement theory. To be valid, a measure must be reliable. What we mean by validity is the extent to which scores on a measure relate to scores on other measures. This is more general than the hackneyed definition that a measure is valid if it measures what it is supposed to measure. It may not do this at all well and still have a great deal of validity in the larger sense meant here.

As with reliability, instruments may be said to be valid in different ways. A measure has face validity if it looks to the subject like it is appropriate for the purposes at hand. It has content validity if it looks to experts like it contains the type of stimulus material appropriate to the variable being assessed. Content validity refers to how well the measure samples the universe of content relevant to the construct or behavior being assessed, so how items were selected, categories defined, and so on, are key issues. An instrument has criterion-related validity if its scores allow prediction of scores on other measures, usually of a practical variety. If scores on the criterion are available at the same time as scores are obtained on the instrument being validated, we refer to concurrent va lidity. If they have to be obtained some time in the future, we refer to predictive validity. An instrument has construct validity if its scores have been found to enter relationships required by the theory underlying it. It has convergent validity if it relates to other ways of assessing the same behavior or construct. It has discriminant validity if it does not relate to measures from which theory would require it to be independent. It has discriminative validity if its scores have been shown to produce expected mean differences between groups, and so on. Which of these types of validity will be necessary for your measures? Perhaps your study is designed to provide just this information. If so, what type will it be addressing and why?

The types of validity you need to show depend, as with reliability, on the nature of your subject matter and the specific research questions you are pursuing. If you are studying a psychological construct (e.g., hostility, anxiety, altruism, or chauvinism), you will need evidence for the construct validity of your instrument, at a minimum. For example, if your study deals with altruism, it will examine relationships between altruism and some other variables. What is the source of these anticipated relationships? The correct answer is someone's theory concerning altruism. To test the relationships properly will require using a measure of altruism that meaningfully taps the construct as it is understood in the relevant theoretical writings. This meaningfulness resides in the research literature dealing with the measure's construct validity (cf. Grusec, 1991).

If your subject matter is behavior, especially as studied from a natural science perspective, you will not be especially concerned with construct validity in the sense just described. Instead, you will be more likely to focus on the content of the measure. You will want to be satisfied that it contains stimuli likely to set the occasion for samples of behavior that are representative of larger populations of that behavior that are not feasible for you to study directly. Moreover, you will want to know the extent to which the behavior produced by the instrument is representative of what you might expect to see at another time or place. We discussed how well data generalize to other assessment occasions as temporal stability. How well data might represent what might be expected in other contexts deals with setting generalizability (Cone, 1978). For example, if you observe positive verbal interchanges between spouses in the laboratory, are they representative of what you might have seen had you observed them at home?

As with reliability, it will not be enough to state in your method section that your measure is valid. Instead, describe what forms of validity are important for your purposes and then provide evidence that they exist for your measures. You will most certainly do this if your research just happens to be a validity study itself, because to make the case for doing the research, you will have provided an extensive review of the measurement literature relevant to the device you plan to use. Any study needs this scrutiny, though. You always need to know whether a measure assesses the variable of interest and whether it does so consistently. In the absence of this vital information, research findings are extremely hard to interpret.

You will find information about the psychometric properties of measures in four places: (a) manuals describing the measure, (b) chapters or review papers evaluating the measure, (c) articles specifically evaluating the psychometric properties of the measure, and (d) articles that use the measure. Be aware that the last of these may not even mention in the abstract or introduction the fact that they collected psychometric data. The information may, instead, be hidden in the method section. In addition, some studies that do not even mention psychometric issues may provide findings relevant to the validity issue. For example, repeated findings that self-report measures of anxiety and depression correlate highly (see Barlow, 1988) cast doubt on the discriminant validity of these measures, at least as assessment instruments of distinct affective domains.

Look Broadly for Decent Measures

We have described the assessment methods you can select among to operationalize the variables in your research. We have also discussed important characteristics good measures will have. Where do you look for such measures? If you are working in an active research area, you will probably use measures that are common to it. If you are braving new frontiers, it might not be clear from the existing literature just what the best measures would be. Several published compendiums provide valuable information about assessment instruments. The best known of these is the *Mental Measurements Yearbook* (Kramer & Conoley, 1992). Published by the University of Nebraska Press, this volume reviews approximately 900 tests of various types. Now in its 11th edition, the *Yearbook* has been around since 1938 when it was initiated by Oscar K. Buros. It is common to refer to the collection simply as *Buros*. In addition to descriptions of the measures, the over 500 reviewers in *Buros* provide commentary on their psychometric adequacy.

Another good source of information about potential measures is *Tests in Print II* (Buros, 1974). Unlike *Buros*, *Tests in Print* does not provide actual reviews of the instruments. It does include more listings than *Buros*, however, and is a good source for locating addresses and journal articles relevant to a particular measure. Unfortunately, it is a bit dated and will not have listings for instruments appearing after 1974.

A more up-to-date alternative, especially useful if you are planning to use a more behaviorally focused measure, is Hersen and Bellack's *Dictionary of Behavioral Assessment Techniques* (Hersen & Bellack, 1988). This volume provides descriptions and reviews of 286 devices and is a very good source of introductory information about a measure. Over 200 researchers provide reviews and references to writings in which the original instrument can be found. The measures themselves are not presented in this or in any of the sources we describe here. Do not be put off by reference to *behavioral* in the book's title. There are many instruments included that would hardly be considered any different from traditional, trait-oriented forms of assessment long familiar to personality and clinical psychologists everywhere.

Sweetland and Keyser published an extensive collection of references to tests in 1983 (Sweetland & Keyser, 1983). They indexed and provided descriptive information on more than 3,500 instruments. The measures are divided into those relevant to business, education, and psychology. The book does not include psychometric information, but it can be a good source for identifying promising instruments and consulting the references associated with each to find out more about them. Supplementary updates to this volume appeared in 1985 (Keyser & Sweetland, 1984) and 1990 (Sweetland & Keyser, 1990). These volumes provide much information on reliability, validity, and norming procedures that was missing in the initial book.

If you are working with a clinical population or variables common thereto, the *Handbook for Psychiatric Rating Scales* (Research and Education

Figure 9.1

```
HAPI 1985-APR 1991 (9104)
BRS SEARCH MODE—ENTER QUERY
        1_: (babies or newborns or infants or fetal or fetus) same (alcohol or
             substance) same (use or abuse or dependence or withdrawal or syn-
             drome)
        RESULT    4 DOCUMENTS


        2_: ..p all/2

              2
AN      3873. 8904.
TI      Dysmorphia Checklist for Fetal Alcohol Syndrome. (FAS
        Checklist).
AU      Fernhoff, Paul M.; Smith, Iris E.; Coles, Claire D.
YR      1979.
SO      Coles, C.D., Smith, I.E., Lancaster, J.S., & Falek, A. (1987). Persistence over
        the first month of neurobehavioral differences in infants exposed to alcohol
        prenatally. Infant Behavior and Development, 10, 23–37.
DE      Fetal-Alcohol-Syndrome. Infant. Infants. Symptoms.
NQ      NUMBER OF QUESTIONS: 61.
ST      SUBSCALE TITLES: X.
AB      The Dysmorphia Checklist for Fetal Alcohol Syndrome (FAS Checklist) is
        designed to be used in the clinical evaluation and diagnosis of children
        prenatally exposed to alcohol. This checklist consists of a list of clinical
        features associated with Fetal Alcohol Syndrome. Individual features are
        scored present or absent and are assigned weights of 1, 2, or 3 corre-
        sponding to the reported frequency of their occurrence in FAS children.
RE      RELIABILITY: REPORTED Y/NOT REPORTED X.
        Internal Consistency: X.
        Parallel Forms: X.
        Test-Retest: X.
        Inter-Rater: X.
VA      VALIDITY: REPORTED Y/NOT REPORTED X.
        Content: X.
        Criterion: X.
        Construct: X.
RF      REFERENCES: Coles, C.D., Smith, I.E., & Falek, A. (1987). Prenatal alcohol
        exposure and infant behavior: Immediate effects and implications for later
        development. Advances in Alcohol and Substance Abuse, 6, 87–104.
        Coles, C.D., Smith, I.E., Fernhoff, P.M., & Falek, A. (1984). Neonatal ethanol
        withdrawal: Characteristics in clinically normal non-dysmorphic neonates.
        Journal of Pediatrics, 105, 445–451. Smith, I.E., Coles, C.D., Lancaster,
        J.S., Fernhoff, P.M., & Falek, A. (1986). The effect of volume and duration
        of prenatal alcohol exposure on neonatal physical and behavioral devel-
        opment. Neurobehavioral Toxicology and Teratology, 8, 375–381.
AT      ANALYST: Ms. I.E. Smith, GAPPP, 1256 Briarcliff Road NE, Atlanta, GA
        30306.
```

Sample listing from *Health and Psychosocial Instruments (HAPI)* database of assessment instruments

Association, 1981) might be worth consulting. Reliability and validity information is provided for each of the rating scales included, along with descriptions of the scales, the types of client for whom the scale would be relevant, and references to consult for further details. Additional books to consult for information about specific measures include those by Corcoran and Fischer (1987) and Robinson, Shaver, and Wrightsman (1991).

A particularly good source if you have access to a computer outfitted with a modem is an on-line database of instruments produced by the Behavioral Measurement Database Service called *Health and Psychosocial Instruments* (*HAPI*). *HAPI* includes information on over 8,000 instruments and is updated quarterly. An example of the type of information provided about a measure can be seen from the sample record obtained from *HAPI* using *BRS™* (see appendix C for detailed information concerning on-line databases, including *HAPI*) presented in Figure 9.1. *HAPI* is now distributed on compact discs for CD-ROM players, and regular updates will be available to libraries and others that subscribe to the service.

Finally, if none of these sources proves helpful, you can always fall back on *Psychological Abstracts* or its compact disc version, *PsycLIT*. Searching these databases using terms describing your variables or synonyms thereof will at least put you in touch with relevant research. If you are lucky, some of the references might even provide ways of measuring the variables. A list of databases for this purpose is provided in appendix C.

Know What to Do If Vital Psychometric Information Is Unavailable

Suppose you have selected your measure and searched high and low for evidence to support its psychometric adequacy and have not found any. Suppose further that no alternative measures exist that you can use. What do you do? If you have understood the material presented earlier, you are pretty clear about the types of generalizability your measure needs to show. Let's look at some of the more important of these and see how you might proceed if they are lacking.

Scorer Generalizability

A reliably scored instrument is essential to any research. Even if the literature shows that your measure *can* be scored reliably, you will want to provide evidence that it *has* been in your particular study. We mentioned this point earlier and repeat it here for emphasis. If you are using a self-report method, have a second person independently score some portion, say 25%, of the answer sheets. If the two sets of scores disagree, identify the problem and correct it. If you are using structured interviews, record them all, if possible, and have independent coders score the tapes themselves or their transcripts. As mentioned in chapter 8, at least 20% should be double scored. If the 20 to 25% you check show problems, intervene. Maybe the two coders have different definitions of the categories you are using. Maybe one or both have just gotten careless. Retraining or increased incentives for accuracy might be needed, and everything coded thus far (not just the reliability data) should be rescored after intervention. If you are using ratings by others, compare the ratings of two independent raters on 20 to 25% of the same subjects. You might do this with a simple correlation, although more precise information will be provided by a percentage agreement measure of some type. For example, you might define an agreement on each rating-scale item as both raters marking the same point on the scale. Or, you might be more liberal and require only that they be within one scale point of each other. Count up the number of agreements and divide by the total number of ratings to obtain percentage agreement. Even better is a kappa coefficient that corrects for chance agreement.

If you are using a direct-observation coding system, consider supplementing it with video or audio tape recording to produce permanent records of the subjects' behavior. Multiple observers working independently can code these, and you can compare their data. Again, some percentage of the observations should be selected randomly, and agreement calculations performed. If video or audio tape recordings cannot be made, it is best to use independent observers working in pairs, continuously checking their agreement. Train a cadre of observers to be available at any time so that the same observers are not always working together. This will prevent consensual drift by the observer pair in their definitions of the behavior. If you cannot take such seemingly elaborate precautions, you can use a single observer, periodically checking this person with a second observer. This is not the ideal arrangement, however, as the primary observer's behavior is often affected by the presence or absence of the "checker" observer (Romanczyk et al., 1973). If you go this route, train observers to very high levels of agreement so that even if they observe better when assessed for agreement than when alone, they are good enough that you can tolerate some slippage.

Just because you obtain your data from some archival source (e.g., patient files in a hospital or records from a county courthouse) do not assume you can skip the important assessment of scorer generalizability. You might think it is a routine matter to determine chronicity of schizophrenia by subtracting a person's date of first hospitalization from the current date. The file might have different dates of initial hospitalization depending on where you look in it, however. Or, you or your assistants may not reliably perform the simple tasks of recording such a date or subtracting one date from another. Always check such steps in the production of data for accuracy.

A key element in assuring that your data are scored reliably lies in rater and observer training. Get lots of practice stimuli (e.g., pilot data) that are very similar to what you expect your "real" subjects will provide. Work the bugs out on this material before letting your raters or observers loose on your precious research data. Ensure that your judges, working independently, show good agreement on practice material before you give them real data to score. It is wise to train them so their agreement is 10 to 15% higher than the lowest you would accept in your study, because agreement frequently drops when raters and observers begin collecting "real" data (Romanczyk et al., 1973).

Temporal Generalizability

You can take several steps if the temporal stability of scores on your measure has not been established and is required by your particular research question. One would be to perform repeat administrations of the measure over the appropriate interval of time before beginning your actual study. Then, correlate the scores of your group of subjects between the two assessment occasions. In other words, establish its temporal stability yourself. Alternatively, you could design your study to control for the possible effects of score changes associated merely with the passage of time. For example, you could include an untreated, assessment-only control group. Or, you might use a more sophisticated design that would include such a group and others (e.g., Solomon four-group). Another possibility would involve repeated assessment of your subjects over time before and after the introduction of your independent variable. In this within-subjects approach, each subject serves as his or her own control for changes in scores associated merely with practice or the passage of time.

Item Generalizability

Internal consistency estimates are among the easiest characteristics to establish for new instruments, so your particular choice is likely to have this important information. If not, you can usually calculate it yourself from existing normative information. Use Kuder-Richardson Formula 21 (Nunnally, 1967) to do this. If the internal consistency of the scale is low, you have a problem. If you go ahead and use the scale anyway, you will have some difficulty interpreting your data. This is because an instrument with low internal consistency measures multiple things. The same score that is based on responses to different items in the scale will mean different things.

You cannot protect yourself by going ahead, running the study, and then computing internal consistency estimates. Suppose they are low? It will be too late to modify the measure to improve matters, and you might not want to do this anyway. To improve internal consistency, you would have to organize elements of the instrument in new ways, fundamentally altering the structure of the instrument and rendering available norms and validity information inapplicable. The reasonable thing to do under the circumstances would be to use a large enough subject sample to permit you to factor analyze the scale after the fact. You could then develop scores for your subjects on each of the emerging factors. The factors that are most conceptually consistent with your theoretical and practical understanding of your constructs would then be used as your dependent variables. Of course, there would be no norms or validity information for these newly developed scales. Moreover, a reasonable factor analysis requires between 7 and 20 subjects per variable, as mentioned in chapter 8. This might be a formidable number if your analysis involves many items or measures.

This discussion applies largely to the use of self-report ratings and ratings by other methods, but it is applicable to all assessment methods, at least on a conceptual level. Space does not permit us to wander into this interesting arena here. Suffice it to say that homogeneity of an assessment instrument is important regardless of method and of whether your subject matter is a psychological construct or actual behavior itself. For example, even if you are performing direct observations of the predatory behavior of free-ranging tarantulas, you will be assuming the several specific responses you code are all members of the same predatory behavior class. If some deal with nesting, some with foraging, and some with reproduction, how will a single score be meaningful?

Method Generalizability

We mentioned convergent and discriminant validity earlier, but did not discuss them in detail. These are especially relevant when self-report measures are being used to tap psychological constructs. This is because new self-report measures often correlate substantially with already existing measures of pervasive individual difference variables. Some of these pervasive variables include intelligence, SES, years of education, and the tendency to say socially desirable things about one's self. Purveyors of new measures must show that they are not simply additional ways of measuring these variables (Campbell, 1960). Because of the pervasiveness of social desirability response sets, for example, new self-report measures must be shown to be independent of social desirability (Edwards, 1970). There are already plenty of good measures of social desirability in the literature, and we do not need another one. Make sure your scale has been correlated with social desirability and shown to be unrelated or at least to have only a modest relationship. In doing this, be alert to the fact that different ways of assessing social desirability (e.g., Edwards, 1957; Crowne & Marlowe, 1960; Wiggins, 1959) are not interchangeable (Edwards, 1990). Only the Edwards version of this variable has been shown to pervade self-report assessment. Because of its derivation from *MMPI* items, it is especially pervasive when assessing psychiatric populations. Thus, it is this version that your measure should have been compared with to establish its discriminant validity. There may be other response sets (e.g., need for approval; Crowne & Marlowe, 1960) you want to compare your measure with, but the most pervasive is social desirability.

If your instrument has not been shown to be independent of social desirability, you should address this in your research. One way to do this would be to include a measure of social desirability along with your other measures and compute the correlation between them yourself. If the correlation is insignificant, social desirability can be eliminated from the interpretation of your results. If there is a correlation, however, you first want to consider what degree of relationship between social desirability and your measure you would expect on the basis of previous literature and theory. For example, depressed individuals are known to distort information in a negative direction (Beck, Rush, Shaw, & Emery, 1979), and therefore a negative correlation between self-reports of depression and social desirability might be expected and even tolerated. Of course, a very high correlation would make your measure suspect. If social desirability is not supposed to correlate with your measure, you may want to control for the effects of social desirability statistically, using partial correlation or ANCOVA procedures.

If your study involves psychological constructs, make sure that you use alternative measures to assess them. Campbell and Fiske (1959) articulated this requirement in the literature many years ago. Noting that scores on any instrument are, in part, a function of the characteristics of the instrument itself, these authors suggested multitrait–multimethod matrixes be used to sort out this method variance, establishing convergent and discriminant validity at the same time. The importance of convergent validity for measures of constructs cannot be emphasized enough. The structure of our language builds in relationships between concepts automatically. When we use language-based assessment instruments, constructs will likely relate to one another at least partially because of this structure. The validity evidence for a given measure should involve more than correlations resulting from the fortuitous use of common assessment methods. If there really is a construct underlying the scores on a given instrument, logic requires it to be assessable in more than one way. That is because, if a single measure completely operationalizes (i.e., defines) a concept, the concept is no longer hypothetical. Because being hypothetical is a cardinal characteristic of psychological traits, without it, one is not dealing with a trait. This is the basis for saying that relationships between assessment alternatives establish the convergent validity of the alternatives and extend the construct validity of the underlying psychological variable at the same time.

If convergent validity has not been shown for your selected measures, you will have to address this in your own research. The simplest way to do this would be to provide alternative ways of assessing your variables and then to compare these after you collect the data. If different methods correlate, you can use them interchangeably or in some combination in your data analyses. If they do not, the data from each may have to be treated separately, leading to some interesting material for your discussion section.

By alternative assessment methods, we are not referring to a second self-report measure, a second rating by other, and so on. Self-report data should be supplemented with ratings by others or direct observation data, for example. Sometimes collateral data sources can be used effectively. If, for example, self-reports of drinking are one of your measures, you might compare these with spouse or roommate or friend reports. Or, you might use unobtrusive measures such as the number of empty beer cans in the trash (Webb, Campbell, Schwartz, & Sechrest, 1966). Some behaviors have fairly direct products or traces that can be used for corroboration. Self-reported homework completions or time spent working on one's dissertation are fairly obvious examples. Look at the problems completed correctly or the pages written to support the verbal measure.

Setting Generalizability

Perhaps previous research has shown that data collected with your anticipated measure in one situation can safely be generalized to others. More likely, you will have to show this yourself. Alternatively, you could rely on one of the researchers' most used caveats that "caution should be exercised in interpreting these results since it is not known whether subjects would have performed similarly in their homes (classrooms, neighborhood, etc.)." If your study is an applied one, you are probably doing it in the setting of eventual interest anyway, and setting generalizability is a moot issue. If you are dealing with psychological constructs, their cross-setting generality is often assumed and rarely tested. This is an issue worth pondering, especially if you are concerned with the ecological validity of your research.

Adapt Others' Measures With Caution

What if you wish to adapt others' measures for your own purpose? For example, you may have found a wonderful scale for assessing assertiveness and wish to alter it for use with individuals diagnosed with multiple personality disorder by asking the person to fill it out with reference to each personality. This, of course, means altering the instructions and focus of the instrument.

Will its original psychometric properties be relevant? You cannot be sure. Logically, the less you change an instrument, the more you should be able to assume that its properties would stay the same. Administering only certain MMPI subscales could reasonably be expected to yield subscale scores that would be the same as subscale scores derived from the same items embedded in the full MMPI. But you cannot be sure unless you gather some data to assess whether this is so. One way to do this would to conduct a pilot study. Scores on the shortened versus full MMPI could be correlated (as when assessing alternate-form reliability). Temporal and item generalizability could be established for ratings of the assertiveness of one's alternate personalities as well as of one's primary personality. And, as indicated previously, additional measures that would help you assess the validity of the altered instrument could be built directly into your research project itself.

Avoid Common Errors in Evaluating and Selecting Measures

Several common errors pervade descriptions of measuring devices. Avoid these. First, do not assume that the name of an instrument captures what it measures. Many fledgling and even some experienced researchers assume that the name of a measure indicates what it assesses. This is not necessarily the case. Examine the content of the measure carefully: It may be misnamed, at least as you understand the construct being assessed.

Assuming that a name mirrors a measure's content is a particular problem with questionnaires that have subscales derived with factor analytic techniques. Putting it simply, a factor analysis looks at the data, sorts out what is most closely associated with what, and shows the investigator what these relationships are. The investigator determines which items are associated closely enough to be considered a factor. Item content has nothing to do with the mathematics of factor analysis. What this means is that items that load on the same factor may (or may not) tap widely different content. The investigator then must inductively figure out a name that seems to fit the items. Unless the creator of the measure has used confirmatory factor analysis to test whether a group of conceptually related items hang together, the name is the researcher's a posteriori creation. Do not assume that it reflects scale content adequately.

Second, do not assume that a significant correlation is a high correlation. Many consumers of psychometric literature make this error. A significant correlation between two measures of the same construct may or may not support the validity of the measure being investigated. The magnitude of the correlation, not its statistical significance, is important. A self-report measure of work productivity and a mechanized assessment of the same variable may correlate .20 and be significant at $p < .05$, but the measures have only 4% of their variance in common. Does this really indicate that one can be substituted for the other?

Third, do not assume that a self-report measure assesses behavior because it correlates with other self-report measures. As we indicated earlier, Campbell and Fiske (1959) long ago pointed out the fallacy of assuming that correlations between measures that used the same method to assess the same construct "proved" the validity of a new measure. Method variance (i.e., the tendency for some of the variation in scores on measures to be a result of the measuring instrument itself) could explain the results. Because two self-report measures involve the same method, their scores may be related as a result of this shared approach to assessment. The true test of an indirect measure of behavior (e.g., self-report) is whether it correlates with a more direct assessment of the same phenomenon. In general, correlations between different ways of assessing the same thing should exceed those between different things assessed with the same method.

Finally, do not use single-item measures. Single-item measures of any construct or behavior are notoriously unreliable. However, beginning researchers often persist in assuming that a subject's answer to a question such as "Was either of your parents an alcoholic?" is a good way to classify the individual as one who grew up in an alcoholic family! This is a particular problem when measuring subject characteristics, either to describe the subjects or to classify them (e.g., as an independent variable). Similarly, designers of new questionnaires often want to analyze each item one by one. Unless you can show that individual items are reliable and valid, do not do this.

Get Copies of Instruments

To examine the content of a measure you are considering using, you need to obtain a copy of the measure. This often turns out to be surprisingly difficult. Journal articles rarely publish copies of measures, and although some are available from commercial publishers, many are not.

To obtain a copy of a measure that interests you and that is not commercially available, contact the creator of the instrument and request one. Make sure to find out the person's current address. Professional directories such as the *APA Membership Register* and member listings of other professional organizations (e.g., Society for Research in Child Development and American Psychological Society) are updated regularly and should help you locate the individual. When you find the person, inquire whether the instrument is copyrighted. If so, you must obtain permission in writing to use the measure.

If you cannot find the author, if the author fails to respond to your request, or if you just want to hedge your bets, find someone else who has used the measure in published research. This person must have found a copy of the measure, right? Ask your chairperson, too, about colleagues who might use the instrument. Then, track down the user and ask for a copy. Use your advisor's name (with permission) to enhance the chances that the person will respond to your request.

Summary

All researchers should provide evidence that their data are from reliably scored instruments, at a minimum. Other forms of generalizability (e.g., temporal, item, method, and setting) will vary in importance depending on the particular study being conducted. Be aware of these, and consider whether and how they must be addressed in your study. We have provided a few suggestions in this regard. If you are in doubt about whether a particular concept applies, ask your chair or other committee members. Do this after thoroughly familiarizing yourself with the issues, consulting some of the references in this section and in appendix D, if necessary. The heart of any research is its instrumentation. Without reasonable choices here, you might as well not do the study. Spend the time needed to make these choices wisely.

> ✔ **To Do . . .**

Selecting Appropriate Measures

☐ Operationalize your variables

☐ Evaluate the reliability of prospective instruments

— Interrater reliability (scorer generalizability)

— Test–retest reliability (temporal stability)

— Alternate form reliability

— Internal consistency (item generalizability)

— Determine which forms of reliability are most appropriate for your study

☐ Evaluate the validity of prospective instruments

— Face validity

— Content validity

— Criterion-related validity

• Concurrent validity

• Predictive validity

— Construct validity

• Convergent validity

• Discriminant validity

• Discriminative validity

— Determine which forms of validity are most appropriate for your study

☐ Look broadly for decent measures

— Use measurement compendiums

— Use computer-based databases

— Use the published literature

☐ Plan what to do if vital psychometric information is unavailable

— Scorer generalizability (interrater reliability)

— Temporal stability

— Item generalizability (internal consistency)

— Convergent and discriminant validity (method generalizability)

— Setting generalizability

☐ Adapt others' measures with caution

☐ Get copies of measures

10 Selecting the Appropriate Statistics

Nothing strikes terror into the heart of many beginning researchers like the word *statistics*. Even students who breezed through requisite graduate statistics courses in rigorous training programs sometimes profess total ignorance of all things numerical when asked to select appropriate statistics for their own research.

Why do even the best students sometimes have difficulty with this topic? Methods typically used to teach statistics are part of the problem. Statistics teachers often take one of two approaches: (a) mathematical or (b) cookbook. The mathematical tradition teaches derivations of formulas and the conceptual underpinnings of statistical analyses. The cookbook tradition teaches how to do statistical computations. In our experience, neither addresses the important issue of matching statistics to research designs—a topic on the cusp of traditional research design and statistics courses.

Another part of the problem is "mathematics anxiety," a repertoire fostered by early disparagement of one's math ability or failure experiences in mathematics classes (many of which may have resulted from poor teaching and not poor student skill). Math anxiety, in turn, can lead students to avoid opportunities to use numbers and thereby miss the chance to develop self-confidence in this area. Avoidance and a resulting lack of practice lead students to depend on others to select statistics for their projects. As a result, they never learn to become independent in this area.

This chapter will help nervous students sort out which statistics are most appropriate for their research designs. We assume that you have taken the average statistics course and are familiar with at least the names of different statistics and their general uses. We do not go into how to calculate, derive, or program particular analyses. Furthermore, we cover primarily statistics related to basic group-design procedures. The strategies we recommend that you follow to select appropriate statistics assume that your study involves identified independent (or predictor) and dependent (or criterion) variables. These strategies will be confusing if your study explores only the underlying structure of a set of variables.

In addition, we do not cover each and every one of the hundreds of statistical tests available. Among the more common procedures we omit are path analysis, sequential analysis and other time-series procedures, structural equation modeling, survival analysis, and statistics for calculating effect sizes. Nor do we cover all of the controversies involved in using particular statistics. Instead, we overview widely used statistics and their potential functions. To the statistical sophisticate, our coverage will likely seem too simple. To the less educated, it may seem extremely complex.

Our goal in this chapter is to help you get some idea of potentially appropriate statistics for your research. Once you select what might be appropriate for your study, you will need to supplement the material here to make sure you really understand the statistics you have selected and to ensure that they are the best ones for the analyses you have to perform.

Beef Up Your Statistical Knowledge Early

How can you prepare to deal with the statistical analyses you will be conducting? If you are at an early stage in your graduate career, get involved in actual research and volunteer to take some responsibility for data analyses. Then, work closely with the faculty member or research director. Ask questions about why particular analyses are more appropriate than others. Taking responsibility for handling the statistics of a study will also force you to learn about parameters and options relevant to the statistics you use.

In addition, start looking for statistics books that speak your language. Dozens of books cover every conceivable statistical topic. These vary in complexity, focus, balance between mathematical and explanatory material, depth of coverage, and (sometimes) symbol systems. As a consequence, different books will be more or less user-friendly. Your task is to find texts that are relatively easy for you to understand. Throughout this chapter, we refer to statistics books that we find useful. We also provide suggestions in appendix E. Bruning and Kintz's (1987) book provides a particularly user-friendly source of computational formulas for many basic statistics. In addition, some manuals for major computer programs provide good statistical information. The key is finding resources that explain what you need in ways that you understand. Even the two of us disagree sometimes on the statistics books we find most comprehensible!

Examine Your Study First

As a first step in choosing appropriate statistics, identify the purposes you want your statistical analyses to serve. Initially, you should specify clearly the various questions you want your statistics to answer. The logical place to start is with your research questions and hypotheses. You need to go beyond this, however, because you will probably use statistics for more than just testing your hypotheses. For example, you may wish to examine the relationships among various dependent variables or to check that your three experimental groups do not differ in demographic characteristics. Below, we itemize a series of steps for figuring out what kind of analyses may meet your needs. We suggest that you proceed through the steps listed below for *each* analysis you plan.

Next, make a list of each and every variable you plan to analyze. If you will look at demographic characteristics of your sample, list each piece of demographic data and determine how you will get a number for each subject on each variable. Do the same thing for your dependent and independent variables.

Don't be surprised if you get confused. Confusion can be a signal that you need to clarify exactly how each measure will generate numerical data. If so, pull out a copy of each instrument, make up mock data for a few subjects, score the data, and examine the results. At the end of this process, you should have one list of questions you intend to answer with statistics and a second list of variables that those statistics will use in one way or another.

Next, choose one of the questions you intend to answer with statistics. Indicate the specific independent and dependent variables (scores) involved in answering this question. For example, if your question is, "Do attention-deficit hyperactivity disorder (ADHD) and non-ADHD boys and girls differ in their recall of social material?" you would list gender (scored as boy or girl) and diagnosis (ADHD vs. non-ADHD) as the independent variables, and the recall score as the dependent variable. Then, ask yourself (a) Will this question be answered by comparing scores for groups of subjects? or (b) will it be answered by relating scores on the different variables to one another in a single group of subjects? With the example just given, the answer would be "yes" to the first question: You want to compare boys and girls, ADHD and non-ADHD groups, and so on. This will require some sort of statistic that compares the scores the different groups obtain. Statistics that compare groups are typical of between-groups, within-groups, and mixed experimental and quasi-experimental designs. Note that a group comparison statistic can be appropriate if you are comparing either (a) the scores of different discrete groups of individuals (e.g., males vs. females) or (b) the scores of the same group of individuals but taken at different points in time (e.g., pre- vs. posttreatment) or under different conditions.

Designs that require group comparison statistics use independent variables that the researcher defines in ways that require subjects to fit into discrete groups. Each group is called a *level* and has a name. In the example above, gender has two levels (boy and girl), because you want your analyses to consider boys and girls separately and to compare them. Diagnosis also has two levels (ADHD and non-ADHD). If the researcher had not been interested in gender differences, gender would not have been an independent variable and the researcher might not have examined gender differences in the analyses.

If you want to treat your subjects as a single group and examine associations among scores, a correlational design might be most appropriate. This would be the case, for example, if the research question asked, "What is the relationship of health beliefs (assessed by a single score on a multi-item questionnaire), social support (assessed by a single score on a multi-item questionnaire), and adherence to a medication regimen (assessed by the average of periodic blood level assay values)?" This research question treats all subjects as a single group. They are not sorted into separate discrete groups (levels). Subjects' scores on social support and health belief measures will be related to their adherence scores. In correlational designs, variables can be continuous or discrete, although they are most often continuous. We will look for correlational statistics to answer association or relationship types of questions.

Many students have trouble at this point because they have not completely worked out their design. Some research topics can be approached with either a group comparison *or* a correlational design. Suppose, for example, you are interested in whether children with high IQs experience more problems with their peers than children without high

IQs. You could study this in two ways: (a) collect IQ scores and peer interaction scores and examine the relationship between them (i.e., correlate them) or (b) sort children into IQ groups with two or more levels (e.g., high IQ and average IQ) and look at differences between the groups in their peer interactions using a group comparison statistic.

If you are not certain which you are doing, look again at the design section of your proposal (see chapter 8), and clarify what you intend to do. One of our colleagues (Dalenberg, personal communication, September 18, 1992) recommends as a rule of thumb that correlational designs are often most appropriate when you conceptualize your independent variables as natural continua (e.g., intelligence) or if you wish to examine the best combinations of independent variables to predict a single dependent variable. Some also hold that correlational designs are more appropriate than group comparisons when you do not manipulate your independent variables. In addition, creating groups by dichotomizing or trichotomizing on continuous measures and then using group-comparison instead of correlational statistics results in loss of statistical power (Cohen, 1983). Group-comparison designs are more appropriate than correlational designs when the independent variables are natural categories (e.g., gender) or are based on variables combined in a nonlinear fashion (e.g., psychiatric diagnosis, which is usually based on presence, absence, or degree of several behaviors). Group comparisons are also generally more appropriate when you manipulate the independent variable.

The second thing to figure out is which of your dependent variables are suitable for parametric statistics. Parametric statistics involve assumptions that the underlying distribution of scores in the population you are sampling is normal and that data from different subjects are independent. (Particular parametric tests have additional requirements, as well.) An oversimplified but common rule of thumb is that categorical data cannot meet these assumptions and should be analyzed using a nonparametric approach. Exceptions to this rule exist (e.g., Myers, DiCecco, White, & Borden, 1982), however. Nonetheless, continuous data are more likely to meet the requirements of parametric statistics than are categorical data. Thus, look at parametric analyses first when dealing with continuous data. If the characteristics of your data violate the assumptions of the parametric analysis, you will need to consider nonparametric alternatives if the analysis is not robust to your particular violations of its assumptions and if you cannot correct for these violations (e.g., by data transformations).

Examine each dependent variable one by one in this process. Not all variables will have the same characteristics. A common error, for example, is to assume that you can use the same analysis to test whether experimental groups are equivalent on age, ethnicity, gender, years of education, and other demographic variables. Age and education are ordinarily analyzed with parametric statistics. Gender and ethnicity are usually examined nonparametrically because they are categorical variables. Similarly, you may use entirely different statistics to answer different questions in your study. Don't assume one test will do it all!

At this point, you should have a list of questions you will use statistics to answer. You will also have a list of independent and dependent variables for each question. For each dependent variable, you will have indicated whether a parametric or nonparametric test is more appropriate. Finally, you will have indicated whether the question involves grouping the subjects and comparing the groups (group-comparison statistic) or relating scores on one or more measures in a single group (correlational statistic). In the pages that follow, we consider each of these options in turn: group-comparison statistics (parametric and nonparametric) and correlational statistics (parametric and nonparametric).

Consider Group Comparison Statistics

Parametric Statistics

Analysis of Variance and t Tests

The *t* test and the ANOVA are widely used parametric statistics for examining differences between groups. If you decide one of them is appropriate for your analysis, you must then select among their numerous variations.

To assist in this process, first, ask yourself how many independent variables will be involved in answering your particular research question. Next, ask yourself how many levels (conditions or groups) will be included with each independent variable. To do this, break each independent variable into the discrete groups it includes (e.g., condition: priming for recall, priming for recognition, no priming [three levels]; time: pre, post, follow-up [three levels]). Finally, for each independent variable, ask yourself whether the different levels involve *different* groups of people being compared with each other (as with the "condition" independent variable above) or the *same* group being compared with itself on the same variable under different conditions (e.g., at different points in time, after exposure to different experimental stimuli; as with the "time" type of independent variable on page 178). Once you have answered these questions, you can use the flowchart in Figure 10.1 to identify the most appropriate statistic for your analysis.

Following the steps in Figure 10.1 leads you to the most appropriate initial choice. The flowchart then instructs you to examine whether your data meet the assumptions of the statistic. If not, you must ascertain whether the statistic is robust to any violations of assumptions (i.e., does not produce misleading conclusions if you use it anyway) you might be making *or* whether there is some way of transforming the data or adjusting the statistic to alleviate the problem. Although many students approach data transformation warily, using a logarithmic, square root, or other sort of transformation to meet the assumptions of a nonrobust statistic is not cheating. In fact, it may help guard against Type I or Type II errors.

If you cannot figure out a way to compensate for assumptions that you violate, the flowchart directs you to seek an alternative statistic that will have fewer assumptions. Of course, along with fewer assumptions may come lower power. Usually, parametric statistics are more powerful than nonparametric ones, so you will generally want to use a parametric test. Maxwell and Delaney (1990) point out, however, that this—like most rules of thumb—is an oversimplification: In some cases, a nonparametric approach can be more powerful than its parametric alternative. Which is the more powerful will depend on the characteristics of your data set. If it's a toss-up and if you are a statistical novice, let pragmatic considerations prevail: Pick the one that you or your statistics consultant knows better.

Let's work through the steps listed so far in this chapter with an example. Suppose, as a preliminary way of examining your data, you wish to see whether men and women differ in their responses to a management style questionnaire (on which scores can range from 30 to 150). For the purposes of this analysis, you have one independent variable (gender) with two levels (male and female). Because you will be comparing groups, your probable analysis will be either a *t* test or an ANOVA. As you only have two groups to compare, a *t* test will be most suitable. Moreover, because different subjects are in the two groups, a *t* test for independent samples will likely be appropriate. Incidentally, with only two groups, *t* tests and ANOVAs are mathematically equivalent.

Now, do your data meet the assumptions of a *t* test? Those include homogeneity of variance in your groups (i.e., the standard deviations in

Figure 10.1

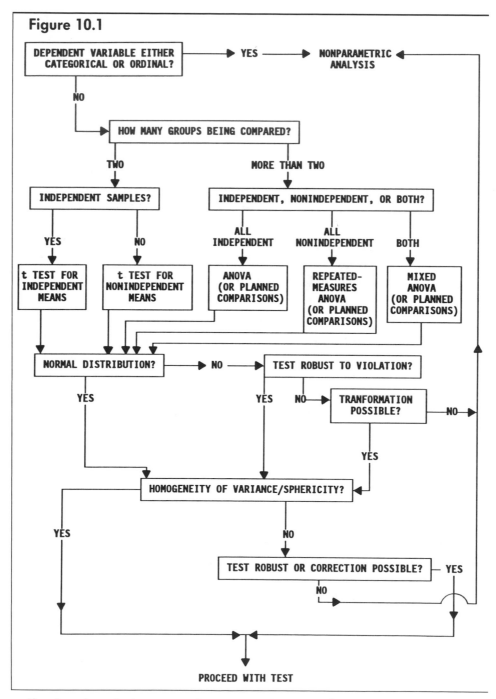

Flowchart for selecting appropriate parametric statistics for group comparison studies (assumes analysis of a single dependent variable). ANOVA = analysis of variance.

the two groups are roughly equal), independence of observations, and a normal distribution of your dependent variable (management style scores) in the population to which you wish to generalize. If you have produced a frequency distribution of the scores for each of your groups, you will have a pretty good idea whether the homogeneity and normality assumptions are tenable, and you can also do specific statistical tests for homogeneity and normality (e.g., to examine whether your distribution has problems with skew or kurtosis). If your data meet these assumptions, you can then proceed to perform the analysis. Table 10.1 lists the assumptions of some of the most common parametric statistical tests and some of the conditions under which the tests are and are not robust to violations.

Now, let's take a more complex example. Suppose your research involves testing whether insight-oriented individual therapy leads to better marital satisfaction than problem-solving individual therapy. Your dependent variable is the score on a marital satisfaction scale. The two independent variables are type of treatment (two levels: insight-oriented versus problem-solving therapy) and time (three levels: pre- versus post-treatment versus follow-up). The first independent variable involves comparing different groups of participants; the second involves comparing the same group with itself at different points in time. If you follow the flowchart in Figure 10.1, you will find yourself at the "mixed ANOVA" box: one between-subjects factor (treatment) and one within-subjects factor (time). Your likely analysis is a 2×3 mixed ANOVA.

By looking at Table 10.1, you see that, although the results of the treatment comparison are likely to be robust to violations of the assumptions of homogeneity of variance, the analyses involving the time factor are not. Thus, you will need to examine your variances for homogeneity. You can do this by using one of a number of tests described in most statistics books (e.g., Keppel, 1991; Kirk, 1982; Maxwell & Delaney, 1990; see appendix D for additional suggestions). Standard statistical software programs such as SAS and SPSS-X will calculate most of these tests (see appendix C for additional software suggestions). If group variances are not homogeneous, you can adjust your degrees of freedom to accommodate this problem using one of several procedures (see Maxwell & Delaney, 1990). The result is that the statistic often becomes more conservative (i.e., decreases the probability of a Type I error) as a way of protecting against the bias introduced by heterogeneity of variances. This means you will have to have greater differences between your groups to achieve the same level of statistical significance you would have had if

Table 10.1

Assumptions of Common Parametric Statistical Tests

Statistical Test	Assumptions
t test	Homogeneity of variance; underlying normal distribution (generally robust to violations of both of these but *not* with repeated measures and unequal *n*s); independent scores within cells (not robust if this is violated)
Analysis of variance (ANOVA)	Homogeneity of variance; underlying normal distribution. Repeated measures ANOVA also assumes sphericity (also called *circularity*; this involves homogeneity of variance and of correlations between pairs of cells involving repeated measures). Mixed ANOVA also requires homogeneity of treatment—differences variances. ANOVA generally robust but *not* with repeated measures and unequal *n*s; may also not be robust with small samples (Tabachnick & Fidell, 1989); independence of scores within cells (not robust if this is violated)
Analysis of covariance (ANCOVA)	Homogeneity of variance (violation leads to interpretive difficulty and biased *F*; see Huitema, 1980, for solutions); independence of scores within cells (not robust); underlying normal distribution (generally robust with relatively equal cell sizes, > 19 *df* for error, two-tailed test, and no outliers; Tabachnick & Fidell, 1989); linear relationship between covariate and dependent variable (DV); homogeneity of regression (i.e., relationship between DV and covariate is the same in each cell); covariates are reliably measured (violation of this assumption leads to loss of power); independence of covariate and independent variables (IVs) highly recommended; random assignment of subjects to conditions highly recommended; repeated measures ANCOVA also assumes homogeneity of covariance
Multivariate analysis of variance (MANOVA)	Multivariate normal distribution; homogeneity of variance for each DV and variance—covariance matrix (not robust if cell sizes are unequal); linear relationships among all DVs; absence of multicollinearity (among DVs) and singularity (among DVs)

continued

Table 10.1, continued	
Statistical Test	**Assumptions**
Discriminant function analysis (DFA)	Same as MANOVA
Pearson product– moment correlation	Continuous DVs; independent observations
Multiple linear regression	Absence of multicollinearity (not robust) and singularity; multivariate normal distribution; homoscedasticity; linear relationships between predictors and criterion; cannot be used for time-series data without compensating for autocorrelated residuals (i.e., each residual may be related to the one before it)

the assumptions had not been violated. In addition, the $F*$ and W tests (Maxwell & Delaney, 1990) are alternatives. These variations of the F test produce unbiased results when variances are unequal, both with equal- and unequal-n cells. These are not appropriate if your design involves repeated measures, however.

Planned Comparisons

But wait! The box in the flowchart also says "planned comparisons" are an option. As an alternative to the standard ANOVA approach, you can select in advance a certain set of comparisons you wish to make among pairs of means, before you collect the data. In doing this, you basically state that you expect certain means to differ and wish to test only these differences. No other comparisons are important to you. You then have the option of doing planned comparisons in place of an omnibus or overall ANOVA. This has the advantage of giving you more statistical power, because you restrict in advance the number of tests you will do. It has the disadvantage of making it more difficult to snoop through the data later on for something interesting that did not involve an a priori hypothesis. This is because you must pay the piper. That is, you get more powerful tests to use first for your planned comparisons, but the trade-off is that you can only snoop later using stringent tests. In general, planned comparisons make sense if you have well-defined hypotheses with good support in the literature, as we recommend in this volume. They may also make sense if you have a complex design in which only a few means are expected to differ and most are not (e.g., if you are running a lot of control conditions). If your study is more exploratory, you may prefer not to restrict yourself in exchange for greater power. Most statistics books that discuss ANOVA also discuss how to do planned comparisons (e.g., Keppel, 1991; Kirk, 1982; Maxwell & Delaney, 1990). Note that several different ways of doing planned comparisons exist, depending on how you select among groups you wish to compare.

Post Hoc Tests

What if you elect not to do planned comparisons? Don't put away your statistics books yet! You need to select a post hoc test. This will allow you to see what mean differences are contributing to any significant effects you find. For example, suppose with the treatment outcome study described earlier, you find a significant main effect for time and an interaction between time and mode of treatment. You will need post hoc tests to see (a) what contributed to the main effect for time (your main effect for time tells you that differences exist among pretreatment, posttreatment, and follow-up means, but not which pairs differ) and (b) which difference in group means contributed to your interaction effect.

An interaction means that the differences between groups are not the same at all of the levels of the independent variables. In this example, a Time × Treatment effect could mean that changes between pretreatment and posttreatment means are not the same for both treatments. It could mean that differences between posttreatment and follow-up means are not identical in the two treatments. It could mean that the two treatment groups differ at one point in time but not at another. Somewhere among the six means the interaction examined (pre–insight, pre–problem-solving, post–insight, post–problem-solving, follow-up–insight, follow-up–problem-solving) are some significant differences. You will need to untangle where these are, however. A post hoc test will help you do this.

Many post hoc tests exist. You can evaluate them in terms of their power, their robustness to violations of their assumptions, and the situations in which each is most appropriate from a conceptual point of view. Maxwell and Delaney (1990) and Kirk (1982) provide good overviews of different options and compare and contrast these options. If you are using either within-subjects or unequal-n designs, which are not robust to violations of homogeneity of variance and normality assumptions, look for a post hoc test appropriate for these designs. Jaccard, Becker, and Wood (1984) surveyed multiple comparison tests, examined which are most accurate and powerful when data violate assumptions of homogeneity of variance, and concluded the following: (a) With repeated measures and nonhomogeneous variances, the Tukey honestly significant difference (HSD) test or the Bonferroni test is appropriate; (b) with unequal sample sizes, no repeated measures, and nonhomogeneous variances, the Games and Howell test is preferable; (c) with nonhomogeneous variance in a mixed design (some within-subjects and some between-subjects independent variables), use the Bonferroni test for post hoc tests with the within-subjects (repeated measures) variables and the Games and Howell test for the between-subjects variables. Under optimal conditions (equal sample sizes and no violation of assumptions), Jaccard et al. concluded that the Tukey HSD and the Peritz test perform best; with unequal sample sizes but no violation of assumptions, they recommend the Tukey–Kramer test.

ANCOVA and MANOVA

But, what about ANCOVA? MANOVA? Should I be using them? Analysis of covariance (ANCOVA), multivariate analysis of variance (MANOVA), and multivariate analysis of covariance (MANCOVA) all provide alternatives to t-test and ANOVA strategies. We consider each below.

An ANCOVA is basically an analysis of variance with the statistical influence of one or more variables (called *covariates*) removed from the dependent variable. In theory, an ANCOVA is what you would get if you could do the ANOVA with the level of the covariates controlled. (In practice, this situation is more complex, as we shall see.) Thus, an ANCOVA may make sense as an alternative to an ANOVA if you know a strong relationship between your dependent variable and another variable exists. Because an ANCOVA decreases your error variance by extracting variance that is due to the relationship between the covariate and the dependent variable (Tabachnick & Fidell, 1989), your independent variable may be more likely to show a significant effect. For example, suppose you investigate the effects of three different reading programs on reading scores. You know, however, that IQ correlates highly with reading scores. It may have such a strong relationship that, unless you control for it in some way, this relationship will prevent you from seeing any differences between your three interventions. In essence, doing an ANCOVA with IQ as a covariate will allow you to extract the relationship between IQ and reading from your analyses, making an effect of your independent variable easier to detect.

Researchers sometimes also advocate use of ANCOVA when some variable emerges after the fact as a potential confound, and you want to remove its influence statistically. As an example, consider the outcome study comparing insight-oriented and problem-solving treatments described earlier. Suppose you found that, despite random assignment, the insight-oriented group had significantly more years of education than the other group. Suppose further that education level correlates with therapy outcome, so that any differences favoring the insight-oriented group could be due to education and not therapy. In such a case, you might want to use education as a covariate. This, so the argument goes, removes the potential impact education may have on, say, marital satisfaction, so you can see the effects of your treatment independent of the effects of education. Some dispute the appropriateness of this procedure, however, because ANCOVA can produce hard-to-interpret or even misleading results in certain cases, as we discuss below.

There are several other things you should know about ANCOVA. First, ANCOVA only makes sense if there is a significant correlation between the covariate and the dependent variable being analyzed. If there is no correlation, the suspected confounding variable has no relationship with the dependent variable and is unlikely to be a viable counterexplanation for any differences between your treatment groups. Furthermore, the results of the ANCOVA will not differ much from the ANOVA results (and you will lose a degree of freedom—i.e., a bit of power—by including the covariate). Second, ANCOVA only controls for a linear relationship between the covariate and the dependent variable—a confound could still exist if there is a curvilinear relationship between the covariate and your dependent variable. Third, using ANCOVA when your covariate may be related to or caused by differences in your independent variable poses major interpretive problems (see Maxwell & Delaney, 1990, for an extended discussion). Fourth, interpretive problems also emerge if you use ANCOVA and your groupings do not involve random assignment (i.e., your study is not a true experiment), an issue Huitema (1980) explores in detail.

Perhaps because of these interpretive problems, some recommend that ANCOVA only be used to extract variance between the dependent variable and the covariate and not to control for unanticipated (or anticipated) confounds. Finally, an ANCOVA cannot be used for nominal covariates with more than two levels (e.g., ethnicity, scored as one of five possible groups), although it can be used when the nominal variable is dichotomous (e.g., gender, scored as male vs. female).

Thus, although ANCOVA can be a powerful and useful procedure, interpreting its results can be less than straightforward. If ANCOVA seems like a possible analysis to you, examine what it can and cannot do. Huitema (1980), Maxwell and Delaney (1990), and Cook and Campbell (1979, chapter 4) all cover ANCOVA. In addition, Huitema (1980) provides formulas for several post hoc tests that can be used with ANCOVA.

What about MANOVA? A MANOVA resembles an ANOVA, except that multiple dependent variables are examined all at once. A MANOVA for the insight-oriented vs. problem-solving study, for example, might examine reported satisfaction with communication, sexual interaction, and instrumental tasks (three dependent variables). A MANOVA basically asks the question, "Do the various factors (independent variables) make a difference for this *group* of dependent variables?" Conceptually, the MANOVA procedures create a synthetic variable that combines the information in all the dependent variables that are included in the analysis, then analyze the synthetic variable, and finally tell you about the significance of main effects and interactions for that synthetic variable. This means you will know whether your independent variable affected the synthetic variable, but not whether it affected any one of the individual variables making up the synthetic one.

Frequently, investigators attempt to control inflated Type I error rates by doing a MANOVA. Type I error can increase when you do many statistical tests on numerous separate dependent variables, thereby increasing the likelihood that at least one will be significant solely as a function of doing so many tests. Because MANOVA treats those dependent variables as a group, the investigators conduct fewer analyses and thus reduce the likelihood of Type I error. If the MANOVA is significant (so the logic goes), the investigator can then proceed to do a series of individual ANOVAs on each of the dependent variables to see what produced the significance, much as one can do a post hoc test comparing specific groups following a significant ANOVA. Alternatively, the investigator can follow a step-down procedure, eliminating variables one by one to see which accounted for the effect (Tabachnick & Fidell, 1989).

Huberty and Morris (1989) challenged the logic of this approach, however. They asserted that MANOVA does not uniformly protect against Type I error and is appropriate primarily when the investigator is interested in the dependent variables as a system or when the dependent variables are conceptually related and assess the same or similar underlying constructs. Multiple ANOVAs, so their argument goes, are preferable when dependent variables are conceptually independent, when doing exploratory research, when previous studies have used separate univariate analyses (so your data will be comparable with those of previous investigators), and when examining whether groups are equivalent (e.g., on possible confounding variables).

So, what is our recommendation? If your dependent variables are conceptually related, a MANOVA may make sense if you can meet its assumptions or if the particular type of MANOVA (e.g., repeated measures) is robust with regard to violations of its assumptions. If your dependent variables are *not* conceptually related, remember that you can correct your alpha level to protect against Type I error (e.g., using the Bonferroni procedure described in most texts that cover ANOVA) if you are doing lots of statistical tests. If you still choose MANOVA in this circumstance, make sure you have a good reason and can counter Huberty and Morris's (1989) excellent points.

Caution Regarding ANOVAs

Some students mistakenly believe that significant ANOVAs mean that the independent variable "caused" the changes in the dependent variable. Not so. Yes, differences in levels of the independent variable *relate* to differences in the dependent variable. Whether you can say the independent variable *caused* the differences, however, depends on your design. If you didn't manipulate the independent variable, you cannot legitimately ascribe causal status to it. Your design, not your statistic, determines whether you can say that your independent variable caused changes in your dependent variable.

Nonparametric Statistics

Your data do not fulfill the assumptions required for an ANOVA. What do you do now? Nonparametric statistics, fortunately, may come to your rescue.

If you were planning to use a between-subjects ANOVA, the Kruskal–Wallis test is a nonparametric alternative, used for ordinal data. When only two groups are being compared, this is equivalent to the Wilcoxon Rank Sum and the Mann-Whitney U tests (Maxwell & Delaney, 1990). Although the Kruskal–Wallis statistic makes no assumptions about underlying distributions, it *does* implicitly assume homogeneity of variance, leading Maxwell and Delaney (1990) to recommend the F^* and W tests when variances are not homogeneous, particularly with unequal cell sizes. Joint ranking or pairwise ranking tests (Maxwell & Delaney, 1990) can be used to compare pairs of cells, in the same way that post hoc mean comparisons are used with ANOVAs.

If your design involves repeated measures and only one (repeated) independent variable, Friedman's test may be appropriate. Like the Kruskal–Wallis test, it analyzes rank orders of subjects' scores and so requires ordinal data.

With categorical data, the most appropriate analysis is often a chi-square (χ^2) test. When there are several levels of an independent variable or when you have more than one independent variable, you may wish to do the equivalent of a post hoc test if your chi-square is significant. This can be done using z tests for proportions. Alternatively, the more complex nonparametric equivalents of ANOVA strategies (logit or log-linear analysis) may be appropriate.

Consider Correlational Statistics

If your design is a correlational one, the first step in selecting a statistic is to decide what is being related to what. If you have two variables that you wish to relate, a bivariate (i.e., two-variable) correlation will be appropriate. If you have a set of variables (i.e., more than one) that you wish to associate with a single different variable, a regression strategy may be the best choice. If that single variable is categorical, perhaps you should use discriminant function analysis or logistic regression.

Bivariate Correlations (Parametric and Nonparametric)

The simplest measures of association are bivariate correlation coefficients. If your data on both variables can be considered interval or ratio, a Pearson product-moment correlation (r) may be appropriate. Keep in mind, however, that the Pearson correlation involves rank ordering, and will not take into account systematic mean differences in the two sets of data. Such differences may be important. For example, suppose you wish to correlate the data of two persons who independently observed the same individuals' head-banging behavior. You would be interested not only in whether they saw the same individuals as higher or lower in head banging but also in whether both observers reported the same amounts of head banging for each individual they both observed. In such a case, you might prefer a correlation that takes into account mean differences. The intraclass correlation coefficient (Winer, 1971) does this.

If *one* of your variables involves ordinal data and the other is ordinal, interval, or ratio in nature, a Spearman rank order procedure would be more appropriate than a Pearson correlation. If one of the variables is dichotomous, a point-biserial correlation will be appropriate. If both are dichotomous, the correlation between them is called the phi (ϕ) coefficient. Note that the formula for r produces the point-biserial and phi coefficients (as special cases), so telling a computer to give you an r statistic with dichotomous data will produce a correct point-biserial or phi coefficient (Cohen & Cohen, 1983).

Regression Strategies

Regression analyses basically select one variable called the *criterion variable* (also sometimes termed the *dependent* or *outcome* variable) and one or more *predictor (independent) variables*. When two or more predictors are used, regression procedures develop an equation that describes the best way of combining the predictors and indicate how well you could guess a person's score on the criterion variable if you knew the scores on the predictors and used the equation to combine them. Regression might be appropriate, for example, if you wished to analyze whether rates of particular therapist behaviors were associated with treatment outcome; whether age, social competence, GRE (Graduate Record Exam) scores, and undergraduate GPA (grade point average) were associated with graduate school GPA; whether various demographic and cognitive measures were associated with rate of recovery from cancer surgery; and so on. Although it can be used with a single predictor, regression more commonly involves multiple predictors. Thus, this parametric version of regression is called multiple regression.

Parametric Multiple Regression

Parametric versions of multiple regression analysis basically produce a list of those variables that enhance your ability to predict the criterion over your best guess if you knew nothing about your subjects' scores on the predictors (this best guess, by the way, would be the mean of the criterion variable). The analysis procedures take into account the fact that some of the predictors may correlate with each other and are therefore redundant. Thus, each significant predictor variable contributes unique (non-redundant) information (i.e., information that goes beyond that which the previous predictors added). Dichotomous as well as continuous variables can be used as predictors, but for parametric versions of multiple regression procedures, the criterion must be a continuous variable. (Non-parametric versions of regression [logit analysis and logistic regression] are mentioned later.) Nominal variables that have more than two levels can also be used as predictors, but these must be treated specially (see Cohen & Cohen, 1983). More complex variations of regression even allow you to assess the effects of interactions between different predictor variables.

Many different forms of regression exist. Most have to do with the order in which you enter your predictor variables into the regression equation. They can be entered one by one or in one or more groups. Different forms of regression also vary in the ways the analysis tests each variable to see whether it contributes any new information (above and beyond the information contained by other variables in the equation) in predicting the criterion variable.

In *hierarchical multiple regression*, you specify the order in which the variables go into the equation in advance, on theoretical or methodological grounds. The analysis extracts the amount of variance associated with the first variable, then goes on to do the same with the second, and so on. You can either specify the order in which each and every individual variable will be entered or group variables into subsets and then enter the subsets, letting the analysis sort out the order within each set. For example, one of our students wished to predict in-law satisfaction on the basis of parental marital satisfaction and the quality of the relationship (cohesion) between the parent and child. "In-law satisfaction" was his criterion variable. He first entered several demographic variables (as a set) in a hierarchical multiple regression analysis. Then, he entered a single measure of social desirability. Finally, he entered the marital satisfaction and cohesion measures (as a set). He chose this order of entry because he wished to control for demographic characteristics and the tendency to respond to self-report measures in a socially desirable way and because he wanted to look at the relationship between marital satisfaction, cohesion, and in-law satisfaction, holding demographic and social desirability variables constant. Put another way, his results told him whether knowing the marital satisfaction and cohesion scores gave him any new information, over and above that provided by the demographic and social desirability measures. He had no reason for ordering his variables *within* sets, however.

An alternative to hierarchical multiple regression is *stepwise regression*. In this procedure, purely computational decision rules identify which variable predicts the criterion variable best, then which variable adds significantly after that, and so on. Whereas with hierarchical multiple regression you specify the order in advance, with stepwise regression the computer does the ordering. If the student in the example just cited used a stepwise procedure, he would have entered all of his variables and let the computer tell him the order in which they predicted in-law satisfaction.

There are various ways of doing this ordering, and you will need to instruct the computer which procedure to use. With *forward entry* procedures, the variable that accounts for the most variance is entered first. The variable that accounts for the second most variance (given that the first is already in the equation) is entered next, and so on. A problem with this analysis is that once the first variable makes it into the equation, it stays there. Later variables that can't get into the equation because of the first variable might, in combination with each other, be better predictors than the first variable, however. *Forward stepwise* procedures solve this problem by testing the variables already entered to see whether they still contribute nonredundant information when new variables are considered. *Backward deletion* procedures start with all of the variables in the regression equation, then delete variables that account for little variance, again going one by one. Some backward stepwise procedures retest the resulting equation with each entry.

Most, but not all, stepwise approaches use procedures that add and delete variables, testing as the analysis proceeds. A crucial point here is that regression analyses can be performed in many different ways. A stepwise regression is not a stepwise regression is not a stepwise regression. Examine the options and their pros and cons in light of the purposes of your analyses, and then make an informed decision.

Cohen and Cohen (1983) point out several disadvantages of using stepwise procedures. First, when large numbers of predictors are used, the approach seriously capitalizes on chance. Second, the results using these procedures may not replicate in a second sample. Third, depending on the rules used to enter and remove predictor variables, results may be quite misleading. Finally, using stepwise procedures means you can avoid having to think through the logical relationships among your predictors and criterion variable. This is a bit like using ANOVAs and post hoc comparisons to snoop through your data rather than making the effort to preplan and specify exactly what you want to examine in advance.

Stepwise procedures may be more readily justified when the sample is large, when replication is possible (either with a second sample or by randomly splitting the sample in two), and when the research goal is not based in theory (as in some applied research, when the goal may simply be to predict a phenomenon and not explain it; Cohen & Cohen, 1983). Tabachnick and Fidell (1989) characterize stepwise procedures as model-*building* techniques; early studies in an area would use these. Hierarchical procedures are model-*testing* techniques;[1] investigators would use these when enough is known to make reasonable predictions.

Regression procedures, like all parametric statistical tests, have certain conditions which, if you fail to meet them, can cause problems. First, multiple regression procedures assume the absence of multicollinearity. Multicollinearity occurs when two or more of the predictor variables are highly intercorrelated—a situation that produces an unstable regression equation (i.e., the weights associated with each of the predictor variables are unlikely to be replicated in a new population).[2] If you have a multicollinearity problem, you could select the most important predictor from among the correlated variables or explore whether you can legitimately combine the correlated variables into a single score.

A second condition you must satisfy in using multiple regression is that predictor variables cannot be combinations of other predictor variables (this is termed *singularity*). In other words, you cannot use scores for hitting, swearing, punching, and total aggression as predictors: The last is a combination of the first three. Third, regression assumes linear relationships between each predictor and the criterion. Fourth, multiple regression assumes an underlying multivariate normal distribution. This means that not only is each predictor normally distributed, all possible combinations of the predictors are as well. A fifth assumption involves homoscedasticity: The prediction made by the regression equation is comparable at different points on the regression line. Fortunately, the last three assumptions can all be checked by examining the residuals. An analysis of residuals basically looks at the difference between each score as predicted by the regression equation and the score you actually got in your data (each difference is called a *residual*). Different patterns of residuals at different points on the regression line have indications for the

---

1. You can also combine hierarchical and stepwise procedures. That is, you can enter a series of subsets of several variables hierarchically but use stepwise procedures to figure out the order of variables within each subset.

2. Tabachnick and Fidell (1989) suggest that bivariate correlations above .7 indicate a possible problem. Note that a low bivariate correlation does not guarantee the absence of multicollinearity, however: Two predictor variables could be only moderately correlated with a third predictor when looked at individually but might be highly correlated when combined. SPSS-X and SAS can calculate indexes to test combinations of variables for multicollinearity.

assumptions of multiple regression (see Tabachnick & Fidell [1989, p. 132], for graphic representations of patterns that indicate difficulties).

Nonparametric Versions of Regression

Logistic regression resembles multiple regression in that a number of predictors are related to a single criterion variable. Predictors can be continuous or not, but unlike multiple regression, the criterion variable is categorical, not continuous. In addition, the mathematics underlying logistic regression are more closely aligned with nonparametric than parametric statistics and differ greatly from those underlying parametric versions of multiple regression. Thus, nonparametric regression statistics tell you about how well *obtained* frequencies in a particular cell fit the *expected* frequencies, rather than about how much of the variance each predictor variable accounts for in the criterion. A similar procedure, *logit analysis* (a version of log-linear analysis) is more restrictive than logistic regression in that all variables (predictors and criterion) must be categorical variables.

Discriminant Function Analysis (Regression's and MANOVA's Relative)

Discriminant function analysis (DFA) has many of the same uses as logistic regression but involves parametric statistics. DFA is most useful when you wish to predict discrete group membership (considered the dependent variable) from a set of variables (considered the independent variables or predictors). For example, you may wish to assess how well MMPI scores predict psychiatric diagnosis or whether you can derive a way to combine demographic data with scores assessing attitudes toward work and the company to predict which prospective employees will and will not quit during the first year on the job. These questions resemble group-comparison questions in that you will divide your sample into two or more discrete groups to form your dependent variable (e.g., antisocial personality disorder versus control; those who leave the company versus those who stay). They resemble regression questions in that you want to examine whether a combination of variables will allow you to separate the groups. A DFA can be useful in these situations, if you meet its assumptions (see Table 10.1).

Basically, DFA examines the predictors (independent variables) and formulates an equation that weights each one to maximize correct classification of subjects into groups (the dependent variable). As with regression, variations of DFA exist. Mathematically, DFA is closely related to

MANOVA. One important consideration involves whether you want the computer to test certain variables before others (hierarchical DFA) or whether you want the computer to order the variables statistically (step-down DF or direct ["standard"] DFA; see Tabachnick & Fidell, 1989).

Factor Analysis

We assumed in the previous pages that you have some variables you designated as independent variables and some as dependent variables, and you are interested in how the independent variables and dependent variables relate to one another. Maybe that is not the case, however. Another set of correlationally based statistics do not sort independent from dependent variables. Instead, they examine the relationships or structures among pieces of data.

Factor analysis and its sibling, principal components analysis, summarize patterns of correlations among a set of variables. Investigators often use these to reduce a large set of variables or items to a smaller number or to test hypotheses about the underlying structure among variables. For example, an investigator developing a new questionnaire may wish to reduce the 50 items to a few homogeneous subscales before looking at differences between groups.

Issues involved in using factor analysis are too numerous and complex to cover here. One issue warrants mentioning in particular, however: sample size. To use factor analysis and related techniques, you will need a minimum of about 5 subjects for every item or variable that will enter the factor analysis, with the more precise number depending on the strength of the relationships among the variables you assess (Gorsuch, 1983; Tabachnick & Fidell, 1989). Thus, you would need at least 250 subjects to analyze the 50-item questionnaire described earlier. In addition, many investigators recommend replicating a factor analysis to be sure of the findings. Are you really willing to recruit enough subjects to do the analysis right? If not, you should not try to solve the problem of too many variables by promising blithely to conduct a factor analysis to create a more manageable number of scores. A better solution is to think through whether all those measures are really necessary.

Use Consultation Prudently

At this point, you may have some idea of which statistics could be appropriate for your study. You may, nonetheless, wonder whether you have selected correctly. You may need to go to the library and read about some of your potential statistics in more depth than we have discussed them here or look up statistics we do not cover.

What should you do if you need additional help? Are you allowed to get help or consultation on statistics, and for what purposes? The answers to these questions depend on the degree of consultation involved. "Consultation" can range from asking your chairperson, another graduate student, or a statistics professor on your faculty a few isolated questions about particular aspects of your analyses to hiring someone to select, program, and run the analyses for you. These extremes are very different in how much of the work is actually done by the consultant versus by you, the one who is earning the degree.

Consultation is healthy. Most faculty members consult colleagues with greater statistical expertise than their own about data analysis and learn from the experience. Even seasoned researchers sometimes write statistical consultation into the budgets of their grants. We consulted with several colleagues in writing this chapter. Consultation with faculty or graduate students to point you in the right direction about the ins and outs of particular analyses generally falls within the boundaries of accepted professional practice. In fact, figuring out what you do not know and then finding out the answer by reading and consulting with a colleague is an important professional skill.

What about greater involvement by a consultant? This is a complex question. Ideally, students would do all of the work themselves, with occasional advice. Unfortunately, at some schools, the statistics classes may not have taught the students well. In addition, the student may have had a great deal of difficulty with the material, the student's chairperson may be as frightened of statistics as the student, or the computer facilities and consultation needed for complex analyses may not be available. In these cases, to ask the student to figure out what to do with the data and then conduct the analyses without assistance may be beyond the student's preparation.

Assume Responsibility for Your Statistics

If you use a consultant, remember that you ultimately must be responsible for the statistics in your project. This means that you must know why one particular statistic and not another is appropriate, what computer program was used and what choices were made in analyzing your data, how things such as missing data were handled, what the computer output means, whether the analyses were done correctly, and how to interpret the findings. In other words, whether you actually perform the analyses or not, you must know what was done, inside and out, and be responsible for the accuracy of the results. Remember, your consultant will not be present during your proposal meeting and oral defense.

What should you do if you need more than occasional advice? First, we recommend that you do as many of the analyses as you can. Thus, if you have appropriate computer resources but no understanding of the particular statistic, you might consult with someone regarding choosing the statistic, programming, and reading the output. You would score, reduce, and enter the data yourself, and run the analyses (perhaps with the assistance of a computer consultant who can help you find errors in your program statements). Second, we recommend consultation specifically aimed at teaching the skills you lack. This might be more appropriately termed *tutoring* than *consultation*. At the end of this tutoring, you should be prepared to pass an examination on what you did, why you did it, the assumptions and characteristics of the statistics you used, and what you found.

In fact, just such an examination may occur in your oral defense! "Well, I really am not sure about exactly what was done; I'll have to ask the person who ran the statistics," is *not* a good way to answer a statistics question in your final orals. You and you alone—not the person who assisted you—must defend your thesis or dissertation before your committee. It is your competence to do research, not your consultant's, that your committee assesses. You, and not a helper, will be earning your degree. Therefore, get the assistance you need to learn and understand what you are doing, but do as much as you can on your own and take full responsibility for ensuring that the statistics have been selected and calculated correctly.

Even if someone will assist you with all of your analyses, prepare your data yourself. Code the data you will use in analyses onto a columnar pad or spreadsheet, after talking with your consultant about how to do it. This will help you understand what the raw data look like. It will also prompt you to think about important issues, such as how to handle missing values. You can also detect outliers—extreme scores that can distort your results and that you might want to handle carefully. We also recommend that you do preliminary analyses yourself, looking at means, standard deviations, frequency distributions, and so on. As mentioned earlier, frequency distributions help you determine whether various statistics are appropriate, and they can alert you early on that you need to alter your statistical plans. You should produce preliminary analyses as the very first step in your data analyses. Most can be done by hand if you do not have access to statistical software. We will say more about preliminary analyses in chapter 11.

Seek Additional Assistance If You Are Still Confused

Still confused after reading this chapter? You probably are not alone. Statistical material is not equally comprehensible to all readers. We could not cover every statistic or even every variation on the basic ones we mentioned. Undoubtedly, many of you will need additional assistance at this point.

Your chairperson, statistics professor, graduate student colleagues, and local consultants may provide further assistance. In addition, several other sources may assist you. Andrews, Klem, Davidson, O'Malley, and Rodgers (1981) provide an extensive decision tree for selecting appropriate statistics. Their material includes correlational, nonparametric, and parametric tests, provides a reference for each statistic they mention, and refers you to statistical packages that will do the analyses you select. They cover repeated measures (within-subjects) statistics only minimally, however. Yates (1982) provides a more limited but useful table to help students select appropriate statistics. Tabachnick and Fidell (1989, pp. 30–31) provide a decision tree for multivariate techniques, including correlational strategies.

Finally, software developers have begun to produce programs to help researchers select statistics. One interesting example is *Statistical Navigator* (see appendix C). This new program provides names, references, and brief descriptions of literally dozens of different statistical tests. It also takes the user step-by-step through a series of questions about a study and provides suggestions about possible statistics.

A problem with this program, as with other written and computer aids, lies in understanding the language the writers use to ask you about your study and your data: One incorrect answer because you do not understand the question can lead you to select a completely inappropriate statistic. Thus, we recommend that you use these tools like you use this chapter—as a way to get ideas that you later confirm or reject through appropriate reading and consultation.

✔ To Do . . .

Selecting Appropriate Statistics

☐ Beef up your statistical knowledge early

— Find comprehensible statistics books

— Get experience doing statistical analyses

☐ Examine your study

— Identify questions you wish statistics to answer

— Make a list of variables you plan to analyze

— Identify independent and dependent variables for each question

☐ Select among group-comparison statistics

☐ Select among correlation statistics

☐ Use consultation prudently

☐ Assume responsibility for your statistics

☐ Seek additional assistance if you are still confused

11 Collecting, Managing, and Analyzing the Data

You've finished the proposal, your committee has approved it, and now it's time to collect the data—to do what you promised to do in your method section. The promises may have been easier to make than to keep, however. How much difficulty you have keeping them will depend in part on careful planning to minimize potential hassles. Chapter 4 described planning steps you could take early in your project. Here, we provide additional advice for avoiding and coping with common problems fledgling researchers encounter as they put their plans into practice.

Before you rush out to recruit subjects, take time to pilot test and fine-tune your procedures, train any research assistants (RAs) you have working with you, develop a data storage and management plan, and arrange for equipment and facilities. In this chapter, we discuss each of these steps in more detail. In addition, make sure you obtain *written approval* from your IRB for the protection of human (or animal) subjects before you even advertise for or recruit human subjects.

Pilot Test Your Procedures

If you have not already pilot tested your procedures, now is the time to do it. Pilot work is important because what you plan to do may look good on paper but not work very well when you actually try it out with real subjects. For example, the procedure you thought would take 15 minutes may take an hour for some subjects. The equipment may not work the way you thought it would, or subjects may not understand your carefully crafted instructions. Even if your procedures run smoothly, pilot work will alert you to issues you need to train your RAs to handle. It is hard to train someone to use procedures that you do not know intimately yourself.

Who should serve as pilot subjects? If you will have no problem recruiting a sufficient sample for the research, the first few subjects you recruit may be designated as *pilots*. Their data should not be included in the study, because ordinarily you will treat them differently than later subjects. If subjects who meet your criteria are in short supply, use individuals who have characteristics that match your target population as much as possible but who would not qualify as subjects in your actual study. For example, in our work with children, we often recruit children of colleagues or of graduate students to serve as pilot subjects. Other graduate students, undergraduate RAs, and friends may be willing to serve as pilot subjects for some or all of your procedures.

The specific purposes of pilot testing are (a) to ensure that subjects will respond in accord with instructions, (b) to uncover and decide how to handle unanticipated problems, and (c) to learn how to use and to check the adequacy of your equipment. Now is the time to fine-tune your procedures and work out the bugs. To facilitate this, you will want to ask your subjects to give you feedback, something that usually will not be done during the actual study. Ask your subjects whether the instructions were clear, what difficulties they had following the instructions, whether anything about the environment or the experimenter's behavior interfered with their performance of the task, and so on. In addition, observe your subjects as they complete your procedures. Do they perform as you instructed them? On the basis of their feedback and your observations, make appropriate changes and run the next pilot subject. Again, ask for feedback. Keep adjusting your procedures until you are satisfied that the study will run smoothly. Keep written notes to use in training any assistants you might involve.

If you are using human judges or observers to rate or record subjects' responses, you should collect pilot data to use when you train these individuals. Thus, you should videotape the kinds of interactions observers will be recording on the playground or collect samples of written open-ended responses that raters will later code. Having these samples will allow your assistants to practice during training on real data. This is important because real data often pose difficulties you may not anticipate when you make up training materials. Perhaps as a result, interobserver agreement often drops when observers begin to observe "real" subjects after training (e.g., Taplin & Reid, 1973). You want to train assistants to deal with these problems *before* you start collecting the data you will use in your thesis or dissertation.

Pilot testing occasionally turns up a problem that requires a major change in design or procedures. Your clever use of an experimental confederate, for example, may be blatantly transparent to the pilot subjects. Your experimental manipulation of subjects' motivation may not be motivating, and so on. All changes in procedures and design must be approved by your chairperson. If you propose a major change, you may need to meet again with your entire committee. At a minimum, you should circulate a memorandum outlining the proposed changes and asking committee members to agree to the changes in writing. In addition, changes in procedures may require you to alter your consent form and to apply to your IRB for approval of the changes.

Recruit and Train Assistants

Ordinarily, you will not conduct your research alone. You may need others to serve as experimenters, raters, observers, confederates, and the like. These individuals may be undergraduate students working for credit, paid assistants, other graduate students, or friends and relatives who have a perverse interest in your being indebted to them for life.

These assistants should first be told—preferably in the form of a written agreement, which you and they sign—exactly what will be required of them and what they will receive as a result of their role in the project. This should include the full nature of their duties, the times they will be asked to work; the duration of their involvement; compensation for services (if any); and, if they are students working for credit, how they will be evaluated. We also recommend letting these people know the conditions under which they may be "fired" from the project.

Be honest, direct, and realistic with prospective assistants. Remember that collecting data may take longer than you plan, that subjects may not show up, and that training takes time. Leading prospective assistants to believe that their duties will be minimal and later dumping extra work on them can create resentment. Let people who do not have time to fulfill your requirements opt out in the beginning. Better this than having them commit themselves to the project and later quit (after considerable time spent training them!) because the project is more work than you told them it would be.

Timing is important. A common error involves recruiting assistants too early. They then have nothing to do for several weeks or months. When the project is finally ready to go, typically several can no longer participate. A good rule of thumb is to begin recruiting assistants after (a) your committee has approved your proposal, (b) you have a source of subjects arranged, and (c) your training materials are ready and your initial pilot testing is complete. An approved proposal ensures that your procedures will not change markedly as a result of a committee member's whim, and a source of subjects usually means that you can begin collecting data as soon as you train your assistants.

Your proposal may dictate certain types of assistants, for example, a female confederate, a graduate-student therapist, or a child model. In addition to screening for qualities that relate to your design, select RAs who are dependable. You want RAs to appear when they say they will and to otherwise meet their commitments. With undergraduates, we sometimes assess this by asking about their job experience, on the assumption that individuals who have held long-term part-time or full-time jobs have had to learn and demonstrate reliable performance. Another quality to look for is good judgment: Ideally, your RAs should do what you would do when an unanticipated problem confronts them. For example, if RAs will be observing in the school setting, they will need to dress appropriately, interact professionally with the school office staff and teachers, and refrain from complaining if a teacher asks them to leave the classroom because it is time for a test he or she neglected to tell them about earlier. Although high-level general intellectual functioning is a wonderful quality in an RA, dependability and good judgment may be more important.

Once you have recruited your RAs, train them well. Research has shown that several procedures contribute to skill acquisition and performance: instruction, modeling, rehearsal, and feedback. You should explain the task to your RAs, show them (though role playing, film, or other means) how to do the task, and have them practice as you give feedback. If your assistants must perform complex duties, break the task down and have them learn and practice small steps that cumulate to mastery of the complete task.

For example, Sharon Foster and some of her students (Dumas et al., 1992) trained other graduate students to interview second-, fifth-, and eighth-grade students about incidents involving peer provocation. Interviewers had to learn a complex coding system for scoring the children's responses as well as the format for conducting a semistructured interview. The first step was for interviewers to review the written coding manual. They then practiced coding pilot responses, beginning with easy responses and progressing to more difficult ones. The research team had previously coded each series of responses. Trainers checked interviewers' responses for accuracy against these criterion coding decisions and provided feedback to the trainees. After interviewers demonstrated 85% or higher agreement with the master coding on all categories on a series of examples, they learned how to interview the children. Trainers described and modeled each of the skills (e.g., asking precise questions and paraphrasing the child's statements) for the interviewer-trainees. Trainees then role-played portions of interviews with trainers (who provided feedback) to learn the skill on which they were being trained. After mastering all of the component skills, interviewers practiced complete interviews with pilot subjects and with the investigators. They were considered competent to interview actual subjects when they completed two different mock interviews with two different investigators and required minimal correction.

Because knowledge of experimental hypotheses has been tied to biased data (e.g., Rosenthal, 1969), keep your RAs as blind as you can to the different conditions of your study. If you cannot keep them blind to your conditions, at least keep them blind to your hypotheses. At the same time, tell them enough to enable them to perform their duties adequately. To figure out whether a piece of information is inappropriate to share, ask yourself, "Could this information conceivably influence in a negative fashion the way this assistant interacts with subjects or scores the data?" If the answer is "yes," do not give the assistant the information.

With students working for credit, you also need to make the experience an educational one. This can be done by teaching assistants fundamentals related to design and procedures, without revealing your hypotheses. Thus, students can learn about the importance of standardized procedures, the concept of experimental control, why and how data on interobserver agreement are collected, and so on.

Do not forget to inform your assistants about the importance of confidentiality. They should not talk about human subjects' data or behavior with others outside the project. In clinical settings, be sure to tell them not to chat about subjects with fellow assistants in public places— prospective participants may overhear their comments.

Schedule Settings and Arrange Materials

After you finalize your procedures and establish a timetable for actually starting the project, work out final logistic details. Exhibit 11.1 provides a

---

Exhibit 11.1

Checklist for Preparing to Implement the Research

_____ Obtain approval in writing from your institutional review board (IRB)
_____ Complete subject recruitment arrangements
_____ Complete subject recruitment forms
_____ Initiate subject recruitment or order animals
_____ Recruit research assistants
_____ Train research assistants
_____ Complete pilot testing
_____ Get changes in procedures approved by your chair, committee, and IRB
_____ Duplicate consent or assent forms
_____ Duplicate other forms
_____ Compile subject files
_____ Develop system for keeping track of subjects and data
_____ Develop system for scheduling assistants, subjects, rooms, keys, equipment, etc.
_____ Develop stimulus material
_____ Complete preinvestigation manipulation checks
_____ Obtain location for study
_____ Schedule location for study
_____ Obtain equipment for study
_____ Develop back-up plan for equipment failure
_____ Write and post rules for equipment use
_____ Make arrangements for running subjects during vacations
_____ Obtain locked data storage facility
_____ Develop data filing and storage system
_____ Schedule regular meetings with assistants
_____ Develop system for recording data for later analysis
_____ Write up system for coding data into computer
_____ Develop data verification plan
_____ Secure data analysis facilities

---

planning checklist for preparing to run subjects. This checklist prompts you to anticipate how you are going to keep the project running smoothly from week to week, and to plan accordingly. Such planning involves ensuring that you have a physical location to run subjects at the times subjects and you or your RAs will be available. If you are running animals in a long series of trials over a specific period of time, make sure someone will be available to run the animals during weekends and vacations.

If you need equipment, make sure it will be available when you need it and have a backup plan in case equipment suddenly fails or disappears. If several people will take equipment to different sites, make rules for checking out and returning equipment so that equipment will be returned to a central spot in a timely fashion and that you can locate missing tape recorders, and so on. Have a plan for preventive maintenance, such as cleaning video- or audiotape heads and replenishing batteries.

You should also get forms copied and organized. Ideally, when a subject arrives, the experimenter should pull out a file with all the forms and information for that subject arranged in the order they will be needed. This file would ordinarily contain copies of the consent or assent form, any special instructions to the experimenter (e.g., a note designating the subject's condition), questionnaires to be completed, and the like. Write the subject's code number on all pieces of data, in case these pieces get separated later on. If your procedures are complex, the file could even contain a checklist (e.g., stapled to the inside of the file) listing the tasks and measures to be completed. As the subject completes each task, the experimenter can check the appropriate spot on the checklist. This arrangement is particularly helpful if data must go through several steps of processing (e.g., be transcribed and coded, and the coding recorded).

Arrange a place to store the data as they come in. To ensure confidentiality, keep data in a locked room (at a minimum), and preferably in a locked filing cabinet. Make sure RAs know the rules and the procedures for filing data (e.g., all data must be filed immediately after a subject has been run—not carried around in a car; no raw data may leave the building).

Think, too, about easy ways of keeping track of how many subjects have been run as the study progresses (a publicly posted cumulative graph of accomplishments motivates everyone) and of informing others involved in the project about what is happening that week. For example, one of us often conducts research involving individual sessions with children in school settings. Sometimes schedules must change from week to week because of teacher requests, RA availability, and the school schedule. When a master schedule to be followed every week is impossible, on Thursday or Friday the experimenter schedules RAs for the following week, after checking with the school secretary about field trips, teacher conference days, and so on, when children will not be available. Late Friday or early Monday, the experimenter or the lead RA takes the schedule to the school and verifies it with the teachers, making last minute changes if needed and also leaving copies with the teachers, the principal, and the school secretary. A finalized copy goes in RAs' boxes and on the lab wall that morning. Next to the schedule is a list of children who have parental permission to participate and have not yet participated. RAs cross off the names of children they saw when they bring in the data each day.

Another detail to think about involves transferring the data to computer-usable form. Unless you are doing a single-organism study with no statistics involved, eventually you will need to do this. Although some researchers like to wait until all data are collected, we prefer to get data ready for and into the computer as they come in. That way, individuals running subjects can also be responsible for recording their own data, and the process is not as tedious as it is when all data are recorded at once. We discuss methods for recording data later.

One exception to our "do it as you go" advice arises if observers or raters will code videotapes or written responses. Unless a coding scheme is carefully implemented, such data can be distorted by observer (rater) drift (i.e., when a team of human judges gradually drift consensually in how they use a coding system over time [Romanczyk et al., 1973]). This can occur if they discuss problems using the coding scheme and evolve implicit decision rules that change over time. If everyone "drifts" as a group, interrater or interobserver agreement figures will be high, and drift will not be detectable from these data. Most important, data that come in later in the project will be coded differently than early data, creating a potential confound for longitudinal, time-series, and pre–post designs. Thus, assembling all the data first and coding tapes or responses in random order later ensures that any drift is not confounded with the time the data were collected. In addition, continuing to meet as a group and to score stimuli that were criterion scored before the study began, along with providing feedback regarding agreement with the criterion, can offset observer drift (DeMaster, Reid, & Twentyman, 1977). This process is called *recalibration*. Recalibration is important for any project involving human judges, and it is crucial when data must be coded as they come in rather than in random order at a later time.

Collect the Data

Finally, the first subject arrives, or you run your first animal. The procedures run smoothly, the subject stays for the entire session, and everyone is where they should be at the right time, doing what they are supposed to do. Time to kick back and have some fun while the RAs take over, right? Well, not quite.

A key to keeping the process running smoothly is to *supervise it closely*.

This does not mean that you should hover vulturelike over your RAs. But you do need to make sure that duties are being accomplished correctly and in a timely fashion. This ordinarily entails setting objectives and arranging a schedule for yourself and your assistants, then regularly assessing progress toward those objectives and compliance with the work schedule. Reward RAs with positive comments and other signs of appreciation for successful performance. Similarly, talk with RAs about any performance problems in a courteous but firm fashion early in the process, to prevent problems that can easily occur without adequate supervision. Encourage RAs to bring up any difficulties they encounter early on, too. Problems in procedures, data coding, and other aspects are best handled as soon as you discover them. Regular meetings of project staff provide good forums for discussing progress and logistics.

Be sure, too, to check your data as they come in to see that they have been collected correctly. If you do this in the presence of RAs, control your desire to exclaim positively over data that look great and to weep over those that do not. These behaviors can prompt the assistants to produce biased data that may make you happier but may not reflect subjects' actual performance (O'Leary, Kent, & Kanowitz, 1975).

If you collect your data in an applied setting, check periodically with contact people in the setting to make sure everything is running smoothly. Doing so will catch potential difficulties early in the process. We cannot emphasize this enough: One RA who fails to attend to protocol may sour those in the setting on research and even get you tossed out! Keep key personnel in the setting appraised of changes in schedules and thank them formally (we do it in writing as well as in person) when you complete your data collection. If you have promised to show them the results, let them know when you should have the data analyzed, and be sure to go back and present your findings. Your performance as a researcher can have important consequences for whether an applied setting allows future students and faculty to use their facilities.

Score, Check, and Analyze the Data

As you get ready to start data collection, think through how you will score your data and transfer them to computer-analyzable form. A good rule of thumb is that the fewer the steps between the raw data and the computer, the better. One good idea, therefore, would be to have your subjects put their answers on computer sheets. Even better would be for them to respond to computer-generated (and scored) questions while sitting directly at the computer. If subjects use computer-readable forms, check them before reading them into the computer to make sure that all marks are dark enough and marked correctly for the computer to read. Also make certain that the computer assigns the correct values to each mark (e.g., "1" for "a," etc.).

Computer scoring during data collection is sometimes impossible or may require resources that you lack (e.g., you may need a form reader to read the data into the computer). If computer scoring is not feasible, you and your assistants could enter the data directly from questionnaires or scoring sheets into the computer. To avoid the many errors associated with this kind of direct entry, however, you should program the computer to provide prompts that indicate the kind of data to be entered next, and you should reenter some percentage of the data to check on consistency.

As an alternative, you (or your RAs) can record data on spreadsheets or columnar paper. Spreadsheets are remnants from the days when data had to be entered into computers on cards, and they contain boxes arranged in 80 columns (designating the 80 spaces available on a computer card) and a number of rows. Each column provides a place for a single digit, a character, or a blank. A piece of data or a space to separate data goes in each column. You can copy data directly from the spreadsheet to a computer file. Although spreadsheets add an extra step to the raw-data-to-computer path, they provide an easily transportable copy of the raw data. Of course, you should always print a copy of raw data entered directly into the computer to make sure you have a hard copy.

Regardless of whether you enter data directly into the computer or use a spreadsheet, write out instructions (i.e., a coding book) to be followed in entering data. This would specify how each variable is scored and where it goes; for example, it might indicate that "male" is to be recorded as "0" and "female" as "1" in Column 5. If you are recording on spreadsheets, leave a blank space every once in a while to separate variables. This will make it easier to check for entry errors in the computer file: You can spot misaligned blank spaces easily.

Consider the computer program you will be using as you plan how to code your data in computer-readable form. Each program has different rules about how the data should be arranged. For example, some will let the same number stand for more than one variable (e.g., be part of the subject number *and* designate the subject's experimental condition), and some will not. If you are collecting the same measure over time on each subject, be sure to check how your program handles repeated-measures data. Some programs require variable transformations to do repeated-measures analyses if you record all your repeated measures on the same line. Be sure to check how your program handles missing data. If you intend to extrapolate values for missing data, do you need to figure out these figures and insert them into your computer file, or can the computer do these steps for you? If you are a computer neophyte or are unfamiliar with the program you plan to use, consult with someone more knowledgeable about your particular analyses for suggestions about how to set up your computer data file.

Similarly, if you are not familiar with software packages and plan to use your own personal computer to analyze the data, shop carefully. Appendix C provides a brief listing of many of the more popular statistics packages available for home computers. Be aware of your analyses, and ask questions that pertain to them before purchasing anything. For example, certain analyses are very complex and take a long time for the computer to run. Unless your computer has a math coprocessor, the statistics may proceed at a snail's pace. The computer will run other analyses fast enough without needing this extra bit of equipment. Some analyses may require more memory than your computer has (in particular, check about memory requirements for calculating repeated-measures statistics and multivariate procedures, if you will be using them). Be sure to ask about the memory requirements for your particular sample and design: Although the program may do the analysis and your computer may have enough memory for the program, the amount of memory required by the program to analyze your data set may exceed the capacity of your computer. If this is the case, you may be wiser to use a mainframe computer or minicomputer with more memory.

What data, and at what level, should be recorded in a computer file? Basically, we recommend putting in anything that you could conceivably want to analyze, whether you planned an analysis with the variable or not. For example, we always code the identity of the person who ran the subject, although we rarely use this variable in analyses (but we just might, if the data looked strange and we wanted to find out if one particular experimenter was responsible). Code individual items of questionnaires if you want the computer to derive subscales, if you wish to compute internal consistency scores on your scales, or if you think you might want to group items in a different fashion at some later date. If none of these is relevant, you may choose to record only summary scores. A good rule of thumb is to record data at as molecular a level as your resources will allow. You can always aggregate later, but you can't always disaggregate.

In addition, figure out how you will handle missing data (e.g., how will you extrapolate a score if your subject failed to answer a few questions on a questionnaire? or how many questions can be omitted before you exclude the scale or the subject?).

Data must be verified for accuracy *every step along the way that involves human recording*. Thus, if you score your questionnaires to get summary scores, someone should check the scoring. If you record data on spreadsheets and then type them into the computer, these steps should be checked. Now is the time to be obsessive-compulsive. We personally have detected major errors in recording, even among some of our most competent assistants—errors sufficient to change the results and interpretation of the analyses. Remember, the computer cannot tell you whether you scored the data correctly. It will only analyze what you give it. As the saying goes, garbage in—garbage out.

After you have recorded and verified your data, it is time to perform the analyses. If this is your virgin journey into a program or type of analysis, *be prepared for frustration*. Some of the most powerful computer programs have user-unfriendly manuals loaded with technical jargon but short on the details of how to handle common types of data. You might as well anticipate that you will run into difficulties and be pleasantly surprised if you do not. And remember, you are not alone, and you are not stupid because you cannot get the machine to do what you want. We have had to learn several computer programs in our combined three decades as faculty members, and rarely do we complete the analyses correctly and without errors the first time we use a new program. It usually takes about seven tries the first time through a new analysis with a new program!

If you are not computer literate, line up someone who knows the software *and* the analyses you plan to use and who will help you or at least give you an example of their programming statements. Preferably, this will be your chairperson or another student in your program. Do your analyses when that person is available for help. Physical availability is best, because your consultant will probably want to see all the printouts and error messages that you have received.

As you tell the computer what to do, take the time to tell it how to label your printouts and your variables. Give them names you will remember 5 years from now. Labeling the levels of your independent variable as *A* and *B* may make sense to you now, but you will not remember what *A* and *B* stand for next month. It takes some time and imagination, but programming the computer to label the top of each page with the name of the project and to give each independent and dependent variable a meaningful name will pay off later in the intelligibility of your printouts. You will already have arrived at this conclusion independently if you have spent time staring blankly at computer file names several years after you created them, trying to remember what they meant.

A good first step in analyzing the data is to get a printout of raw data, together with means and standard deviations (for parametric data), ranges, and frequency distributions for each cell of the design. Examine the frequency distributions for skew, bimodal distributions, extreme outliers, and other features that may require that you handle your data differently than you planned.

Look over your means, standard deviations, sample sizes, and distributions for unusual values or incorrect sample sizes. Such values can be a sign that someone has entered data incorrectly or something in your programming statements is faulty. For example, one of us recently found that one subject scored 71 on a 1- to 7-point scale! Once you have checked out-of-range values or ones that do not "seem right," you can perform your major analyses.

Check the accuracy of any variable transformation statements you have instructed the computer to follow, too. You can do this by computing a few transformed variables by hand and checking them against computer-generated values, as well as by looking for errors in statements themselves. This is crucial. One excellent student of ours carefully verified and analyzed her data, following all of the checking procedures we outline here except for checking transformed variables. The final version of the study was approved by her committee, and it was submitted and provisionally accepted for publication in an excellent journal. A few final additional analyses showed some strange mean values on one variable, however. When the student tracked these down, she discovered with horror that these strange values resulted from a typographical error in programming the computer to combine several variables. The computer had done as it was told, of course. Garbage in, ... Fortunately, she caught the error before submitting the final version for publication.

In addition to checking for errors, spend some time looking at your data. Get scatterplots of correlations among variables. Look at how each group of subjects scored on major variables, whether the distributions of different groups overlapped, and if so, how much. This kind of early data exploration provides a good feel for the data and will probably help you interpret more complex statistical findings later.

Finally, perform your actual analyses. Figure out what sample sizes and degrees of freedom the computer should be using, and check the printout to see if the computer's figures match your own. If not, look for errors in programming or data entry. Ask your chairperson or someone else more knowledgeable than you are to check your printouts for possible errors, too. Get printouts of your analyses that indicate your programming statements as well as the results. These make it easier to check for errors.

If you are examining groups of subjects, a good place to start your analyses is to see if they are equivalent on demographic characteristics and other potentially confounding variables. If they are not equivalent, you can then correlate the potential confound with your dependent variables. If uncorrelated, the confound is not linearly related to the dependent variable and is unlikely to influence your analyses. A significant and moderate (or higher) correlation, however, will indicate that you need to control for that variable, either through a design change (e.g., using the confounding variable as an additional independent variable) or statistically (e.g., using analysis of covariance; but see chapter 10).

Also check whether your data meet the assumptions of the statistics you plan to use. If not, check whether your proposed analysis is robust with regard to violation of the assumption, and, if not, take appropriate actions (e.g., transform the data or select an alternative analysis). Recall that in chapter 10 we discussed the assumptions of various statistics.

Do not be surprised if, as you analyze your data, you come up with additional questions and need to perform analyses beyond those you originally proposed. The actual results of a study rarely turn out exactly as predicted and often raise questions about why this failed to happen. Additional analyses frequently help you answer such questions. The results of these analyses may or may not wind up in the final version of your thesis or dissertation, depending on what they tell you and how they qualify the interpretation of the analyses you planned.

As you near the end of your analyses, start thinking again about writing. A good way to ease back into writing is to revise your literature review and method sections first and then to work on the results and discussion sections.

Revise Your Literature Review and Method Section

If you did a thorough, high-quality literature review during the proposal stage and gathered your data in a timely fashion, your literature review should need very few changes. Nonetheless, you will need to peruse the major journals that publish articles in your area to add literature that has been published since you proposed your project and to see which in-press citations have been published. In addition, you probably need to make changes that your committee requested during the proposal meeting. If you produced an abbreviated literature review for the proposal, you now must pay your dues and do that comprehensive literature review you put off.

Just as a well-done literature review at the proposal stage means fewer revisions later, a clearly written, well-specified method section in the proposal can be easily revised at this point by doing three things. First, if you wrote your method section in the future tense, change to the past tense now. Second, alter your descriptions of subjects, procedures, and so on, if there are differences between what you actually did and what you had planned to do. Third, add details about your actual population (e.g., a description or table of subject characteristics for each group you included) and about any analyses you conducted relevant to your measures (e.g., interrater agreement data for your study). When these revisions are complete, it is time to make the numbers in your computer printouts come alive, namely, to turn them into cogent prose, tables, and figures that describe your results. The next chapter covers writing the results section.

✔ **To Do . . .**

Collecting, Managing and Analyzing the Data

☐ Pilot test your procedures

☐ Recruit and train assistants

☐ Schedule settings and arrange materials

  —Complete checklist in Exhibit 11.1

☐ Collect the data

  —Supervise assistants regularly

  —Catch problems early

☐ Score the data

  —Verify scoring

  —Enter data into computer

  —Verify data entry

☐ Analyze the data

  —Obtain help if unfamiliar with computer programs

  —Label variables and printouts

  —Obtain printouts of raw data and variable distributions

  —Peruse printouts for unusual values and verify them

  —Check accuracy of transformation programs

  —Examine whether data meet the assumptions of your statistics

☐ Revise your literature review and method section

  —"Freshen" references

  —Alter method section to reflect actual procedures

12

Presenting the Results

You collected all your data, analyzed them (incorrectly, at first; correctly, at last!), and now you are ready to present them to the world. Well, maybe not the world just yet. For the time being, you will be happy to get them down on paper so that this section of your writing will be out of the way and you can move on to the discussion section.

If all has gone well and you have followed our advice closely up to now, the task of preparing your results section should be easy. That is because you should already have prepared it, at least in skeleton form, for your proposal. Remember how shocked (and probably resistant!) you were to the suggestion that you mock up a results section to include in your proposal? Well, now comes the payoff. The mock results section should have been helpful in clarifying your design and planned analyses. Now, it will be useful once again in providing the framework for the "real" results section. In fact, if you took our advice seriously and prepared complete mock results for your proposal, most of your work has already been done. Producing a results section now should be mainly a job of erasing the imaginary data and filling the space with real data. Let's look at the kinds of information you will want to include in your results section and how you might want to organize it for maximum clarity.

Present Relevant Data

The results section is the place to present the major types of data related to the hypotheses you examined in your study. In addition to the data, of course, you will include the statistical treatments you used to make sense out of them. Be complete, but think "lean and mean" at the same time. As a general strategy, state your conclusions, and then follow immediately with the data and statistical analyses supporting your conclusions. For example, you might say "boys were found to spend more time in types of play involving large muscle activity. This can be seen in Table 1, in which the means for boys for all three games involving such activity are significantly higher than for girls (main effect for gender [1, 59] = 4.62, $p < .05$)." The presentation of individual scores or raw data should be avoided, unless, of course, your study involves a single-subject design. Retain the raw data in an appendix for later consultation if needed. As Yates (1982) observed, the archival function of such a placement can be very important, especially for any subsequent analyses that might be requested by editors of journals to which the research is eventually submitted for publication. Confine the results section to data and their statistical treatment. Reserve the implications of the results for the discussion section.

Present data related to the purposes of the study, avoiding the temptation to inject analyses that are interesting but really tangential. Many ignore this suggestion when dealing with the instrumentation needed to produce the data for the major hypotheses. For example, as part of ensuring the adequacy of your measures, you may collect generalizability data of one type or another. (Chapter 9 discussed several instances in which you might address reliability and validity issues in your study.) Suppose, for example, your major dependent variable involves ratings by others. To show these data are adequately reliable for further analysis in examining the major hypotheses of the study, you compare the data from independent raters. The results of these comparisons are important in showing how sound your methodology was. They are not directly relevant to your major hypotheses, however, unless your study was about interrater reliability for this particular measure. The best place for these data is in the method section at the point at which you are describing the measure itself. Similarly, place data related to the characteristics of your sample and the demographic equivalence of any groups you compare in the subjects subsection of the method section. Be aware, however, that some disagree with us on this point, so be sure to check with your chairperson.

Present Results in an Orderly, Logical Way

There is nothing mysterious about results presentation. Once you have decided what to include and what to avoid, the rest is rather mechanical.

Order and Sequence the Results

The results section really started back at the hypothesis-formulation stage. Recall our very strong statements concerning hypotheses. Assuming that you produced some hypotheses before starting your research (as chapter 3 recommended), you most likely listed them in order of importance. If so, you simultaneously produced the general organization of the rest of your write-up, especially the results section, without even knowing it. Now, merely present the results in the order of the importance of the hypotheses. To get things started, it might be useful to restate the principal hypotheses at the beginning of the results section. Then, go into the data used to test each, along with the relevant statistical analyses. If there are numerous dependent measures or analyses for each hypothesis, consider using subheadings. Each subheading could be a shortened reference to the hypothesis being tested. After you present data relevant to your hypotheses, present the findings of secondary analyses.

Some authorities might suggest you organize your results by major dependent measure. This seems to us to be logically less suitable than by hypothesis because you are not studying the measures themselves. Rather, you are using them as a vehicle for testing your hypotheses. If, however, you have several measures related to each hypothesis, you might want to organize them by subheading within hypotheses. Even if you do not use subheadings within subheadings (!), it is a good idea to decide on an order for presenting the results for each measure and then stick with that order when you present the results for the rest of the hypotheses.

Sometimes, the clearest way of organizing your results is by analysis. For example, suppose you have three hypotheses that pertain to the percentage of variance three variables will account for in a multiple regression equation. Here, you may wish to summarize all three hypotheses, then present the results of the one multiple regression. This way you avoid redundancy and still keep your results tied to your hypotheses.

Include Relevant Information

For each analysis you conduct, include the name of the statistic and its particulars. Particulars for ANOVA, for example, include the factors, how many levels of each, whether any factors involved repeated measures, and the name of any post hoc test you used. Include important statistical values (e. g., F, t, and p) for all significant effects. Some will want you to include this information for nonsignificant effects as well, perhaps in an appendix. Also include means, standard deviations, and sample sizes for each dependent variable. For correlational studies, include these for the sample as a whole, unless the sample was not subdivided for analyses (when you will want means, sample sizes, and standard deviations for each subsample).

If you compare groups of subjects, present means, standard deviations, and sample sizes appropriate to each significant effect. For example, if a Gender × Grade ANOVA shows a main effect only for gender, make sure you present these types of data for gender (collapsed across grade). You may also wish to present the same data for each grade–gender cell in an appendix.

Which information should you include in a table or figure and which goes in the text? In general, means and standard deviations most often go in tables, unless there are so few of them they can be accommodated easily in the text. Statistical values (e.g., Fs) may go in the text or a table, depending on which is easier to follow. Place the names of statistical tests and describe their particulars in the text.

Word Your Results Clearly

Remember, the results section is the place for maximum clarity. This is not the time to be creative or to look for the most proseworthy way of saying things. A good rule to follow is "Be monotonously repetitive!" Decide on a particular sentence structure that most clearly presents the results of a particular type, and stick with that structure for all results that are similar. For example, if your study uses a 2 × 2 factorial design and involves three different dependent variables that you analyze using ANOVA, present the results for each dependent variable in exactly the same way. Thus, if gender was one of your independent variables, you might present any results for it first, followed by those for your second independent variable, followed by the interaction, if any. Stick with this order as you lay out the data for each of your dependent variables. Moreover, if you discuss data for females first for the first dependent variable, discuss them first for all the rest. Consistency and symmetry will aid greatly in understanding your results, which may be the most difficult section of your thesis or dissertation. The reader will follow your presentation more easily if you minimize variety in sentence structure and write clearly and concisely, thus eliminating a significant potential distraction from the task of understanding your results. In addition, consistency in presentation allows the reader to return much more easily to previously read sections to check for understanding or comparison against later results.

In addition to being monotonously repetitive, it is a good idea to write English rather than statistical sentences (Yates, 1982). Make it a habit to put the statistics related to a conclusion or finding at the end of the sentence. For example, "Males were less likely to notice differences in facial expression than females ($M_{males} = 5.2$; $M_{females} = 3.5$), $F(1, 29) = 6.49$, $p < .05$." This is much easier to read than "The mean for the males on the Test of Facial Cue Reading was 5.2, which the ANOVA $F(1, 29) = 6.49$, $p < .05$, revealed to be significantly higher than the females' mean of 3.5." Notice in our first example that we also talked about the dependent variable when comparing males and females, not the specific measure of it. This is acceptable when there is a single measure for a particular variable. If there is more than one, it is a good idea to precede the first example with something such as "With respect to differences in facial expression, males were less likely to notice differences in facial expression than females on the Test of Facial Cue Reading." This could then be followed with the results on the second measure, for example, "However, there were no differences on the videotape measure of visual affect ($M_{males} = 12.4$; $M_{females} = 13.1$), $F(1, 29) = 1.56$, $p = ns$."

Follow Conventions Concerning the Presentation of Statistics

There are generally accepted rules or conventions regarding how you are supposed to present the results of statistical tests. Remember our rule about being monotonously repetitive to aid reader understanding? Adherence to conventions in presenting statistics is based on exactly the same logic. Readers should not be distracted from understanding your findings by having to figure out your creative way of presenting statistics. Recommendations about such presentations in psychology (and most of the social and behavioral sciences) have been documented in the *Publication Manual of the American Psychological Association* (1994). We have given you some examples of statistical results presented according to APA style in the preceding section. The general rule when presenting inferential statistical information in the text is to present the symbol of the statistic followed by the degrees of freedom (e.g., $F[1, 29]$, then the value of the statistic (e.g., 6.49), and finally the probability level (e.g., $p < .05$). A zero is not used before the decimal in probability levels. When a chi square is used, the degrees of freedom and sample size are reported in parentheses, for example, $\chi^2(4, N = 86) = 9.67$, $p < .05$. There are numerous other conventions concerning the presentation of statistics in the text of papers, and space does not allow us to discuss all of them here. The APA *Publication Manual* gives more details.

Follow Conventions Concerning the Preparation of Tables

Because tables are more difficult (and therefore more expensive) to typeset, most journal editors will resist including them except for important findings and ones that cannot be presented in the text. In a thesis or dissertation, you have more latitude because they are not going to be typeset.

A well-crafted table can assist readers immeasurably in understanding your results. Skill in constructing such tables takes a good deal of practice. The best advice we can give you about preparing tables is found in the five Ps referred to in chapter 4: Prior Planning Prevents Poor Performance. First, think about the effect you want your table to have on the reader. If you are presenting data on a dependent measure in order to show the impact of one or more independent variables, decide which of the latter you want to emphasize most. For example, suppose you are studying the effects of exposure to disclosing and nondisclosing models on subsequent self-disclosure of therapy candidates. Suppose further that you have included gender as a secondary independent variable. Your data might be arranged in a 2×2 matrix and subjected to an ANOVA. In a simple four-group comparison such as this, you could probably present the data in the text and forego the need for a table. If you use a table, however, you might arrange your data the way we have in Table 12.1. Or, you might arrange your presentation as we have in Table 12.2. Which of these two tables gives more emphasis to modeling?

Table 12.1

Means Levels of Self-Disclosure (and Standard Devations) by Gender Following Exposure to Disclosing or Nondisclosing Models

	Female		Male	
Model	*M*	*SD*	*M*	*SD*
Disclosing	7.60	2.34	4.85	2.02
Nondisclosing	4.76	1.89	2.67	1.93

Note. $n = 12$ per group.

Table 12.2

Mean Levels of Self-Disclosure (and Standard Deviations) by Gender Following Exposure to Disclosing or Nondisclosing Models

	Disclosing model		Nondisclosing model	
Gender	M	SD	M	SD
Female	7.60	2.24	4.76	1.89
Male	4.85	2.02	2.67	1.93

Note. $n = 12$ per group.

If you said Table 12.2, you would agree with most readers. In general, it is easier to make side-by-side than up–down comparisons.

This was a fairly straightforward example. Suppose we complicate it a bit by adding additional dependent measures. For example, we might differentiate types of self-disclosure. We might have content related to (a) sex and intimacy, (b) money, and (c) professional ambition. How would we represent data for all three types of content under the different modeling conditions for males and females? Table 12.3 shows one possibility.

How easy is it to see the impact of the major independent variable, namely, modeling, in this presentation? True, the two model conditions are still presented side by side. But, to make comparisons between the disclosing and nondisclosing conditions, one would need to do this measure by measure. This would require finding a mean on the left and looking across to its counterpart on the right, ignoring the means in

Table 12.3

Mean Levels of Self-Disclosure (and Standard Deviations) for Three Types of Content Following Exposure to Disclosing or Nondisclosing Models for Females and Males

	Disclosing model						Nondisclosing model					
	Sex/ intimacy		Money		Prof'l amb.		Sex/ intimacy		Money		Prof'l amb.	
Gender	M	SD	M	SD	M	SD	M	SD	M	SD	M	SD
Female	5.20	2.01	4.80	1.98	4.75	1.87	3.26	1.67	3.91	1.56	3.84	1.73
Male	3.35	1.77	5.92	1.96	5.87	2.15	2.67	1.78	5.13	2.21	5.46	2.04

Note. $n = 15$ per group. Prof'l amb. = professional ambition.

between. It might help to place your forefingers on the respective columns, but a different arrangement of the table might make the evaluation of the major independent variable more straightforward. Consider the layout represented in Table 12.4.

It is much easier to compare the effects of model disclosure in this arrangement because one can make side-by-side comparisons for females and males on each dependent measure by reading down the columns. Moreover, an overall comparison of disclosing versus nondisclosing model conditions could easily be made by taking the mean of the entries in each column.

In theses and dissertations, it is generally better to use more than fewer tables. Include ones that are central to interpreting your results in the results section; place less central ones in the appendixes. Although the APA *Publication Manual* requires tables to be included at the end of the manuscript after the footnote page (however, when typeset, tables are presented close to where they are discussed in text), schools often allow more latitude in placement. We prefer tables to appear in the text as near to where they are being described as possible. This facilitates reading, as there is no need to be switching back and forth between text and the end of a long thesis or dissertation to find the relevant table.

When constructing tables, keep an eye out for readability. Allow sufficient space between entries, line up columns of numbers on decimal points, and avoid splitting tables across pages if possible. Tables presented

Table 12.4

Mean Self-Disclosure (and Standard Deviations) for Three Types of Content Following Exposure to Disclosing or Nondisclosing Models

Gender	Disclosing model		Nondisclosing model	
	M	SD	M	SD
Female				
Sex/intimacy	5.20	2.01	3.26	1.67
Money	4.80	1.98	3.91	1.56
Professional ambition	4.75	1.87	3.84	1.73
Male				
Sex/intimacy	3.35	1.77	2.67	1.78
Money	5.92	1.96	5.13	2.21
Professional ambition	5.87	2.15	5.46	2.04

Note. $n = 15$ per group.

vertically on a page are less cumbersome than ones presented in landscape fashion, requiring the reader to turn the page sideways. Sometimes, the difference in vertical versus landscape presentation can turn on the need for precision in your data entries. If it is not really necessary to present data to the second decimal place, don't. This will save space and avoid the appearance of pseudoscientific writing. If you do use the landscape format, be sure the title of the table appears along the binding side of the page (i.e., the left-hand side).

Speaking of titles, write one that is brief and explanatory at the same time. Avoid including information in the title that also appears in headings of the table itself. As an illustration, compare the titles of Tables 12.3 and 12.4. These tables present the same information, just arranged in different ways. The title for Table 12.3 errs on the side of excess detail. In part, this is the result of duplicating information that occurs in the headings of the table itself. Note that brevity was purchased in the title of Table 12.4 by omitting reference to the secondary independent variable, gender. This was not a great information loss as the table headings convey this anyway. Also, words like *levels* and *scores* can generally be omitted because they are easily inferred from a glance at the table.

As we said above, the preparation of effective tables takes practice. The APA *Publication Manual* provides many more details concerning tabular presentations. It even includes a checklist specific to tables (see p. 140 of the *Manual*). Consult this valuable resource before beginning your initial drafts. Look at professional journals to see how others have presented tables like yours for analyses and copy the clearest as examples. Also, you will benefit from trying out different arrangements and then having other people look at them and tell you how easy they are to interpret.

Once you have decided on a particular layout, present all similar data in tables set up exactly the same way. Remember our advice to be monotonously repetitious in presenting your results? The same applies to tables. Do not tax the reader or yourself with different formats when the first, painstakingly prepared one can serve nicely as the template for many others. Also, remember to present only the most important data in tabular form. Save the individual subject data and other detailed peripheral information for your appendixes.

Follow Conventions Concerning the Preparation of Figures

The other major type of illustration you will want to consider is a figure. Anything that is not text or a table will fall into this category, including graphs, charts, photographs, and drawings. Because figures typically are more expensive to prepare (in time and money) than text or tables, you will want to use them sparingly. Certain types of information are difficult to convey any other way, however, and you will have to rely on figures for these. For example, one of us had a student who, for his master's thesis, evaluated approaches to teaching mealtime skills to persons with retardation. The professionally prepared drawings that appeared in the thesis as figures greatly facilitated communicating the topography of the utensil grip the subjects learned (Nelson, Cone, & Hanson, 1975). Also, figures portray interactions among independent variables and trends over time or over dosage levels most effectively.

Ask yourself the following questions before you decide to use figures:

1. What do you want the figure to communicate?
2. Can this be communicated effectively by text or tabular presentation?
3. Will the figure be duplicative of information already provided in other ways?
4. How will the figure complement information presented in other forms?
5. What type of figure (e.g., graph, drawing, or photograph) will be best?
6. If using a graph, what type of graph (e.g., histogram, bar, or line) will be best?
7. How will you have the figure produced (e.g., drawn by hand yourself or prepared with software or by a professional draftsperson)?

You are ready to begin preparing your figures once you have answered these questions. As with tables, there are a number of conventions applied with varying consistency to figures. Let's spend a few moments reviewing these. We will not discuss the various types of charts and graphs you might select. Good descriptions of these can be found in the APA *Publication Manual* and in Parsonson and Baer (1978). We will limit ourselves to a few high points of graphic presentation, mixing generally accepted convention with some preferences of our own. Start your graph with cartesian coordinates (i.e., lines at right angles to one another). The dependent variable will be represented on the vertical or Y axis (or ordinate); the independent variable or time, on the horizontal or X axis (or abscissa). A rule of thumb is that the length of the Y axis should be approximately two-thirds the length of the X axis. The Y axis should

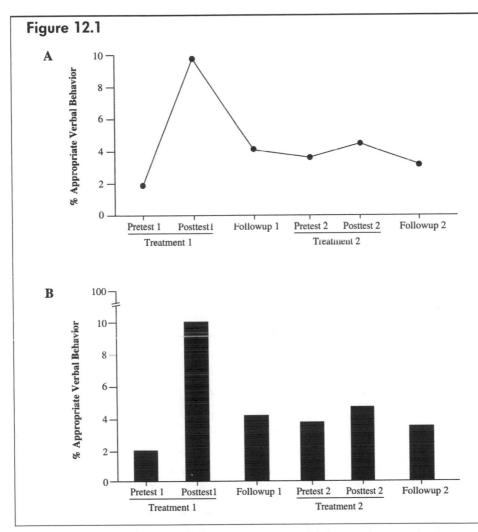

Figure 12.1

(A) Discrete data in line graph format; no scale break on an attenuated Y axis. (B) Identical data in bar graph format, with scale break. From Parsonson and Baer (1978), "The analysis and presentation of graphic data." In T. R. Kratochwill (Ed.), *Single Subject Research* (pp. 101–165). San Diego, CA: Academic Press. Reprinted by permission.

include the entire range possible on the dependent variable. For example, if you are presenting percentages, the intercept of the axes should be at 0 and the last number on the ordinate should be 100. If your scores actually occupy only a portion of the entire range, consider showing a discontinuity or interruption in the ordinate. Figure 12.1 illustrates these points. The data in the top portion of the figure (A) give a somewhat different impression than those in the bottom half (B). This is because they do not emphasize just how far from being 100% appropriate the verbal behavior actually is. In (A), the pre- to posttest changes shown by the first two data points seem quite large. When the "distance to go" is made clear by including the entire range as in (B), the impression of the impact of the intervention is likely to be different.

The units on the axes should be equally distant from each other. On the X axis, this would be true for units showing equal amounts of time passage. Notice in Figure 12.1 that the distances between Pre- and Posttest 1 and Pre- and Posttest 2 are identical. The distances from posttest to follow-up differ from the pre- to posttest distances, however, and reflect the different amounts of time involved.

Units on the axes are indicated by grid or tick marks starting at the axis and extending toward the inside of the figure slightly. Some authorities (e.g., Parsonson & Baer, 1978) prefer the tick marks to extend toward the outside of the figure. Others (e.g., APA, 1983) prefer to extend them toward the inside. In any event, the vertical axis should not extend beyond the last tick mark. Both axes are labeled clearly, giving the name of the variable being measured and the units of measurement. In Figure 12.1, appropriate verbal behavior is the variable, and it is measured in terms of percentage. Axis labels are placed parallel to the axes, whereas tick mark numbers or labels are placed horizontally.

Figure 12.2 illustrates additional conventions. Again, notice the discontinuity in the ordinate. This time we have also shown a discontinuity on the abscissa, as well. Notice that the general layout of the data in Figure 12.2 communicates the type of design (A-B-A-B) used in the study. Notice also that each of the phases is labeled and separated by a dashed vertical line. It is useful to name the phases descriptively (e.g., *feedback*) as this communicates more information than generic labels (e.g., *treatment*). Figure 12.2 presents data from four groups. Generally, four lines in a line graph would be the maximum for readability. If the data are close, however, even four may be too many. Note also that we have included a legend for the groups. It is a good idea to put a box around a legend and include it within the area defined by the axes. If space does not allow this, the next best location is usually to the right of the figure.

Once you decide on symbols for your lines on the graph, be consistent. In Figure 12.2, we used squares for girls and diamonds for boys. The figure could have been even more consistent had we kept these same symbols for both grade levels, using open and filled versions to indicate fourth and second grades, respectively. If you use more than one figure,

Figure 12.2

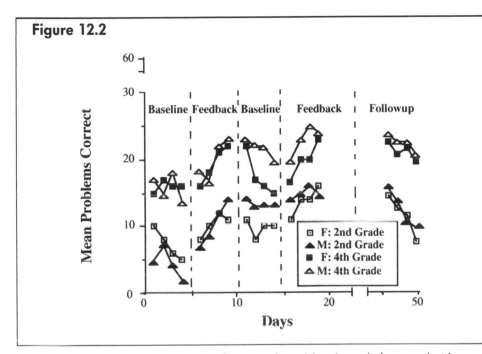

Mean subtraction problems correct for second- and fourth-grade boys and girls across four phases of the study and at follow-up.

keep the symbols consistent. That is, always represent boys with diamonds, girls with squares, fourth grader open, and so on.

Figure 12.2 also illustrates some other useful conventions. Data points are not connected *between* phases, allowing easier evaluation of differences between phases. Missing data would be indicated by a blank space. Points on either side of the missing data would not be connected across the missing day. The lines within the axes should be narrower than the axes themselves.

Sometimes you may wish to present the results for more than one dependent variable in the same figure. This can be tricky when the scale of measurement differs for the variables. Figure 12.3 illustrates a solution for this problem. In this figure, two ordinates are used, with one line of the graph being referred to the left ordinate, and the other to the right. This shows quite graphically the different directions of change associated with the treatment for each of the dependent variables. This presentation makes it easy to compare the variables, and the entire presentation is more economical than drafting two different figures.

Figure 12.3

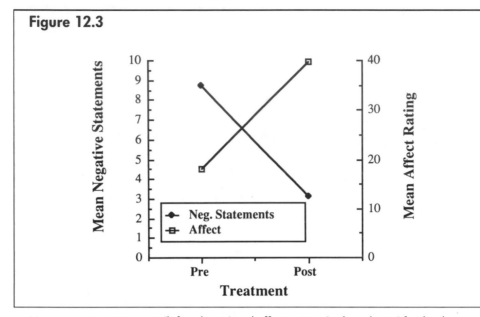

Mean negative statements (left ordinate) and affect ratings (right ordinate) for the depressed clients at pre- and posttreatment assessments.

Finally, the selection of the type of graph appropriate to the data is important. Generally, line graphs are inappropriate for data that are discontinuous. The top half of Figure 12.1 illustrates this. As Parsonson and Baer (1978) point out, the "actual data path between temporally distant plotted points is unknown" (p. 117). In such cases, the bar graph shown in the bottom half of the figure is more appropriate.

The last step for most of us in creating a figure is deciding on a caption for it. In the preparation of manuscripts for publication, the APA requires the inclusion of figure captions on a separate page that is placed at the very end of the manuscript. The figures themselves are similarly placed, so this is not unreasonable. In theses and in dissertations, one has more latitude in placement, however. As with tables, we prefer figures to appear in the text near where they are being discussed. The caption for the figure would then appear just below it.

Figure captions serve two purposes. They provide a title for the figure and explain the figure itself. Figures and their captions are designed to stand by themselves. That is, the reader should not have to search the text to understand the data the figure presents. In composing a caption, describe the contents of the figure. This can usually be accomplished in a brief sentence or phrase. An example of a "too brief" caption for Figure 12.3 is "*Figure 12.3*. Verbal behavior and affect levels pre- and posttreatment." Compare this caption with the one actually provided with the figure.

Just as was true for tables, crafting figures well takes repeated practice. There are many more details to consider than space has permitted us to discuss here. The APA *Publication Manual* covers most of these details. It also includes a useful checklist specifically for figures (see p. 162 of the *Manual*). It is a good idea to try out different versions of figures before committing to final production. Ask friends or your committee chairperson for their reactions. Revise the figure and then draw it or have it drawn professionally.

A really time-effective way to develop alternate forms of figures is with computer software developed especially for this purpose. The advent of personal computers and associated graphics software has made the production of publishable quality figures much easier. Two examples of easy to use and powerful software for graphs are Cricket Graph™ for the MacIntosh™ and Harvard Graphics™ for the IBM™ and compatibles. We recommend that you take the time, preferably early in your graduate career, to familiarize yourself with a computer graphics program. Some are relatively inexpensive (Cricket Graph™ was selling for about $115 at the time of this writing) and well worth their cost given the savings in your time or the cost of having a professional draftsperson do the work for you. Besides, it is always good to have a few graphs lying around the house showing the success of your exercise or weight-loss program!

If you decide to take the old fashioned handdrawn route to figure production, a number of materials available commercially will make your job easier. Among these, the most useful are blue-lined graph paper and rub-on, press-on, or dry transfer lettering systems. The graph paper can be of immeasurable help in lining up and spacing the elements of your figure, and its blue lines will not show when photocopies are made of the finished product. Most university bookstores carry such paper in various sizes and have lettering kits, as well. The latter will often include press-on lines to be used as axes and symbols to be used as points in line graphs. Yates (1982, pp. 165–171) provides some very useful suggestions for the do-it-yourself figure drafter.

✓ To Do . . .

Presenting the Results

☐ Present data related to purposes of the study

☐ Present results in an orderly, logical way

— Order and sequence the results

— Include relevant information

- Name of statistic

- Relevant details about the statistic

- Statistical values for significant effects

- Means

- Standard deviations

- Sample size

— Word our results clearly

— Follow conventions in psychology regarding presentation of statistics

— Create well-crafted, clear tables

— Prepare well-crafted clear figures

13

Discussing the Results

You've written the proposal. You've found enough subjects. You've collected, inspected, and analyzed the data so much that you feel like you know each data point personally. You've finally figured out how to describe in words what your statistics told you about your data. And now the blank sheet (or screen) headed "Discussion" stares back at you.

Students commonly tell us that they don't know what to write in the discussion—they have said everything already. It is easy to understand why they believe this, but it really is not so. In your discussion section, you will interpret your findings, place them in the context of your hypotheses and the literature you reviewed, and examine critically their implications and limitations. In this chapter, we pose numerous questions that may apply to your study. As you read them, think about the answers. Keep notes on your thoughts and consider integrating these points into your discussion section.

Summarize Your Findings

Most discussion sections begin with an integrative summary of the results. This should not reiterate your statistics; you should not state F and p values, nor should you reiterate technical details of the analyses. Instead, describe your results clearly, using as little statistical jargon as possible. A statement such as "Students who were told to expect a later memory test were more vigilant and showed better recall than those who were not" is better than "There was a significant main effect for condition on the vigilance and recall variables." Use the "layperson test": how would you describe your results to educated people in a way that they would understand?

237

One good way to organize your summary of the results is around whether they did or did not support each of the hypotheses or research questions. This summary can lead logically into a discussion of the various reasons *why* you found what you did (or did not) find. Discuss hypotheses in the order that you originally listed them in the subsection on research questions and hypotheses of your literature review, briefly restating each hypothesis so that the reader will not have to turn back to the earlier section. This should mirror the order in which your results section unfolded, as well.

An alternate way of summarizing the results is to present major findings together. If, for example, you studied the effects of therapist self-disclosure on client attitudes and interactions in therapy, you could consider each set of dependent variables in turn. Of course, you will still need to point out whether and how these findings support your original hypotheses and relate to your research questions.

Do not forget adventitious findings—results of analyses that you may not have planned originally or did not expect to be significant. Sometimes the unexpected provides the most interesting outcome. If you compared groups of individuals, did you find any unexpected differences between the groups? Did these differences relate to your dependent variables? For example, one of our students (Sikora, 1989) examined the relationships among divorce, recent life changes, and preschool children's behavior with peers. Unfortunately, the children of divorced parents and of adults who indicated a great deal of life change came from significantly poorer families than the control children. Surprisingly, divorce and reported life change related very little to behavior, but socioeconomic status correlated strongly with behavior. This relationship, therefore, became a major focus of the discussion that followed, despite the fact that Sikora's hypotheses had not even mentioned socioeconomic status.

Interpret Your Findings

Summarizing the results is only one part of their interpretation. What do they mean? What do your results tell you about the relationship between the independent variables and the dependent variables? Were there relationships? Did they apply to several or only selected dependent variables? Were there confounds or mediators that accounted for the findings?

Some of you will be lucky. Your study will turn out exactly as you predicted. You will readily think of an interpretation for your findings, because you thought about that interpretation when you designed the study. If you are among these lucky few, you can progress to discussing alternative explanations for your findings and exploring what they mean for theory, practice, and the world at large.

The majority of you, however, will not be so lucky. You will find that some things turned out as you had hoped and others did not. All this means is that some things did not happen as predicted. Be grateful: This gives you lots to talk about! In this case, you should consider *which* variables showed predicted relationships and which did not. Then consider *why* this was the case. Do significant variables share any commonalities? Point them out. Why did nonsignificant variables turn out that way? In other words, compare and contrast the significant with the nonsignificant findings, examining why the differences exist and what these differences might tell you about the phenomena you are studying.

Consider several explanations for why your measures do not all agree: (a) instrumentation problems (Did you measure the dependent variables well? Were measures reliable enough to detect true effects?); (b) inadequate documentation or manipulation of the independent variable (You *think* you assessed or manipulated it well, but did you *really* do so? Was there a strong enough "dose" of the independent variable to make a difference?); (c) inadequate sample size (Was your sample large enough to detect an effect?); (d) specific procedural aspects of the study that may have suppressed effects of the independent variable; and (e) true relationships between the independent and dependent variables other than the ones you predicted (Do finer distinctions need to be made in how the independent variable works? Do additional mechanisms or mediators need to be proposed?). Each of these can be considered in turn, discussing reasons why it is or is not a plausible explanation for your failure to find what you had expected.

You may also be able to use some of your results or to conduct supplemental analyses of the data to provide evidence for or against some of these explanations. If, for example, you used a relatively new measure for your study, one with minimal reliability and validity information, you may be able to correlate that measure with other measures used in the study that have known reliability and validity data. These correlations could support or challenge the validity of the new measure.

The occasional student will find no significant findings at all, even after months of toil. In this case, you should analyze why this may have occurred, considering the factors just described. Conduct whatever supplemental analyses of your data are possible to check out hypotheses for the lack of findings. For example, if your data are highly variable and you suspect that only a subset of your subjects responded to your independent variable as predicted, analyze data for that subset only. If you suspect that demographic variables were responsible for your lack of findings, correlate the problem demographics with your dependent variables. These analyses, of course, should be presented in the results section and discussed as supplemental (and, if your sample sizes are quite small, preliminary).

Do not despair if you find little to crow about. Science advances through an accumulation of information. Some of that involves failed predictions. Failed predictions can be as important as supported predictions in a well-designed study with adequate sample size and reliable and valid measures. In these cases, failed predictions may suggest that the framework that led to the hypotheses may need revision. Remember, however, that the absence of significant findings does not confirm the null hypothesis, and consider a range of plausible explanations.

In the absence of significant findings in other areas, you can always correlate your demographic variables with your dependent variables, and your dependent variables with each other. This will provide additional information to discuss in the absence of more substantive findings.

Place Your Findings in Context

Your study is not the only research dealing with the issue you investigated. In fact, you probably spent many a page describing related studies when you wrote your literature review. Do not, therefore, write your discussion as though your study was the only one in the field! As you summarize and describe your results, consider how they do and do not fit with the literature you reviewed earlier.

Numerous topics provide grist for this discussion. First, consider how your findings fit with past literature. To do this, think about how your study compares with earlier research in terms of population characteristics, measurement tools, independent variables (and how they were verified), research design, and procedures. Then, think about whether your results converge with, clarify, or contradict past findings.

If your study converges with others, differences between your methods and those of others may indicate ways your study *extends* earlier findings. For example, if researchers repeatedly found that couples' attributions measured in the laboratory correlated with marital satisfaction, and you found something similar using daily logs of attributions, you could discuss how well the relationship held using measures taken daily in the natural environment.

Your results might also clarify contradictions in the literature. If so, point this out. Researchers often can explain contradictory findings as they examine new and finer grained distinctions in population parameters, measurement domains, and independent variables. If you made these kinds of distinctions, your findings can help others understand existing literature better. Suppose, for example, previous studies used men and women as subjects, without looking for gender differences. You examined these gender differences, and they were significant. This not only means that future research should consider gender as an important variable but that past research may have *failed* to find effects when genders were combined, because of the variance attributable to gender. Past samples that were dominated by men would likely show patterns for the male gender, whereas those dominated by women would show patterns for the female gender.

If you failed to find what others found, consider why. Again, appraise differences between your study and others' work. Consider methodological explanations: Could different measures, procedures, or samples account for the discrepancy? In addition, discuss what your failure to replicate others' results says about *limitations* to the generalizability of their findings. Do your findings suggest any new distinctions that need to be made in the literature in the future? If your failure to find what others found is not an artifact of problems with your procedures or measures, you may have discovered something important about the phenomenon you examined.

Consider, as well, what your research contributes to the existing literature. Remember, a dissertation is supposed to be a *new* contribution to knowledge. A thesis may provide less new information but should certainly add to what is already known. Regardless of how familiar the study now seems to you, it adds to the literature in some way. Point this out. What did you do that no one else did? How did this improve on past investigations? And what did this improvement yield in terms of findings?

Consider the Implications of Your Findings

What do your findings imply? How do they improve our understanding of the phenomenon you investigated? How should they alter the way we think about the issues you have researched? In thinking about the implications of your findings, consider how they might speak to theory, research, and practice.

With respect to theory, first think about the prevailing theoretical models in your research area. What do these models postulate? What are their implicit assumptions? What would these theories predict about your results? Are your results consistent with one or more of these theories? Why or why not? Your findings do not prove or disprove a theory: They just support or fail to support it. Although it would be nice if your findings were consistent with only a single theory, they may be explained equally well by more than one. That's fine—discuss this fact and describe how future researchers might design studies to pit the two explanations against one another.

With respect to research methodology, remember, understanding of a phenomenon advances as important distinctions are made. Did your study imply any new distinctions or any factors that are important to control in further investigations? For example, consider Sikora's (1989) dissertation on preschool children described earlier. Her finding that socioeconomic status correlated consistently with social behavior implies that future researchers in peer relations should control for socioeconomic status and describe that characteristic of their subjects.

Research also advances with improvements in design and measurement. Do your results have implications in these areas? If you used observational measures when others used only self-reports, do your results indicate that future studies should follow your lead? In general, research often progresses from general to specific, and from weak designs to strong. Thus, if you used a longitudinal design and failed to find what cross-sectional studies found, you may use your results to lobby for the continued use of stronger designs that yield more conclusive results.

With respect to the practice of psychology, what do your findings have to say for clinical, educational, or industrial/organizational practice? Who might pay attention to these findings, and why? How should these potential readers change their thinking or practice on the basis of your findings? Even disappointing findings may indicate that applied psychologists should consider your issue more carefully than they traditionally do. For example, suppose your findings challenge the customary assumptions about the problems adult offspring of alcoholics experience. Or, suppose they question the accuracy or even the existence of repressed memories. What would this mean for mental health professionals whose interventions are based on these assumptions? What would it mean for the lay public who reads undocumented "pop psychology" books full of these "facts"?

Some studies have more implications for practice than others, of course. Studies that involve clinical or business populations, for example, are likely to have a great many practical applications; basic science investigations in physiological psychology may have none. If your findings have potential implications for applied work, be sure to consider their limitations as well. You may need to speculate about the generalizability of what you found. Be sure in so doing to acknowledge your speculations and to describe the kind of research that would be necessary to bridge the gap between your findings and the applications you discuss.

This brings us to another important issue—the role of speculation in the discussion section. Many students err in their discussion by sticking too closely to their data. As a result, the discussion section has no discussion! In talking about your findings, balance scientific skepticism with speculation and hypotheses about what your data mean and why they turned out the way they did. In practice, this means it is all right to speculate. Just don't stray too far from the data. Furthermore, be aware of the assumptions you make in leaping from the data to your speculations and point them out. If you can justify your logic with your own findings or those of others, that's even better. The keys are to be explicit about your speculations and to discuss evidence for and against them, if such evidence exists.

Include a Humility Subsection

A discussion section is certainly a place to brag (subtly, of course) about the quality of your project and the importance of your findings. This boasting should be tempered by recognition that your study is not perfect, however. Writing what one of our colleagues terms a "humility" subsection allows you to point out the limitations of your study. This not only demonstrates that you understand research methodology and the inevitable trade-offs that accompany research decisions, it can also preempt your committee from tearing your study to pieces.

Limitations of your study generally come from two sources: (a) decisions made about how to conduct the study and (b) problems that came up when conducting it. Decisions about criteria for subject inclusion, procedures, measures, and design all may carry limitations as well as strengths. In this section of the discussion, consider those trade-offs. Of course, you may have anticipated some of the potential problems and taken steps to circumvent them, allowing you to point out (humbly, to be sure) how you dealt with the potential limitation.

Unavoidable problems that limit your findings may also have come up as you conducted the study. Your sample may have been smaller than planned, limiting your statistical power. Consent rates may have been low. Subjects may have dropped out of the study. If you compared different groups of individuals, you may have found that they differed on demographic variables. Perhaps you overlooked a potential confounding variable that you should have assessed. Observations conducted in the natural environment may not have been as reliable as you wished. All of these headaches during the study now provide you with material for your humility section. Remember, the key word here is *discuss*. This is not a complaint section. A litany of the problems you encountered is not likely to be very interesting. A discussion of how they may or may not have affected your findings is.

Think about possible limitations in four major areas. The first lies in the design of the investigation and involves issues of internal validity: limitations in whether you can attribute causal status to the independent variables, potential confounding variables, and so on. The second lies in external validity: generalizing your findings to other populations, tasks or situations, nonexperimental settings, and so on. The third area is in measurement and involves the reliability, validity, and scope of your measures, as well as whether response sets or other measurement problems may have contributed to your findings. The final area is in the statistical analyses you selected. You may not have limitations in all of these areas, but you should consider each as you appraise the strengths and weaknesses of your study.

Note Internal Validity Issues

Design issues always involve compromises. Any design that is correlational/quasi-experimental and does not involve random assignment of the independent variable does not permit you to say that the independent variable "caused" differences in the dependent variable. **Unless you manipulated it, you cannot say unequivocally that the independent variable affected any of your dependent variables**. In nonexperimental research, you need to consider alternative explanations for the relationship between your independent and your dependent variables: reverse causation (the variable called the dependent variable caused the independent variable), third-variable causation (a confound caused both the independent and dependent variable), and reciprocal/circular causation (increases in the independent variable caused changes in the dependent variable; increases in the dependent variable also caused changes in the independent variable). Of course, if you controlled potential confounds, you may be able to rule out some of these possible explanations. This will give you stronger support for a causal hypothesis than if you failed to control these variables, but you still cannot make unequivocal causal statements in such designs.

Problems in attributing causality also occur when a mixed design is used. These designs involve at least one independent variable that is experimental and another that is not. For example, consider a study in which older and younger subjects complete one of two experimental memory tasks. Although differences in performance between the two tasks can be attributed to differences in the conditions, differences related to age cannot necessarily be ascribed to age per se, as age was not manipulated. You can review specific considerations regarding internal validity issues attached to particular designs by looking at Campbell and Stanley's (1963) and Cook and Campbell's (1979) classic books on experimental and quasi-experimental designs.

It may also be that, in retrospect, you failed to collect certain kinds of information that would help you to make sense of your findings. Or there may be a potential confound that you did not control. Here is a good place to mention this, if you did not discuss it earlier.

Note External Validity Limitations

Even the purest, most carefully controlled experimental designs are not without limitations. The control necessitated by true experiments almost always entails some compromises in external validity. Generalizability across situations, stimuli, and procedures to important real-life situations is often an issue for discussion.

Other elements of investigations, regardless of design, can also limit their generalizability. These include the characteristics of the population and the specific operationalization of the independent variable (would your findings generalize to other operationalizations or variations?). In addition, analogue and laboratory studies virtually always raise issues about generalizability of findings in the natural environment.

Note Measurement Issues

Your measures, too, may have limitations. Insufficient reliability and validity information may be one such limitation. Reliance on self-report as an indicator of observable behavior in the absence of data to show that the measure actually corresponds with direct observation is another common problem. Possible reactivity to measurement procedures, less-than-perfectly reliable ratings or observations, missing data, and possible biases that could influence your results (e.g., response sets, such as social desirability) can also be considered if they are potential problems. Finally, consider whether the measures you used adequately operationalized the variables you wished to measure: Did you select an instrument that was less than perfect for your purposes (perhaps because of its established reliability and validity data)? If so, consider the problems associated with the content of the measure for your particular study.

Note Statistical Problems

Problems may be associated with your analyses. Did your data meet the assumptions of the statistics? Were your statistics overly conservative or overly liberal? Did your sample size limit the power of your statistics to detect anything but the strongest effects? Did you control for Type I error by limiting the number of statistical tests you performed, setting your alpha level to control for the number of tests you used, or using appropriate multivariate procedures? Did you use a new statistical procedure that lacks full elaboration of its assumptions and its problems?

Ideally, you encountered none of these statistical problems. If you did, it may be time to revisit your results section and take care of the problem before you place your completed write-up in the hands of your committee. If, for example, you ran dozens of tests only to find a few significant results, you might have found those by chance alone. Go back and reset your alpha level using the Bonferroni correction or a related procedure (e.g., Maxwell & Delaney, 1990). If you ran lots of repeated measures ANOVAs but failed to check for homogeneity of variance, look at your tables of standard deviations and do F_{max} tests (Winer, 1971) to see if you violated this assumption. But, if you've done all of these things and minor statistical concerns remain, discuss these in your "limitations" subsection.

As you humble yourself in writing, you may believe that the many limitations of the study make its findings worthless. This is probably not so. As you write, remember first that no research is perfect. The results of each study must be considered in light of its limitations, and final conclusions are reached on the basis of a body of evidence, not a single investigation. Also, recall that the choices you made seemed the best available at the time. Don't forget the silver lining, either. Every weakness may have a corresponding asset as its flip side. For example, controlled laboratory experiments gain tight experimental control at the expense of external validity, whereas natural-environment and quasi-experimental studies gain generalizability at the expense of easy interpretation. Be sure to consider both the pros and cons of your choices as you acknowledge the limitations of your study.

Include Comments About Future Directions

Ordinarily, your discussion section will end by pointing out directions that researchers need to pursue in the future. This is where you tell others what questions and issues they should examine, given your findings.

Researchers often say that each study raises more questions than it answers. In writing the previous sections, you should have thought of many questions that warrant future research. Pull them together and elaborate them in this section of your discussion.

Most discussion writers think easily of extending the study to other populations. You can go beyond this by thinking about several additional questions. Ideally, the theory underlying your study in the first place will also stimulate these questions. What additional independent variables need further study? What additional levels of existing independent variables should investigators study? What important dependent variables should they examine, and what would be the best way of assessing these? What design improvements are needed? What methodological innovations should researchers make in future studies?

In addition, think about what new distinctions might be made in population characteristics, independent variables, and dependent variables. These distinctions may suggest comparisons that can be made in future studies. For example, perhaps your results lead you to surmise that cognitive behavior therapy affects different types of thoughts in different ways. The logical next steps would be to develop reliable and valid ways of measuring different classes of thoughts and then to implement cognitive behavior therapy and assess its impact on these different measures.

One way to think about future directions is to ask yourself what follow-up studies you would do, given your results. What questions do your findings lead you to ask? What more do you need to find out to understand fully the issue you set out to address in your study? What would you do with unlimited resources? Here is the place to dream. Of course, make sure that your dreams are grounded in reality and that you can justify why the information gleaned from your menu of future studies would be important for theory, research, or practice.

Use These Tips to Organize and Write Your Discussion

Be a Critical Thinker

As you consider your conclusions, play the devil's advocate. What would a critic say in response to your points? Anticipate the criticisms and weave your rebuttals into your discussion. This both fills up pages and demonstrates your intellectual agility—assuming, of course, that your logic is sound!

Remember also to show the reader the steps in your logic. Do not assume that simply presenting your findings will make your conclusions obvious. If you make assumptions in drawing your conclusions, point them out. If your conclusions come from a series of thoughts, show the reader that series. Your conclusions may seem simple once you have arrived at them, but remember how much thought it took for you to figure out what the results mean. Assume that your reader needs to be guided through the same process.

Avoid Common Problems

A series of common problems often characterizes the discussion sections of dissertations, theses, and published articles. Avoid the following errors:

1. *Do not discuss nearly significant or nonsignificant findings with means in the right direction as though they were significant.* They were not. You may, however, consider whether power problems limited your ability to detect effects. Thus, a statement such as "The finding that boys were more active than girls approached significance. Boys' greater activity could be the result of . . ." treats a nonsignificant finding as though it were significant. On the other hand, a statement such as "Boys' activity level failed to differ significantly from that of girls. This may have been due to the relatively small sample size, however, and the difference approached significance. Future studies should explore this question with a larger sample . . ." would be more acceptable.

2. *Do not use causal language to discuss correlational findings.* Many

writers describing correlational studies pay homage to the problems of assuming causation in their obligatory humility section, but they use terms such as *affect*, *influence*, and *produced* throughout the discussion! If your study was not a true experiment, replace verbs that imply causation with words and phrases such as "correlated with," "was associated with," and "related to."

3. *Do not equate statistical significance with effect size.* A *p* value of .05, .01, or .00001 is in part a function of the magnitude of effect relative to chance, but it is also influenced by sample size. With a sample of 100, for example, correlations of .19 will be significant at the .05 level! Yet the two variables share less than 4% of their variance in common! When discussing correlations, be especially careful to focus your discussion on the magnitude of significant correlations. The same applies to differences between means—the magnitude of the *p* value tells you nothing about the magnitude or practical significance of differences between groups.

4. *Avoid language that assumes that self-report of events means the actual events occurred.* Stating that "clinic mothers reported that their children were more deviant than did nonclinic mothers" is preferable to saying that "clinic children were more deviant than nonclinic children." The more precise language also suggests two alternative explanations for your findings: Clinic children may have actually behaved in more deviant ways, or one or both sets of mothers may view or report behavior in biased ways.

5. *Do not present new analyses for the first time in the discussion section or discuss results that were not reported in the results section.* If you wish to discuss a supplemental analysis, describe the test and its results first in the results section.

6. *Do not just reiterate the results section.* As we have repeatedly emphasized, go beyond mere summary to interpret, synthesize, analyze, and critique your findings. Show your reader your logic as you go along, and acknowledge speculation when you engage in it.

Select an Appropriate Organization

Although many ways of organizing the discussion section exist, two common structures work well, in our experience. The first more or less follows the headings listed in the previous sections of this chapter. Thus, you progress from summary to interpretation and implications, to integration with existing literature, limitations, and future directions. The second structure involves organizing the discussion around major findings, and

Exhibit 13.1

Two Hypothetical Outlines for a Discussion Section

Outline 1

I. Summary and integration of results
   A. Hypothesis 1
   B. Hypothesis 2
   ↓
   Z. Additional findings

II. Explanations for findings
   A. Hypothesis 1
   B. Hypothesis 2
   ↓
   Z. Additional findings

III. Integration of findings with past literature
   1. Convergent findings
      a. Description of how findings converge with relevant findings of others
      b. Explanations of convergence
      c. Implications of convergence
   2. Divergent findings
      a. Description of how findings diverge from relevant findings of others
      b. Explanations of divergence
      c. Implications of divergence
   3. Contributions of findings to literature
      a. How findings resolve current issues
      b. What findings suggest about new distinctions and controls

IV. Implications of findings
   A. Theoretical implications
   B. Research implications
   C. Applied implications

V. Limitations
   A. Design and internal validity
   B. External validity and generalizability
   C. Analyses and statistical power
   D. Measurement

VI. Future directions

Outline 2

I. Summary and discussion of findings
   A. Finding 1
      1. Summary
      2. Explanation of finding
      3. Convergence or divergence with past literature
         a. Explanations for convergence or divergence
         b. Implications of convergence or divergence
      4. Limitations related to finding
      5. Specific research needed to clarify or extend finding
      ↓
   Z. Finding *n* (topics covered as above)

continued

Exhibit 13.1, continued

Outline 2, continued

II. General implications of findings
   A. Theoretical implications
   B. Research implications
   C. Applied implications

III. General limitations of study (covers issues not discussed under specific findings)
   A. Design and internal validity
   B. External validity and generalizability
   C. Analyses and statistical power
   D. Measurement

IV. Future directions

---

integrating implications, others' findings, and specific limitations into your discussion of each finding. Exhibit 13.1 presents two hypothetical outlines for a discussion section that follow these different formats.

Be sure to end your discussion section with a wrap-up paragraph. This should pull the discussion together and highlight some of your main points, without being a summary. End the discussion, as you began, with general statements. Be upbeat. One of our favorite endings involves emphasizing the importance of a full understanding of the area under investigation, to remind the reader of how comprehension of the processes or individuals under investigation will improve theory, research, or practice. Then, having written your last sentence, congratulate yourself and celebrate! You deserve it!

✔ To Do . . .

Discussing the Results

☐ Summarize your findings

—Avoid technical detail

—Use clear language

☐ Interpret your findings

☐ Place your findings in context

—Consider how your findings converge with, clarify, or contradict past findings

☐ Consider the implications of your findings

—Theoretical implications

—Methodological implications

—Applied implications

☐ Include a humility subsection

—Consider internal validity issues

—Consider external validity issues

—Consider measurement issues

—Consider statistical issues

☐ Include comments about future directions

☐ Use these tips:

—Be a critical thinker

—Avoid common problems

—Select an appropriate organization

14

Managing Committee Meetings: Proposal and Oral Defense

rdinarily, the thesis or dissertation candidate meets with the committee formally twice: once at the proposal meeting and again during the oral defense. The proposal meeting occurs *before* you begin to collect data. The oral defense occurs *after* you have analyzed your data and written up your project. Although proposal meetings are not always required, oral defenses of the dissertation are. Defenses of master's thesis research are usually required.

During the proposal meeting, committee members and the student meet together to discuss the proposed research. Usually this occurs after the student has prepared a complete proposal (i.e., literature review, methodology, proposed data analyses, references, and appendixes) and the chairperson is satisfied with this product. The student then submits the document to the committee and schedules a 1- to 2-hour meeting.

Proposal meetings generally follow one of two formats: (a) an implicit problem-solving model or (b) a minidefense model. In the problem-solving model, the meeting largely involves committee members asking questions to clarify the proposal, raising potential problems they see with the project, and suggesting alternative procedures, measures, and so on. The underlying theme is cooperative; committee members work with the student and chairperson to produce a better product. In the minidefense model, committee members expect the student to defend the content of the proposal; the focus is on students' skills in articulating the rationale for various aspects of the proposal and defending the choices they have made. In many ways, this resembles the oral defense. With both models, committee members expect that the proposal may be altered as a result of their discussion. Of course, meetings can contain a mixture of problem-solving and minidefense components.

The oral defense is generally more formal than the proposal meeting.

Exhibit 14.1

Information to Seek About the Proposal Meeting and Final Oral Defense

- When does the meeting usually occur in the dissertation or thesis process?
- How far in advance should committee members be given the written document?
- What forms need to be filed before having the meeting? How far in advance?
- What is the general format of meetings? Does each committee member ask all of his or her questions one after the other, or do members take turns?
- Who chairs the meeeting?
- How long is the meeting?
- Does the student make a formal presentation? How long?
- What is included? Are overheads or slides expected?
- Do questions focus only on the research, or do they pertain to other areas as well?
- Who records suggestions regarding changes in the proposal or final document?
- What is the general tone of meetings? Do members respond to your answers?
- What are the rules about absent committee members?
- Who else may attend besides the committee and the student?
- How does the meeting end?
- Do students ever fail? Under what conditions? What happens after a failure?
- What happens after the meeting? How do you alter the document to reflect changes?
- Must committee members approve changes in the document after the alterations have been made, or can the chair do this?

This formality results in part because its major purpose involves evaluating whether you have the research competence to be granted the master's or doctoral degree. This evaluation is based on both the written document and on your performance in the oral defense. Thus, in your oral defense, committee members will ask you to explain what you did, what you found, and what it means, and to discuss your research intelligently in the context of others' findings in the area. They will be looking for evidence that you (a) understand what you did and why, (b) can think about your project from a scientific (as opposed to a commonsense or intuitive) perspective, and (c) can describe what you did to others. In general, faculty members expect more expertise and a more polished presentation from dissertation than from master's thesis students. Although some students believe that these meetings are pro forma exercises, we know of students who have failed their oral defense. Others have been sent back to the drawing board after a disastrous proposal meeting. We therefore recommend taking both the proposal meeting and the defense very seriously and preparing appropriately.

Departments vary widely in how proposal meetings and oral defenses are structured. Therefore, investigating local rules and norms is essential to prepare adequately for these meetings. Exhibit 14.1 presents a series of questions to ask other students and faculty about the proposal meeting and the oral defense. The answers to these questions will give you an idea of the logistics, variability, tone, and scope of these meetings.

Prepare for the Proposal Meeting

Know the Format

The format and length of proposal meetings differ from department to department. At the outset you may be asked, for example, to provide a brief formal overview of your proposal. Such an overview should summarize your rationale for the study and focus primarily on the methodology you intend to use. Following the overview, committee members will ask questions. These will take three basic forms: (a) What do you plan to do? (asking for greater clarity or expanded information); (b) Why are or aren't you doing _____? (inquiring about rationales and decision making); and (c) What will you do about _____? (stating a problem that the member believes likely to arise). Ordinarily, these questions will focus on the study itself, but committee members may also raise questions about why your research question is important; findings in the general area in which you are working; methodological issues related to your measures, design, or procedures; and statistical issues. Committee members will also make suggestions they believe will improve the project.

You, not your chair, should answer these questions and respond to suggestions. The best preparation for questions, of course, is to know exactly what you are doing and why you have selected some methods and not others. Be sure to think about methodological and theoretical reasons for your choices, as well as about practical ones, and present the former responses first when articulating your responses to committee members' questions. Committee members do not respond well to answers such as, "I'm including 15 subjects per group because I need to finish soon and don't have time to run more than that" and other responses that imply that you put convenience above scientific integrity. An answer such as, "I did a power analysis based on pilot data. My pilot data suggest that my effect will be quite strong and the power analysis showed this sample size should be sufficient to detect it" (if this is the case, of course) will come across much better.

Committee members' suggestions about improving the study may vary considerably in quality and in the work required to accomplish them. In responding to these suggestions, ask yourself first whether and how each suggestion would add to the quality of your research. If it would add substantially, you may want to follow it, even if it involves significant extra work. If it involves altering an aspect of the methodology you have already thought about, it is fine to discuss the pros and cons of the suggestion with committee members. Never dismiss a suggestion simply because you are horrified by the amount of work it would entail.

Does this mean that you have to add independent and dependent variables to your study at the whim of committee members? Of course not. You might respond to an unreasonable request by saying, "That would be an interesting aspect of this issue to address, but I believe it is beyond the scope of this study. I will certainly comment on it in the discussion section," and then pray that your chairperson backs you up. In addition, you can raise practical issues, although you should discuss these from a scientific perspective as much as possible, for example, as in the following:

> I agree that restricting my sample to middle-class, married, employed women who have just given birth to their first children and have a reliably diagnosed major depressive disorder (and no concomitant medical or psychological problems) would be the best way to do the study, but such a homogeneous sample is not available to me here in Podunk in sufficient numbers to do the study. I tried to expand the subject parameters in ways that wouldn't jeopardize the findings. Do you see special problems with this, or can you suggest ways that will allow me to recruit a large enough sample?

Responding competently to committee members' suggestions requires that you be a fairly quick thinker and be reasonably articulate extemporaneously. If you have difficulties in either of these areas, take the time you need to think through a suggestion. One way to buy time is to restate the suggestion or question: "So, you are suggesting that . . . ." You can then comment on the pros and cons of the idea. By the end of this process, you may have an opinion. A second way to buy time is to say, "Give me a minute to think about that." Then, sit quietly and think about what you want to say. Either your committee will sit quietly, or—

more likely—another committee member or your chair will jump in with a comment or opinion.

Make Sure Notes Are Taken

You and your committee will undoubtedly agree to changes in your proposal during the proposal meeting. Someone should write down these changes. Before the meeting, clarify with your chairperson who will do this. In addition, having the changes read aloud at the end of the meeting can help make sure everyone concurs with them.

At the end of the meeting, one of several things may happen. You may be asked to leave the room so your committee can discuss the proposal meeting. Your committee may formally approve your proposal (ordinarily with the suggested revisions, which must be either typed and circulated or incorporated into the proposal itself). In some cases, the committee returns the proposal to the student for more work before they will approve it. In rare cases, the proposal may be disapproved. Outright disapproval can occur if the study is fatally flawed, the committee believes that the proposal demonstrates incompetence in research design or scientific writing, or the study poses major ethical problems. The student usually then has the option of preparing another proposal, perhaps with a new committee.

Prepare for the Oral Defense

Know the Format

The oral defense usually begins with a formal presentation that may or may not involve slides or overhead transparencies. Because dissertation orals are open to the academic community, people may be present at the defense who have not read the document. Thus, plan your presentation as though it were a talk you were about to give to a room of professionals at a conference of the American Psychological Association, the American Psychological Society, or a similar group. Just as you would have a strict time limit at a conference, find out your time limit for the presentation and plan your talk so it will not run overtime. Rehearse it to make sure it won't.

After the talk, questions will begin. As in the proposal meeting, you will be asked about what you did, why you did it, what you found, and

---

Exhibit 14.2

Common Oral Defense Questions

- What do you see as the problems in your study? What limitations do these pose in what you can say? How would you correct these in future studies?
- If you want to improve this measure, procedure, and so on, how would you do it?
- Which current theory or model best explains your findings?
- How would someone using a _____ theoretical framework interpret your findings?
- How do you explain the discrepancy between your findings and those of Dr. X?
- What implications do your findings have for future research methodology in this area?
- What do you see your study contributing to the literature?
- What have you learned about this area from doing this research?
- What would be the next logical study to do as a follow-up to this one (or to clarify a hard-to-interpret finding)?
- What implications, if any, do your findings have for applied psychological practice?
- If you had your study to do over again, with unlimited resources, how would you do it?
- What do you plan to do next with your data?

---

why you arrived at your conclusions. You may also be asked to comment on alternative explanations offered by committee members. Finally, you will be asked "thought questions," most of which revolve around the larger issues involved in your research. Exhibit 14.2 lists typical generic questions you might be asked at an oral defense.

At the end of the meeting, the committee will excuse you and any visitors from the room. They will then discuss the written document and your oral performance. Discussions can be brief or lengthy. Lengthy discussions do not mean you are in trouble: Faculty members may be arguing about a minor point of your findings or methodology and not about your performance! Committee members will almost always require changes in the written product after the defense (otherwise some believe they haven't done their job properly), so don't be dismayed. As with the proposal meeting, someone should write these changes down and review them aloud to ensure all agree. After committee members conclude their discussion, they will call you back into the room and tell you the results of their deliberation. You may pass both the written and the oral requirements, pass one but not the other, or fail both. In some departments and schools, failures can be remediated with a second try. If all has gone well, pop the champagne corks and celebrate!

How can you increase the chances that the orals will go well? First and foremost, prepare a well-written document. If the manuscript you hand to your committee is thorough, thoughtful, well written, and carefully prepared (e.g., no references missing, no spelling errors, tables match text, clear readable copy), you will begin your orals with a favorable impression because of your excellent document. Do not let your personal eagerness to finish or your personal timetable mislead you into pressuring your chairperson or committee to meet when your written document needs more work, as this is likely to backfire (Yates, 1982). Second, prepare for the defense by finding out what is likely to happen, planning your talk, and rehearsing how you will deal with probable questions. Finally, develop an action plan for managing excess anxiety that can interfere with optimal performance. The pages that follow explore all of these topics in detail.

Prepare Your Talk

The talk you give to begin your oral defense will set the tone for the rest of the meeting. It is worth your time to write or outline this talk and then practice until you can give a professional-sounding, coherent overview of your study. A 10- to 20-minute time limit for this talk is not uncommon, but in some departments a half hour or more is the norm.

The major parts of your talk will usually parallel the sections of an APA-style journal article and will include an introduction, and method, results, and discussion sections. For a 20-minute talk, allow about 5 minutes per section; for a 45-minute presentation, you might want approximately 10, 20, 10, and 5 minutes, respectively, to cover each of the four sections.

Some polished speakers like to start presentations by telling a joke. This breaks the ice and indicates that you have a sense of humor. If you are not a joke teller, however, this is probably not the time to launch a career as a comedian. Another ice-breaking strategy is to thank the committee for coming and openly acknowledge (with a smile) your sheer terror at standing before them. Make eye contact with members of the audience early and often.

Start at the beginning. Tell the audience how you got interested in this particular research. Keep it professional, though. Your colleagues are not interested in the fact that you have always had a problem with weight yourself or that it runs in the family, and so on. Something more along the lines of "Dr. Bulimarex and his research group, of which I am a member, had been studying _____ for the past 3 years. We had become interested in why it is that some people. . . ."

Then, launch into a brief review of the relevant research in the area, setting the context for your particular study. Recall the discussion in chapter 6 about organizing your literature review using a funnel approach, starting broadly and leading the reader skillfully to the conclusion that the absolutely most logical next study to do in the area was the one you were about to propose. In the short time allowed in your oral presentation, you will not be able to start too far out toward the mouth of the funnel. Instead, assume some familiarity with the general area and concentrate your introduction on the literature most relevant to your own research. Briefly summarize the progression of studies that led up to yours, emphasizing major findings. Give a general integrative overview rather than a boring litany of names and dates. Then, review the shortcomings of previous research and lay the groundwork for your own study, explaining how it was designed to overcome some of these. Be humble here. Every study, including yours, will have problems. Do not go overboard in criticizing others or you might be setting yourself up for a similar fate during the question period following your remarks. If you have included a table summarizing research studies in the literature review section of your dissertation, and if you have enough time to present this material, you might want to use a transparency or slide of it for your oral presentation. Alternatively, you can make a slide or overhead of major findings in simplified form.

When you have skillfully led the audience to the conclusion that your study is the logical next step for research in this area, state your research question and specific hypotheses. An overhead or slide may assist with this. Then move into your methodology. Follow the customary APA format, starting with a description of your subjects and research setting. Describe recruitment procedures and inclusion and exclusion criteria. Mention informed consent. Next, describe your independent variables and dependent measures. Again, slides of any unusual apparatus and transparencies of your tests, checklists, or observation codes may be useful for longer presentations. Mention the reliability and validity of your measures and indicate how you trained raters or observers, if used, and how you ensured their continued high reliability during the data collection phase. Weave in a description of your procedures for handling each subject and for debriefing them after they participated.

Your design likely will have become clear by this time. In case it has not, though, describe it. Verbal description will suffice for straightforward designs. More complex designs may require a diagram on a slide or transparency.

You will obviously not be able to present every detail of your methodology in 5 to 20 minutes. Leave out details that listeners will not be able to follow or that are relatively less important to your study. In an observational study, for example, knowing the word-for-word definitions of each observation category will usually not be necessary. If you are not sure what to include, pick the ten most important facts to mention and then add to this list until you fill your allotted time for the method section.

Next, present your results. Do this in the order in which you introduced your research hypotheses. If you used more than one dependent measure to test each hypothesis, decide an order for their presentation and stick with this order as you come to each hypothesis. As with the method section, you will undoubtedly have more data than time permits you to present. Cull through it carefully, and select only those data that pertained most directly to testing your hypotheses or that yielded the most important findings.

Here, more than anywhere, simple is best. Do not state your F and p values in your talk. Just present the name of the analysis and its findings—in English. One way to keep your presentation simple is to present only those data that relate to your hypotheses and major findings. You need not present every analysis you did. Nor do nonsignificant findings ordinarily warrant more than brief mention. Again, ask yourself what's most important, see how much time it takes to go over those findings, and add on if time permits. It is better to be selective and clear than to throw every number in your study at audience members and confuse them totally.

After presenting your results, discuss the implications of your findings. Do this in the order in which you stated your hypotheses originally (also the order you presented the results). Begin your discussion with a restatement of the purpose of the research and then launch into the first hypothesis. Refer frequently to how your research fits with studies of others, and note how your results might alter the prevalent thinking in the area.

After an enthusiastic discussion of the implications of your findings, include a brief humility section. Here, you should acknowledge some of the inevitable shortcomings of your research and lay the groundwork for future improved studies. Be careful not to be overly self-critical. Acknowledge obvious shortcomings and point out the limits to the generalizability of your findings. The latter is always a safe place to be humble because nearly all studies have some limitations in this regard. Finally, end your presentation with two or three specific suggestions for future research.

Prepare Audiovisual Materials

It is hard to imagine a research presentation that lasts longer than 5 minutes without some form of audiovisual assistance. Audiovisual (A/V) aids help get your message across and keep your audience awake and interested. The number and type of A/V aids you use depends on your setting and the length of your talk. Even a 10-minute presentation, however, can usually benefit from a few overheads, slides, or handouts.

We have developed several guidelines for using A/V assists over the years. First, select a medium of presentation that is readily available and reliable. For presenting textual material, including tables of numbers, figures, and assessment instruments, we use overhead projectors and transparencies almost exclusively. This medium is generally available, transparencies are relatively inexpensive to prepare, and most copiers and laser printers will make them. Their ease of preparation and low cost mean that you can revise readily as new data come in or as better ways of presenting the material occur to you. In addition, the room can often stay fully illuminated when viewing overheads.

Slides are also an effective medium, but they are generally more expensive, take longer to prepare, and thus are not as easily revised. Slides nonetheless convey the research context more adequately than overheads and make the presentation more real to the audience. For example, showing pictures of a child sitting in front of the experimental apparatus or of the traffic intersection where data on seat belt usage were collected can do a lot to bring your presentation to life. These advantages lead some to use a combination of slides and transparencies for presentations. With both, make sure they can be seen clearly throughout the room.

Videotape provides an even better way to bring life to your presentation in longer talks. This especially flexible medium does, however, require the appropriate equipment. For example, with today's digital VCRs (videocassette recorders), it is possible to obtain a flicker-free freeze frame picture, allowing you to mix data presentations with nondata motion presentations on the same videotape. Moreover, indexing systems on the VCR allow you to advance or return to specific locations to reshow a particular table or segment of experimenter–subject interaction. If you decide to use videotapes, however, make sure the tape can be seen and heard clearly throughout the room.

There are even more elaborate A/V assists you could use, of course, including presentations of material directly from your personal computer. Unless you have had sufficient experience with these media, however, our advice is to follow the old military KISS maxim: Keep It Simple, Stupid. The Murphy's Law of research presentations is that anything that can go wrong will, especially where equipment is concerned. The simplest and perfectly satisfactory approach is to confine your visual aids to a portable overhead projector. Most academic departments will have one. Whatever equipment you use, check it out immediately before your presentation. Know where a backup can be found in case something breaks or a bulb burns out during your presentation (it happens, believe us!). Sit in different parts of the room to check sound and picture quality. Coordinate with anyone who will be assisting to dim lights, change transparencies, or distribute handouts.

If you use overheads, slides, or handouts in your presentation, do not merely make transparencies of tables from your thesis or dissertation for your oral presentation. You probably crammed a lot of data into those tables. This information will not be easy to digest when it appears briefly on a screen. Pare down the tables, putting the data in several new overheads or slides if they are absolutely needed to make a point. Keep the composition of tables uncluttered. It is better to use more tables with fewer numbers in them than the reverse. Leave out nonessential statistical details (e.g., F values or beta weights). Then, either type the new version of the table in a larger type size or run the table through an enlarging copier so that any transparency you make will be readable from the back of the room.

Develop Strategies to Handle Questions

Many students are terrified by the thought of being questioned about their research during the oral defense. Knowing something about what committee members will probably ask (see Exhibit 14.2) and writing out and rehearsing your answers can quell much of this concern. Developing strategies for responding to questions can also help. We described some of these strategies in the proposal meeting section of this chapter; others are listed below.

Respond to questions professionally in your role as scientist. Even if you know your committee members well, now is not the time to joke around informally. Also, as Yates (1982) cogently points out, now is not the time to get angry or defensive either, even if a question seems pointless or unnecessarily antagonistic. Again, pretend your committee is a professional audience at a national convention and comport yourself accordingly.

In addition, take your time. As in the proposal meeting, rephrase hard-to-follow questions to make sure you understand them. Give complete answers that show your thought processes. And remember, your committee members may have missed something you said in the document or may ask what seem to you at this point to be very easy questions.

Answer questions succinctly. Do not give long lectures. In particular, do not throw in fancy jargon or mention concepts that you do not understand fully. Using a term incorrectly invites probing questions to see if you understand what you are talking about.

Keep in mind that most students are faced with one or more convoluted, hard-to-follow questions in their oral defense. If you don't understand the question, other committee members may not, either! Take the time to paraphrase confusing questions to make sure you heard them correctly and to allow the questioner to correct any misperceptions you might have.

Expect a few questions with no right or wrong answers. These thought questions may require speculation. It is fine to speculate as long as you acknowledge that you are speculating. Presenting speculations as though they were facts is a sure way to elicit intellectual attacks from committee members.

Do not be surprised if you are not sure of answers to some of the questions. If you really do not know the answer to something, say "I don't know" or "I'm not sure" rather than guessing. An occasional "don't know" won't flunk you (unless, of course, it is in response to questions such as "Who were your subjects?" and "What measures did you use?"). A stupid guess, on the other hand, communicates two things: (a) you did not know the answer, and (b) you failed to recognize your ignorance.

Expect a certain amount of grandstanding. One of our colleagues, Dr. Albert Farrell, tells his students to remember that committee members ask questions during the orals for three reasons. The first, and rarest, reason is that they genuinely want to know the answer to the question. The second, and more common, reason is that they want to know if *you* know the answer to the question. The third reason is that they want to show other committee members that *they* know the answer to the question. Grandstanding, as reflected in the last reason, often takes the form of lengthy questions or responses to your answers and does not imply that you have handled yourself incompetently. Do not try to compete with the grandstander. Just let faculty grandstanders do their thing, make an appropriate comment such as "That's a really important point," and move on.

Reading whether committee members approve of the way you answer questions is hard to do. We recommend that you spend your time trying to provide good answers rather than second guessing what committee members think of your performance. A committee member may smile congenially and nod but be dissatisfied with your response, and another may sit stony-faced and love what you are saying. Sitting in on others' defenses will help you see whether the general tone of these meetings at your school is somber or more lively. The one fairly reliable predictor we have found to indicate that things are going well is the occurrence of frequent, lively exchanges among committee members and between you and them. This probably means that everyone is having a good time and that you are doing fine. The absence of lively exchange, however, does *not* mean that you should start loading the pistol!

Finally, find out what materials you can take with you to your defense. If allowed, we recommend you take your printouts, copies of measures, the articles you used in the literature review, and even copies of notes you made in preparation for your oral defense. Stash these unobtrusively under your table or in a corner. We have heard questions during orals about whether the numbers in Table 462 really were correct, whether Smith and Jones really produced a three- and not a four-factor structure with the XYZ measure, and what items were included on a particular dependent measure. If you suspect you might need to refer to one of these items during your defense, see if you can take it with you.

Rehearse Your Oral Defense

The oral defense is important enough to spend some time rehearsing. If you can, schedule a "mock orals," so you can practice both your oral presentation and responses to audience questions. Fellow graduate students (especially those who have been through or observed an oral defense) and your chairperson are ideal audience members, if you can persuade them to spare the time.

Before giving your mock presentation, ask your chairperson to review a prepared outline of your talk. After suitable changes, prepare your rehearsals. We recommend the two-rehearsal format in which you give the talk once to yourself, audiotaping or videotaping it for later review, and once to an audience. Review the tape of the first rehearsal with timer

---

Exhibit 14.3

Checklist of Important Behaviors for Oral Presentations and Responses to Questions

Yes	No	**For Oral Presentations**
☐	☐	1. Did you make an appropriate opening comment?
☐	☐	2. Did you vary your voice level and intonation throughout?
☐	☐	3. Did you smile appropriately?
☐	☐	4. Did you make eye contact with the audience?
☐	☐	5. Did you look energetic, peppy, and forceful, avoiding leaning your chin on your palm on a table?
☐	☐	6. Did you speak from carefully prepared notes and avoid reading your talk?
☐	☐	7. Did you make major points clearly?
☐	☐	8. Did you use good transitions between sections of the talk?
☐	☐	9. Did you allocate your time appropriately?
☐	☐	10. Were your audiovisual (A/V) assists clear and easy to read?
☐	☐	11. Were any additional A/V materials needed?
☐	☐	12. Did you minimize "uhs," "ahs," throat clears, and other speech interrupters?
☐	☐	13. Did you use advance organizers, namely, tell your audience where you were going at the beginning and at key points during the presentation?
☐	☐	14. Could your audience follow your results easily?
☐	☐	15. Did you keep your talk simple and to the point?
☐	☐	16. Did you avoid unnecessary detail?
☐	☐	17. Did you avoid distracting mannerisms (e.g., excessive movement or fiddling with clothing, mustache, or hair?)
☐	☐	18. Did you use scientific vocabulary appropriately?
☐	☐	19. Did you explain complex procedures clearly?

Yes	No	**For Oral Questioning**
☐	☐	20. Did your answers address the questions?
☐	☐	21. Were your answers concise?
☐	☐	22. Did you appear confident during questioning?
☐	☐	23. Did you qualify your remarks appropriately (e.g., acknowledging speculation as such)?
☐	☐	24. Did you respond nondefensively to antagonistic questions?
☐	☐	25. Did you rephrase hard-to-understand questions before attempting to respond?

in hand before doing the second one. Time the lengths of the various sections and the total talk, and plan where you will expand or economize the next time around.

For both rehearsals, prepare completely ahead of time. Have your notes and A/V equipment ready to use, and use them as you plan to during the actual presentation. Select a place to rehearse that is as much like the orals setting as possible. Conduct the rehearsal at the same time of day. For the dress rehearsal with an audience, you might even want to wear the clothes you plan to wear during your defense. The more cues likely to be part of your actual presentation context that you can build into your rehearsal, the more useful the rehearsal will be.

After your talk, get your audience to ask questions that you anticipate your committee members will ask. Prime your audience to ask questions you fear (e.g., about theoretical or statistical issues): Now is a low-risk time to practice and get feedback.

Build sufficient time into your mock orals for feedback from the audience at the end. Prepare a few items to ask about the talk and about how you handled questions. Review these when you view or listen to your own tape as well. Exhibit 14.3 presents a simple checklist of some important behaviors to note during the presentation and questioning. You might even ask your rehearsal audience to fill out a checklist similar to this as a way of directing their attention to specific aspects of your presentation. In addition, ask them for their general reactions and suggestions for changes.

If a specific portion of the talk concerns you (e.g., how clearly you described the design of the study or presented the results of the factor analysis), solicit the audience's reaction. Ask how it might have been done differently. Be open and reflective, and avoid defensiveness. Remember, these are your friends. They are doing you a favor. Hear their suggestions, and take their comments seriously.

Manage Your Anxiety Constructively

The oral defense (and for some, the proposal meeting) seems to produce at least twinges of anxiety even in the most experienced and eloquent speakers. Some students experience overwhelming anxiety as they think about the oral examination. Some anxiety is normal: The oral defense is the last step toward an important degree, it is an evaluative situation, and the rules for what to expect and how to handle the defense are ambiguous.

Note that we do not say that you must go through the proposal meeting or orals without anxiety. Indeed, we believe the U-shaped arousal function is relevant to the oral defense—a medium level of arousal facilitates performance by helping to focus one's attention on the task. Too much anxiety, however, can impede your ability to think on your feet and to express yourself clearly. One key to a successful proposal meeting and oral defense lies in managing one's arousal constructively.

Researchers (e.g., Lang, 1971) identify three sometimes related but more often nonconvergent elements of anxiety. The first, the cognitive component, involves the subjective experience of anxiety: the things you say to yourself about the situation and how you label your feelings. The second, the physiological component, pertains to the physical substrate of arousal (e.g., increased heart rate and nervous system activity, perhaps experienced as sweaty palms or shortness of breath). The final, the motor component, relates to your observable performance. Managing these three components can help you deal more effectively with the proposal meeting and oral defense.

Manage Your Thoughts

Two general cognitive factors can contribute to "orals anxiety": (a) fear of the unknown (What will they ask? Will I be able to answer?) and (b) irrational thinking (I'm sure I'll fail and be unemployed for the rest of my life). To see if either of these haunts your thoughts, think about the orals. Listen to what you say to yourself. Does this self-talk revolve around fear of the unknown or the potential catastrophic consequences of failure? If so, read on.

If the ambiguity and uncertainty of oral presentations worry you, make the process less ambiguous. Reading this chapter should help. In addition, talk with people about what happened when they went through their oral defense. Gather a list of common questions from other students and from your chairperson, and add these to the ones in Exhibit 14.2. Dissertation defenses are open to the public, so go to some in your department to see what they are like (choose someone who is likely to pass so that you can see a successful coping model). Conduct a mock orals or rehearsal to get some idea in advance of what the experience will be like. All of these preparations together should substantially decrease the ambiguity of the situation for you, and you will feel better prepared.

What about irrational thinking? Over three decades ago, Ellis (e.g., Ellis & Harper, 1961) proposed the notion that irrational beliefs could make us feel more depressed, anxious, angry, and the like. One key irrational belief related to anxiety involves catastrophic thinking: "If things do not turn out as I wish, it will be just awful." A second relates to perfectionism: "I must handle myself flawlessly in all circumstances." Either of these beliefs can be associated with performance anxiety, and together they can be quite debilitating.

The key to dealing with irrational self-talk is to challenge it and talk back more rationally. First, let's look at perfectionism. Do you really have to handle your orals perfectly? Of course not. You just have to handle them competently. Correcting a misstatement, taking time to think through your answers, and encountering occasional problems understanding or answering a question will not lead you to fail your orals. Recognize and plan for the fact that you may not be as articulate on your feet as you are on paper. That is perfectly natural, and no one expects you to be.

What about catastrophes? Some students fear they will not be able to answer questions correctly. They then say to themselves, "I will fail the orals. Then all my work will be down the drain and I will be homeless and unemployable and no one will love me." Let's examine the assumptions behind these thoughts more rationally. First, what is the evidence that you will not be able to answer the questions? You know what you did, right? You know why you did it, right? At this point, you should know more about your specific topic area than anyone in the room, with the possible exception of your chairperson. A reasonable prediction is that you will be able to answer most questions easily and that a few will be more difficult for you. It is also possible to have fun during your orals: It can be intellectually stimulating and enjoyable to have a group of bright individuals discussing a project you know well for a couple of hours.

Will occasional difficulty with a question lead you to fail the orals? Probably not. Overall, you are likely to handle the easy questions well and the difficult questions satisfactorily. After all, the best predictor of future behavior is past behavior, and if you have done well in graduate school, you will likely do fine in the orals, too. Even if you muff a question or two, you are unlikely to fail your orals. Remember, the faculty have an investment in you. They really want you to succeed.

And what if you do fail? What is the worst that would happen? Many schools allow students to retake the orals if they pass the written portion of the dissertation but fail the orals. The worst that would happen then would be that you would be embarrassed by having to retake your exam. Embarrassment is rarely fatal, and no doubt you would survive. Unless you have forged ahead in your program despite repeated feedback that you should hang on to your day job, completely flunking at this point is highly unlikely.

Manage Your Physical Reactions

Another key to managing anxiety is to reduce your arousal level. Working on irrational thoughts may help reduce your arousal. In addition, many techniques work directly to modulate physiological arousal, including progressive relaxation, meditation, autogenic training, self-hypnosis, exercise, and pleasant imagery (see, for example, Poppen, 1988).

To manage the physical components of your anxiety, experiment and find a strategy that works for you. Some like to visualize the threatening scene ahead of time, while seeing themselves performing deliberately and competently. Many athletes are trained in this form of imagery or visualization. Others can lower their anxiety by sitting in a quiet place, closing their eyes, and imagining a relaxing setting such as a favorite beach or place in the mountains. Or perhaps progressive relaxation will work for you, as you move from the tips of your toes to the top of your head, deliberately tensing and relaxing each body part as you come to it. Many medical centers and universities offer instruction in relaxation that may prove helpful, if these skills do not come easily to you. A good way to teach yourself is to use Cotter and Guerra's audiocassette, "Self-Relaxation Training" (order from Research Press, P.O. Box 9177, Champaign, IL 61826).

In addition to selecting and learning a skill to manage your physiological arousal, schedule time to use it right before your oral defense. One student we know planned a doctoral defense so she would have time for a vigorous workout and shower before it started!

Another way of managing one's physiology involves drugs. Taking a pill is easier than learning arousal reduction skills, but some drugs carry the risk of also slowing your cognitive processes. We do not recommend pharmacological coping aids unless you are absolutely certain that they will not create untoward side-effects in the situation.

Manage Your Motor Behavior

The final component of anxiety, the motor component, has to do with how you appear to others. Remember, the motor, physiological, and cognitive components of anxiety need not covary. Thus, although inside you may be shaking, this does not have to show in your behavior. Many of the best performers confess to feeling anxious inside—anxiety that their audience cannot detect.

As with most of our advice, the key to looking like a professional in your orals lies in planning and practice. Remember the five Ps: Prior Planning Prevents Poor Performance. Think of which of your professors

Exhibit 14.4

Timed Behavioral Checklist for Performance Anxiety

Rater: _____

Name: _____

Date: _____ Speech No. _____ I.D. _____

Behavior Time period	1	2	3	4	5	6	7	8	9	Σ
1. Paces										
2. Sways										
3. Shuffles feet										
4. Knees tremble										
5. Extraneous arm and hand movements (swings, scratches, toys, etc.)										
6. Arms rigid										
7. Hands restrained (in pockets, behind back, clasped)										
8. Hand tremors										
9. No eye contact										
10. Face muscles tense (drawn, tics, or grimaces)										
11. Face "deadpan"										
12. Face pale										
13. Face flushed (blushes)										
14. Moistens lips										
15. Swallows										
16. Clears throat										
17. Breathes heavily										
18. Perspires (face, hands, or arm-pits)										
19. Voice quivers										
20. Speech blocks or stammers										

Comments:

Note. From *Insight Versus Desensitization in Psychotherapy* (p. 109), by G. L. Paul, 1966, Stanford, CA: Stanford University Press. Copyright 1966 by Stanford University Press. Reprinted by permission.

comes across very professionally and emulate the behaviors that give you that impression. Remember, you do not have to feel like you are competent—you just need to *pretend* that you feel that way. Rehearsal, too, can help considerably. Exhibit 14.4 presents Paul's (1966) Timed Behavioral Checklist for Performance Anxiety. You can use this to identify and reduce performance cues that make you look anxious. Use it to rate a videotaped version of your talk—you may be surprised at how calm you can appear. Many of us look much more competent than we feel.

Get Help for Serious Anxiety Problems

As we've said, some anxiety during an oral defense is normal, even desirable. If you generally experience *serious* anxiety in public speaking situations, however, you may want to obtain treatment for your speech anxiety before you get to the oral defense. For minor cases of speech anxiety, participating in Toastmasters can be useful. This is an international organization with chapters in many towns and cities. Contact the chapter nearest you. For more serious cases, seek assistance from a qualified, competent professional who specializes in empirically proven strategies for anxiety management.

Summary

Proposal meetings and oral defenses can be terrifying for some, even if they are productive. For others who enjoy lively discussion of academic issues, these meetings can even be enjoyable. Here, as with virtually every step of the research process, some advance investigation and preparation can increase the chances that this aspect of your project will go smoothly and successfully.

✔ To Do . . .

Managing Committee Meetings

☐ Prepare for the proposal meeting

— Know the format (use Exhibit 14.1)

—Make sure notes are taken

☐ Prepare for the oral defense

—Know the format (use Exhibit 14.1)

—Prepare your talk

—Prepare audiovisual materials

—Develop strategies to handle questions

—Rehearse your oral defense (use Exhibits 14.3 and 14.4)

—Manage your anxiety constructively

15 Presenting Your Project to the World

It's over. You've defended your research, made the necessary revisions, and presented the required copies to the librarian. Whew! Now, on with your life, right? Wrong! Well, at least not without ever looking back at your project. You began a research process months and possibly years ago when you started looking for an idea that could be molded into the project you've just completed. That process, as Yogi Berra once said, isn't over until it's over. And research, in a sense, is never really over. Research is a cyclical process that begins with a question and begins again when the answers to that question have been presented to the research community. In truth, your study probably raised additional questions that you or others will pursue in the future. So, research is probably best thought of as an evolutionary process rather than as something with definite boundaries and end points.

When should you present your research to others? Usually, as soon as possible after your oral defense. We encourage speed, because you will have a natural tendency to let down after an oral defense, and you risk never touching your document again. This is a mistake. For one thing, the research process gets aborted if results are not disseminated. If this happens, you never really complete the research cycle. For another thing, you foreclose the opportunity for others to learn from your work. As we said in chapter 3, research is a cumulative process. Each study builds on those that have gone before. If yours is not there for others to see, they cannot build on it. Nor can they come to you with questions that might improve the quality of their own research. In addition, sharing your results with others communicates something important about how you value the time and effort you have expended and the sacrifices you have asked others to make on your behalf. Was it really so bad that you never want to talk about it again? Were all those sacrifices only for the sake of a diploma to hang on a wall?

Finally, on a less lofty note, presenting and publishing your work may help you in the job search now or later on. If you plan an academic career, want to apply for postdoctoral research fellowships, or are interested in research-oriented clinical internships, having some presentations, publications, and submissions on your vita will enhance your credentials. If you just finished a master's thesis and want to apply to doctoral programs, note that most faculty look favorably on students who took the initiative to present and publish their theses.

Although some master's research will lack the necessary scope for publication, most thesis and dissertation work will be suitable for presenting at a conference and publishing in a journal. Assuming we have convinced you to share the good news of your findings, let's talk strategy for a minute. How should you go about disseminating your research to the scientific and other communities?

Present It First, Publish It Later

The ideal progression with respect to research dissemination is to present your findings to groups of professionals and get their feedback, incorporate this feedback into your own thinking about the research, and then prepare a formal submission for publication. This permits the research to benefit from the gradual shaping provided by the peer-review process. In addition, presenting (particularly at conferences) inevitably leads to conversations with others interested in your work, expanding your professional network and providing support and encouragement for your efforts. Think about the Big Names you wrote about. Wouldn't it be a thrill if one of them came up and complimented you on your study?

A continuum of outlets exists for presenting research results. At one end are informal discussions of your findings with other students over coffee. At the other is the formal presentation of your research to the Committee for Nobel Laureates at the Nobel Institute in Stockholm. In between, there are departmental colloquia, research presentations on job interviews, informal media presentations (e.g., as a guest on a radio or television show), and formal presentations at state, regional, national, and international professional conferences. Most of us spend our research careers at the lower end of the continuum, leaving the APA Distinguished Scientist, President's Medal, Nobel Prize, and other high-level presentations for the truly gifted, rare few in psychology capable of reaching such lofty heights.

Many departments routinely schedule colloquia during which students, faculty, or invited visitors present their research to anyone interested in attending. If yours does, we recommend presenting your findings in this forum as soon as possible after completing your defense. You may be thinking, "Okay, okay, I'll present a paper, but I think I'll skip the opportunity for local presentation because the audience is probably not important enough for me to bother." Actually, presentations "at home" are sometimes the most challenging, as members of the local audience are more likely than others to know some of the real issues and to feel comfortable discussing them with you. Thus, they are less likely to pull punches in questioning you about your research procedures and findings. You might be thinking, "I have to see these people every day. What if my research presentation is absolutely horrid? Do I want to have to slink along the hallways or come to school only at night to avoid the scorn or pity of my colleagues?" These considerations lead some to say that if you can present at home, you can present anywhere.

Beyond the department, there are state-level professional meetings, as well as regional, national, and international meetings. Where you choose to submit your research will depend on a number of factors, including whether the meeting invites research presentations, the schedule (i.e., time of year the meeting is held), the cost of attending, and professional advantages. Assuming the meeting welcomes research presentations, the most important of these considerations may be the professional advantages that can accrue. If you are likely to be looking for a job immediately after completing your study, you should consider submitting your research to a meeting that may help you find a position. If your interest is in an applied position and you have definite geographic requirements, consider a state or regional meeting. These often have placement facilities and procedures for arranging interviews with representatives of agencies currently hiring in the geographic area represented at the meeting. Even if no formal placement facilities exist, presenting at a state or regional meeting will expose you to persons in the desired geographic area and increase your chances of hearing about suitable positions.

If your career aspirations tend toward the academic, consider submitting an abstract to a national convention. The annual meetings of the American Psychological Society or the American Psychological Association include job placement functions, as do meetings of disciplines and of specialized groups such as the Society for Research in Child Development, the Association for the Advancement of Behavior Therapy, and so on. You can find out about the timing of these conventions by looking through recent issues of publications from these organizations. Be warned that abstracts often must be submitted long before the conference. For example, the Association for the Advancement of Behavior Therapy, which meets in November each year, requires that submissions be received by early April. The American Psychological Association Convention in August each year requires submissions to be received by mid-December. Presenting your study in a forum such as these obviously takes some advance planning. This is such an important part of the dissertation–job-finding sequence, however, that we strongly recommend that you build such a presentation into the time schedule you developed in chapter 4.

When you begin exploring presentation possibilities, you will find that most professional organizations entertain a number of different presentation formats. These include poster presentations, individual papers presented orally, papers presented as part of organized symposia, workshops, panel discussions, and invited addresses. For research presentations, the first three will be the most relevant. Submissions of individual projects such as a thesis or dissertation are often most appropriate for poster sessions or paper presentations. If your study is part of a research program, you may be able to talk your chairperson into organizing a research symposium that includes several presentations around a particular theme. Your study might be included as one of the submissions.

In general, symposia are reserved for more seasoned researchers, each of whom has a program of research and summarizes one or more studies from that program in the presentation. We will therefore focus our suggestions in the following section on paper presentation and poster session formats.

Pare to Prepare for Presentation

Did you notice the subheading for this section? We emphasize "paring" because much of getting a thesis or dissertation ready for dissemination involves just that, paring it down to a manageable size. The dictionary defines the process quite appropriately: "to cut off, or shave off the superficial substance or extremities of," "to remove or cut away the outside part," "to pare away redundancies" (*Webster's New International Dictionary*, 1950).

If you wish to present your research at a conference, you will have to submit an abstract of your study. Producing a good abstract requires

Exhibit 15.1

Sample Abstract for a Poster Presentation

Abstract: Effects of a Positive Behavioral Context on the Social Impact
of Aggressive Behavior

Although aggression correlates highly with peer rejection, not all aggressive children are rejected. Why not? Dyadic aggression occurs in the context of a relationship defined by numerous and varied interactions, and possibly this behavioral context modifies the impact of aggression on peer acceptance. Thus, a child may react quite differently to a peer who hits and pushes than to a second peer who hits, pushes, helps, shares, and initiates enjoyable activities.

This study tested the hypothesis that the positive context of aggressive behavior would influence its social impact. Sixty-six 4th- to 6th-grade girls were randomly assigned to one of six conditions. Each girl saw a series of fifteen 30-second videotaped vignettes of the same two 10-year-old girls interacting. In five of the six conditions, subjects viewed 4 vignettes in which one girl (the "target") displayed verbal or physical aggression. They also saw between 0 and 16 positive vignettes depicting the same target actress (a) saying "yes" to a request, (b) initiating an activity, and (c) giving or loaning something, or doing an unsolicited favor. Numbers of positive vignettes varied across conditions such that 0, 20, 43, 60, or 80% of the vignettes were positive. A sixth condition contained only positive vignettes (100%).

Four different random orders of positive and negative vignettes were used for each condition. To control for primacy and recency effects, each series began and ended with two neutral vignettes (e.g., playing or working alone). Time from initial to final vignette was constant across conditions. As manipulation checks, undergraduates correctly coded 97% of the behaviors in the vignettes, and in a previous study, 5th-grade girls' liking ratings increased after seeing positive vignettes (viewed individually, not as a series) and decreased after seeing negative vignettes.

After viewing the videotapes, each girl rated how much she (a) liked the target and (b) would like to be the target actress's best friend (1- to 7-point scales). These correlated .87 and were averaged. Girls also chose terms that they would use to describe the target actress to a friend from a list of nine positive and nine negative global trait/construct labels related to friendship choice and peer status (e.g., "nice to other kids" or "selfish").

The ANOVAs for the sociometric ratings, number of positive descriptors, and number of negative descriptors all showed significant effects. For all variables, Tukey post hoc tests showed that the first four conditions (0–60% positive) did not differ from each other but did differ significantly from the last two conditions (80 and 100% positive); these last two conditions did not differ. Results indicated a marked discontinuity in both liking and trait-oriented judgments with a shift from 60 to 80% positive behaviors.

continued

Exhibit 15.1, continued

Results supported the hypothesis that a prosocial social repertoire can offset the negative social impact of aggressive behavior, but only when aggression occurs in a highly positive context. Shifts in liking were all-or-none in this study and were accompanied by differences in other social judgments, implying that liking is one component of a set of covarying social cognitions. In addition, the results challenge the implicit linear model underlying social-skills training, which assumes that increasing positive behavior and decreasing negative behavior will influence peer liking in proportion to the change. Instead, improved acceptance may not occur until the child's behavior change reaches a certain threshold or ratio of positive to negative responses.

Note. Abstract submitted by D. Nangle, S. L. Foster, and J. T. Ellis for presentation at the biannual meeting of the Society for Research in Child Development, Seattle, WA, 1991. Adapted by permission.

that you pare your 100 or more pages to just one or two. The abstract should contain the rationale for your research, methodology, results, and brief reference to its significance and implications. Roughly 60% of the allocated words should describe method and results. These sections should communicate the most important details of the study, because this is what the program committee will use to decide whether to accept or reject it. For this reason, make clear to the reviewer what you did and the methodological soundness of your procedures. Exhibit 15.1 presents an abstract that was submitted and accepted for presentation at a meeting of the Society for Research on Child Development. It was based on a student's master's thesis (Nangle, Foster, & Ellis, 1991). It is fairly typical of such submissions and might be a useful model in planning your own.

Assume that a program committee or group recognizes the worth of your research and schedules you to present your paper at a conference. Or, someone invites you for a job interview. The next round of paring involves producing your talk or poster. Preparation for these two events differs somewhat.

Oral Presentations

First, consider how much of your study you should present. That depends on a number of factors. How much time will you have? Who is likely to be in the audience? Will A/V equipment be available? These are some preliminary questions you should ask before preparing any presentation. Regional or national meetings will allow you 10 to 20 minutes for your talk and usually provide overhead or slide projectors. On job interviews or during local departmental research colloquia, expect an hour to be allocated. In these cases, plan to hold your remarks to 45 minutes to allow time for questions, late starts, equipment hesitancies, and so on. Chapter 14 presented lots of suggestions for preparing an oral presentation, and we won't repeat them all here.

When we discussed the oral defense, we emphasized the benefits of practicing your talk. The same logic applies here. Because all you need at this point is a group to listen to you, the audience can consist of practically anyone. The most useful include your chairperson or other faculty members, graduate student colleagues, and significant others. Other good possibilities for dress-rehearsal audiences would be undergraduate classes you or your colleagues are teaching, or research seminars or journal clubs at the agency in which you are doing a practicum or internship.

Poster Presentations

Most regional or national professional organizations are more likely to accept individual studies for presentation during poster sessions than during a series of oral talks. For a poster session, you will need to prepare a visual layout of your study that parallels the organization and content that you would present orally or in a formal journal submission. The various sections of your paper, namely, abstract, introduction, method, results, and so on, are typed and attached to a large (approximately 3 × 5') poster. Poster presentations are usually grouped around a particular theme (e.g., human learning; assessment and diagnosis). Numerous presenters display their posters for a period of time (e.g., 1.5 hours) in the rooms of the conference center dedicated to poster presentations. As the author, you are expected to stand beside your poster and discuss it with members of the audience as they wander by.

The rules governing poster presentations vary somewhat from conference to conference. In general, most poster guidelines specify that (a) the type size must be readable at a distance of 2 to 3 feet; (b) handouts of the complete presentation must be available at the poster site; and (c) at least one author of the paper must be present throughout to discuss the poster.

To decide what goes into your poster, first set some page or word limits. We suggest a maximum of one page for the introduction to and rationale for the study; two pages for the method; one or two pages for the results, supplemented by no more than three tables or figures; and one page for discussion. Sometimes, results and discussion can be combined. Here we refer to pages with large type, so concise, clear prose is essential. Remember, your readers will want to walk by, read the paper quickly, and get the gist of the study. They can look over your handout (which should provide a more detailed description of the study) some other time. We find it useful to use the abstract as a basis for the poster and build up, adding additional details in order of importance until we have met our page or word limits.

If you have attended poster sessions already, you have probably been dazzled by the variety of presentation styles. Remember, when you give such a presentation, you represent not only yourself but your coauthors and school as well. The visual appearance of your poster makes an important statement that complements its written content. Most of us have seen handwritten or poorly typed poster presentations and been thankful that they did not have our school's name attached to them. At the other extreme, we have all seen brightly colored Las Vegas-style posters that clearly represent style over substance. Taste, clarity, and ease of reading are the most important criteria applicable to posters, given that their content has been considered important enough by the program committee to be accepted in the first place.

Our suggestions for successful posters conform with these criteria. First, follow the guidelines provided by the program committee. This is not the place to get creative. Remember, they have their rules for a reason. Second, keep it simple. You will have to carry your poster with you to the conference, often on an airplane. You will have to set it up and take it down in approximately 15 minutes. The only materials you can count on being provided will be the poster board to which you attach your materials. Be sure to take a supply of push pins or tacks with you.

Unless your school has a department that will produce a beautiful poster for you, the low-tech approach may work best. Prepare your poster elements as typed pages with enlarged print attached to a stiff colored backing that permits a half or three-quarter inch border around the entire page. Use the same colored backing throughout. As a rule, keep each section (abstract, introduction, etc.) on a separate page. If two pages are needed, consider using a large enough backing to include both typed pages on the same backing. Grouping in this way helps browsers read the presentation. Tack or pin your material to the poster board in the usual left to right sequence. If diagrams, figures, or other elements differ in size and a smooth left-to-right flow is difficult, consider using large arrows between sections to guide the reader's eye.

Do not forget the title and authors. These should be in a type size much larger than the rest of the poster and should be capable of being read at a distance of approximately 15 to 20 feet. In addition, presenters commonly run out of handouts. Plan for this by having a tablet or other means by which interested persons can leave their address so that you can mail information to them later.

Publish Your Study After Presenting It

After you have presented your findings to various professional audiences and received feedback from them, plan to submit your study for publication. Speed and brevity are again two important considerations at this point. As discussed above, avoid the temptation to shove your document in a drawer and forget about it. Capitalize on the completion momentum and write it up for publication as soon as possible.

Select a Journal

Prepare your research for publication by first selecting an appropriate journal. Your committee chairperson may suggest an appropriate outlet. Possibly, your study is part of a research program that normally directs its submissions to one or two journals. You also probably became familiar with one or more outlets for research of the type you have completed when doing your literature review. In which journals does most of the research in this area appear?

Journal "pecking orders" exist, with some journals being harder to publish in than others. Many journals of the APA, for example, handle hundreds of submissions each year and have 80% or higher rejection rates. Editors of these journals often are looking for reasons to reject manuscripts. If your study did not turn out as well as you wanted or had some obvious problems, you might want to try a less selective or more specialized journal and avoid the pain of an almost-certain rejection from a selective journal. If your findings and methodology are solid, and if you have a thick skin and don't mind the fact that you may have to revise and submit the article to your second-choice outlet, you may want to try for a more prestigious or widely circulated journal. Chairpersons and committee members with experience publishing in your area can advise you about how likely different journals are to accept your submission.

When you have selected the appropriate journal, get a copy of its instructions to authors. These can usually be found toward the front or back of each issue and describe the type of work the journal publishes, along with format and submission requirements. For most journals in the behavioral sciences, these will be pretty standard, and many format requirements conform closely to those of the *Publication Manual of the American Psychological Association* (APA, 1994). Pay attention to the types of work considered appropriate by the journal, however. You will save yourself considerable time by not sending your manuscript to inappropriate journals. It usually takes 60 to 90 days for your paper to be reviewed. You certainly want to avoid delays of this length when a rejection is a foregone conclusion because you have sent your paper to an inappropriate journal.

Prepare the Manuscript

As with preparing a presentation, paring will be essential in readying your study to submit to a journal. Many research-based journal articles contain a maximum of 25 double-spaced manuscript pages of text. Journals that publish primarily reviews of the literature (e.g., *Psychological Bulletin*, *Developmental Review*, *Psychological Review*, and *Clinical Psychology Review*) often accept longer papers. Some data-type journals (e.g., medical publications) require considerably shorter articles. In any event, your submission will require shortening your thesis or dissertation. Examine your target journal to estimate average article length. Assuming you follow APA style, you can estimate how many journal pages your paper might take by taking the total number of pages in your submission (including title page, references, etc.), and dividing by three (APA, 1994).

An important warning: Do not simply cut and paste from your thesis or dissertation. This leads to disjointed papers. As we mentioned earlier, one idea is to build up from your poster presentation or abstract rather than pare down from your thesis or dissertation. To create a very compact poster, you had to include only the most important details. Add the next most important points, then the next, and so on, until your paper approximates the target length.

As you write, consider the specific requirements and typical content of articles appearing in the journal you have selected. How much emphasis do authors give to theoretical issues, to methodological ones, to discussion? Tailor your paper to the specific requirements of the journal, both explicit and implicit, whenever possible.

Be sure to attend to details. If a phrase or sentence is not clear to you, it will not be clear to the reviewer who has never heard of your work. Have a colleague read your paper, checking in particular for inadequate or unnecessary detail and for clarity. In addition, proofread and follow APA publication requirements meticulously. A sloppy paper leads many to wonder how carefully the research was conducted.

Discuss with your chairperson and other coauthors how to orchestrate the write-up. Often, the student writes a first draft, and coauthors edit it and make comments. Making a publicly agreed-to schedule for completion of drafts helps get the manuscript ready in a timely fashion.

Decide Authorship

Standard 6.23 of the *Ethical Principles of Psychologists and Code of Conduct* (APA, 1992; reprinted in appendix A) governs authorship issues. Usually, dissertations and theses are submitted for publication under the joint authorship of the student and the chair of the student's committee, with the student as first author. As noted in the APA *Publication Manual* (1994), authorship is accorded those who make "substantial scientific contributions" to the research and is not reserved for those who do the actual writing. In general, the term "substantial professional contributions" includes activities such as suggesting the problem or hypotheses, writing major portions of the paper, conducting the statistical analyses, suggesting the research design, and so on. Minor intellectual contributions and clerical and other forms of nonintellectual contributions (e.g., building an apparatus, collecting data, and making suggestions for statistical analyses) can be acknowledged in footnotes. The significance of the contribution each person makes generally determines the order of authorship, with the person making the greatest contribution listed first.

The Ethics Committee of the APA has indicated that second authorship for committee chairs may be considered obligatory if they designate the primary variables, make major interpretative contributions, or provide the database. It also noted that authorship is a courtesy if the chair suggests the general research area, is substantially involved in the development of the design and dependent measures, or contributes substantially to writing the published report. It goes on to say that authorship is not acceptable if the chairperson's only contributions consist of editorial suggestions, encouragement, or the provision of physical facilities, financial support, or critiques (APA Ethics Committee, February 19, 1983).

Refer to authors in the text of the paper (for example, "All children were observed by the first author") by ordinal position of authorship, not by reference to professional seniority. This is obvious when the requirement to order authors by significance of contribution is remembered, because it is quite often the case that junior authors make greater contributions, especially to doctoral dissertations.

It is sometimes difficult to ascertain the relative significance of contributions among authors at the completion of a particular research endeavor. As a result, disputes about authorship or order of authors are common, and they are not very pleasant. A very good way to avoid them is to decide at the *beginning* of a collaborative research effort just who is going to do what and what the relative contributions mean in terms of authorship.

In fact, dissemination is such an important part of the research process that it is unwise to leave issues regarding presentation and publication unspoken. Especially with dissertations, a good deal of both the student's and faculty's time will be devoted to the research, and its completion demands some form of presentation at least, and publication at best. After deciding on your research question, think about making a formal agreement with your chairperson (perhaps in writing) covering jointly determined plans for dissemination. The agreement should state what forms dissemination will take, the approximate time after completion these forms will be pursued, individual responsibilities of the student, the chair, and any others who will be involved, and the order of authorship you anticipate. The agreement should also provide contingencies should one or more of the parties alter level or timing of their participation. A clear, written agreement produced in advance can do much to prevent strained relationships later.

Submit the Manuscript

When you are ready to send your slimmed-down opus to the previously selected journal, consult the journal's guidelines for authors once again to determine the exact submission procedures to be followed. Submit the required number of copies to the address provided in a recent issue of the journal (most journals change editors every 3 to 5 years). Be sure that your copies are legible and complete, and that pages are in the proper order. Do not staple or otherwise bind pages together. A paper clip will suffice. Accompany your submission with a cover letter indicating that the paper is not simultaneously being considered by any other journal. If the journal has a provision for anonymous (or blind) reviews and you are requesting one, state this in the letter. Mention that all subjects (human or animal) have been treated in accord with the ethical standards of the APA concerning research. If any copyrighted material appears in your submission, be sure to enclose copies of any permissions you have for its use. Finally, indicate a phone number and address where you may be reached. If your address changes while the article is under review, notify the editor handling the paper promptly.

Editors of most journals assign papers to an associate editor with expertise in the general area the paper covers, reserving a few papers to handle themselves. The associate editors then seek comments from between two and five reviewers, among whom will usually be an expert in your specific topic. These individuals provide written comments about the strengths and weaknesses of the paper and recommend whether they believe the journal should publish it.

Most editors will acknowledge receipt of your manuscript in writing. Some will tell you who is handling the manuscript (i.e., the editor or one of the associate editors) and a date by which you can expect to receive the reviews and a decision about whether the journal may wish to publish the manuscript. About 90 days turnaround time is not unusual, but journals with many submissions may have longer delays.

If you have not heard from the journal within a week or two of the target date, call or write to the person handling your manuscript and inquire politely about its status. The associate editor may have had trouble finding reviewers, a reviewer may be late, or the associate editor may be behind. Polite, repeated inquiries at 2-week intervals can prompt a slow editor to complete the review process on your manuscript in a more timely fashion.

When you receive an editorial decision on your manuscript, your work is not over. Journal editors ordinarily use four categories of response. The rarest is an outright acceptance with no requirement for additional changes. The most common is a rejection, accompanied by one or more reviews, usually anonymous, detailing the reviewers' reactions to the paper. A third type of decision involves conditionally accepting the paper provided that you are able and willing to make certain changes. The fourth type of decision is really no decision at all. It involves telling the authors that the reviewers and editor could not decide. The paper had a number of strengths, but it also had enough weaknesses that an acceptance, even with the promise of changes, could not be rendered at this time. The editor encourages the authors to revise the paper along the lines suggested by the reviewers and resubmit it for additional consideration. In such cases, the paper will often be treated as a new sub-mission and sent through the entire review process again.

The "revise–resubmit" verdict often devastates first-time submitters, who conclude that their paper is ultimately doomed. In actuality, with a good journal that has a high rejection rate, a revise–resubmit decision can be excellent news. It means your paper was good enough to get a second chance! You may nonetheless prefer to revise and submit the paper to another journal in which the probability of early acceptance is more likely.

Don't Let Criticism Get You Down

Because approximately 80% of the papers submitted to the best journals are rejected, it is reasonable to assume that *your* study may meet a similar fate the first time you submit it. Even if the study is not rejected, it will likely receive criticisms. First-timers often react to such criticism with excessive anger or depression.

In interpreting reviewers' comments, keep in mind that editors ask reviewers to indicate how the paper can be improved. In addition, whereas a strength can often be stated in a brief phrase, it takes more space to explain a weakness. Finally, the review tradition emphasizes critical rather than laudatory commentary. Thus, most comments you receive will focus on weaknesses of the manuscript. Even papers that are published in excellent journals usually go through at least two revisions to handle reviewers' criticisms. Don't take the comments personally.

The high likelihood of initial rejection is another good reason for getting your project written up in submissable form as soon after your defense as possible. The bad news is that you may have to try again, revising your paper and sending it out one more time. The good news about a rejection is that it is usually accompanied by excellent suggestions from experts in your area as to how the paper can be improved. If you attend to these carefully and make the changes that are appropriate, you will increase your chances for acceptance of your next submission con-siderably.

Incidentally, it is considered professionally unacceptable to submit your manuscript to a second journal without revision. Different journals sometimes use the same reviewers, and these hard-working colleagues do not take kindly to seeing paper a second time when its authors have not bothered to respond to suggestions for improving the first version. The peer-review process is an important mechanism for the advancement of science, and it behooves all of us to respect it.

If you do receive a rejection the first time you submit the paper, you may be inclined to put the paper away and forget about it. After all, although some of the comments of the reviewers simply reflected their misunderstanding of what was done or found, some were rather telling criticisms of the study as well. You might be tempted to conclude that the research is so flawed it is not worth disseminating further. Avoid this temptation. Remember, a committee of scholars at your school approved what you have done. It must have *some* merit. Most carefully conceived and conducted research efforts have something worth sharing with the professional community. When you get your reviews, read them and show them to your chair. Set a time to discuss them after a week or so. Then, put the reviews away and forget about them until just before meeting with your chair. At this point, you will have a fresh, somewhat less defensive perspective. You will be ready to offer suggestions about how the reviewers' concerns can be addressed in a revision. When you do meet with your chair, decide how each of the concerns will be handled and who will be responsible for each. Decide where to send the revision and consult that journal's instructions to authors.

Consider Dividing Major Projects for Multiple Submissions

It is useful to approach the process of submitting your research for publication systematically, particularly with a dissertation that can produce multiple scholarly products. In fact, you might have a publication program worked out from the very beginning. You might decide at the outset that your literature review will be of such comprehensiveness and quality that it will warrant submission to a discussion or review-type journal, such as *Psychological Bulletin*. In addition, you might develop a piece of apparatus or computer software for conducting your study that could be described in a separate paper submitted to an appropriately specialized journal. You might produce treatment manuals describing your intervention programs in sufficient detail to warrant publication as a short book. Or, you might develop and produce sufficient information about a new assessment instrument that you could write a stand-alone article describing it. All of these spin-offs from the major thrust of your research could be parts of your publication program.

If you consider submitting more than one paper from your dissertation, you will want to consult the APA's warnings about duplicate publication (APA, 1983). Duplicate publication involves work that has been "published in whole or in substantial part in another journal or in any readily available work" (APA, 1983, p. 167). If, for example, you submit the literature review section of your thesis or dissertation separately, it must be substantially different from the introduction or other sections of the research paper submission. Prudence dictates informing the editor receiving either submission of the second paper so that the editor will have the opportunity to decide whether duplicate publication is an issue.

Note that we are talking about submitting papers describing relatively independent parts of the larger project. We do not advocate "piecemeal publication of several reports of the results from a single data base . . ." (APA, 1983, p. 168). This practice often constitutes duplicate publication (because of substantial overlap). There are legitimate instances (e.g., results of individual assessment occasions in a longitudinal study) in which multiple publications from the same database would be warranted, however, and you are encouraged to consult the APA *Publication Manual* for more discussion of these.

Weigh the Benefits of Dissemination in the Popular Press

So far we have restricted our discussion to disseminating your findings to professional audiences. The general public may be an appropriate audience, as well. Not only does the profession generally benefit from informing the public of significant research in the academic community, but you may benefit personally. For example, as mentioned earlier, one of us currently works with a student on the development of a measure of personally destructive spending. The student is interested in a career as a human service professional and sees herself doing workshops and consulting individually with people with "shopping addictions." When the student's dissertation is complete, media interviews could inform the public of this relatively new research area and of the potential for help for persons experiencing these problems. Having her name mentioned as an expert in this area should help her beginning career in the community, as well.

Students pursuing academic careers can also benefit from having information about their work appear in the popular press. If the research requires cooperation of local agencies, schools, and so on, a good way to be introduced can sometimes be a newspaper story about the "fascinating

research of Dr. Blank, newly appointed assistant professor at O.U.K.D."
Timing the appearance of such a story to precede your contacting the
agencies might go a long way toward opening some doors.

We speak here of stories in local newspapers and appearances on
radio or local television talk shows. These do not usually involve publication of major portions of your findings. There are more formal popular
outlets (e.g., magazines or trade books), however, in which a substantial
part of some types of applied research might be published. These may
or may not be appropriate to your professional objectives.

Warnings are in order, however. These are not peer-reviewed journals and, thus, will not carry much weight in the academic community.
Moreover, previous publication in popular outlets such as these might
foreclose publication in professional journals because of the duplicate
publication prohibition. Consider your dissemination options carefully.
Develop a plan or program that involves multiple publications, if appropriate, and multiple dissemination outlets, both professional and popular,
if appropriate. If you decide to reach the public through the media, be
sure to follow the APA guidelines for appropriate public presentation.
Include sequencing and time lines in your plan and consider using the
project planning software discussed in chapter 4.

Summary

Dissemination is the important last step in the research cycle. Do not
avoid it in your natural inclination to get the entire process behind you
as soon as possible. This chapter has covered many important issues
involving sharing your research findings with the professional and lay
communities. One of the most central is the need for a dissemination
plan that you implement as soon after your defense as possible. Just as
you learned from the work of many other graduate students, others who
follow will want to learn from you. Give them that opportunity.

✔ To Do . . .

Presenting Your Project Publicly

☐ Present it first, publish it later

   —Identify outlet

   —Submit abstract

☐ Pare to prepare for oral and poster presentations

   —Identify format and length of oral talks

   —Identify page limits for posters

   —Create clear, readable poster

   —Prepare handouts to accompany poster

   —Obtain tablet, push pins, etc., to use during poster session

☐ Publish your study

   —Select a journal

   —Prepare the manuscript

   —Decide authorship

   —Submit the manuscript

   —Don't let criticism get you down

☐ Divide major projects for multiple submissions

☐ Weigh the benefits of dissemination in the popular press

Epilogue

There it is! We've said it all! We have successfully disgorged years of accumulated wisdom concerning theses and dissertations. Now we never have to say these things again, right? We can simply *require* prospective students to read this book, thereby making a small contribution to our retirement funds and saving us the tedium of repeating these bon mots one more time. Perhaps. We hope the book helps students. That was our purpose.

We hope it helps our colleagues as well, because many of them have no doubt heard echoes of their advice to students from time to time in their own offices as well. Let us hear from you. We welcome your comments and suggestions. Who knows, the revision urge may strike even us one of these days. Writing theses and dissertations—and even books—can become addictive.

Appendix A: Selected Ethical Standards Relevant to the Conduct of Research in Psychology

1.14 Avoiding Harm

Psychologists take reasonable steps to avoid harming their patients or clients, research participants, students, and others with whom they work, and to minimize harm where it is foreseeable and unavoidable.

1.16 Misuse of Psychologists' Work

(a) Psychologists do not participate in activities in which it appears likely that their skills or data will be misused by others, unless corrective mechanisms are available. (See also Standard 7.04, Truthfulness and Candor.)

(b) If psychologists learn of misuse or misrepresentation of their work, they take reasonable steps to correct or minimize the misuse or misrepresentation.

1.19 Exploitative Relationships

(a) Psychologists do not exploit persons over whom they have supervisory, evaluative, or other authority such as students, supervisees, employees, research participants, and clients or patients. (See also Standards 4.05–4.07 regarding sexual involvement with clients or patients.)

(b) Psychologists do not engage in sexual relationships with students or supervisees in training over whom the psychologist has evaluative or direct authority, because such relationships are so likely to impair judgment or be exploitative.

1.22 Delegation to and Supervision of Subordinates

(a) Psychologists delegate to their employees, supervisees, and research assistants only those responsibilities that such persons can reason-

From *Ethical Principles of Psychologists and Code of Conduct* (American Psychological Association, 1992).

ably be expected to perform competently, on the basis of their education, training, or experience, either independently or with the level of supervision being provided.

(b) Psychologists provide proper training and supervision to their employees or supervisees and take reasonable steps to see that such persons perform services responsibly, competently, and ethically.

(c) If institutional policies, procedures, or practices prevent fulfillment of this obligation, psychologists attempt to modify their role or to correct the situation to the extent feasible.

1.23 Documentation of Professional and Scientific Work

(a) Psychologists appropriately document their professional and scientific work in order to facilitate provision of services later by them or by other professionals, to ensure accountability, and to meet other requirements of institutions or the law.

(b) When psychologists have reason to believe that records of their professional services will be used in legal proceedings involving recipients of or participants in their work, they have a responsibility to create and maintain documentation in the kind of detail and quality that would be consistent with reasonable scrutiny in an adjudicative forum. (See also Standard 7.01, Professionalism, under Forensic Activities.)

1.25 Fees and Financial Arrangements

(a) As early as is feasible in a professional or scientific relationship, the psychologist and the patient, client, or other appropriate recipient of psychological services reach an agreement specifying the compensation and the billing arrangements.

(b) Psychologists do not exploit recipients of services or payors with respect to fees.

(c) Psychologists' fee practices are consistent with law.

(d) Psychologists do not misrepresent their fees.

(e) If limitations to services can be anticipated because of limitations in financing, this is discussed with the patient, client, or other appropriate recipient of services as early as is feasible. (See also Standard 4.08, Interruption of Services.)

(f) If the patient, client, or other recipient of services does not pay for services as agreed, and if the psychologist wishes to use collection agencies or legal measures to collect the fees, the psychologist first informs the person that such measures will be taken and provides that person an opportunity to make prompt payment. (See also Standard 5.11, Withholding Records for Nonpayment.)

3.03 Avoidance of False or Deceptive Statements

(a) Psychologists do not make public statements that are false, deceptive, misleading, or fraudulent, either because of what they state, convey, or suggest or because of what they omit, concerning their research, practice, or other work activities or those of persons or organizations with which they are affiliated. As examples (and not in limitation) of this standard, psychologists do not make false or deceptive statements concerning (1) their training, experience, or competence; (2) their academic degrees; (3) their credentials; (4) their institutional or association affiliations; (5) their services; (6) the scientific or clinical basis for, or results or degree of success of, their services; (7) their fees; or (8) their publications or research findings. (See also Standards 6.15, Deception in Research, and 6.18, Providing Participants With Information About the Study.)

(b) Psychologists claim as credentials for their psychological work, only degrees that (1) were earned from a regionally accredited educational institution or (2) were the basis for psychology licensure by the state in which they practice.

5.01 Discussing the Limits of Confidentiality

(a) Psychologists discuss with persons and organizations with whom they establish a scientific or professional relationship (including, to the extent feasible, minors and their legal representatives) (1) the relevant limitations on confidentiality, including limitations where applicable in group, marital, and family therapy or in organizational consulting, and (2) the foreseeable uses of the information generated through their services.

(b) Unless it is not feasible or is contraindicated, the discussion of confidentiality occurs at the outset of the relationship and thereafter as new circumstances may warrant.

(c) Permission for electronic recording of interviews is secured from clients and patients.

5.02 Maintaining Confidentiality

Psychologists have a primary obligation and take reasonable precautions to respect the confidentiality rights of those with whom they work or consult, recognizing that confidentiality may be established by law, institutional rules, or professional or scientific relationships. (See also Standard 6.26, Professional Reviewers.)

5.03 Minimizing Intrusions on Privacy

(a) In order to minimize intrusions on privacy, psychologists include in written and oral reports, consultations, and the like, only information germane to the purpose for which the communication is made.

(b) Psychologists discuss confidential information obtained in clinical or consulting relationships, or evaluative data concerning patients, individual or organizational clients, students, research participants, supervisees, and employees, only for appropriate scientific or professional purposes and only with persons clearly concerned with such matters.

5.04 Maintenance of Records

Psychologists maintain appropriate confidentiality in creating, storing, accessing, transferring, and disposing of records under their control, whether these are written, automated, or in any other medium. Psychologists maintain and dispose of records in accordance with law and in a manner that permits compliance with the requirements of this Ethics Code.

5.07 Confidential Information in Databases

(a) If confidential information concerning recipients of psychological services is to be entered into databases or systems of records available to persons whose access has not been consented to by the recipient, then psychologists use coding or other techniques to avoid the inclusion of personal identifiers.

(b) If a research protocol approved by an institutional review board or similar body requires the inclusion of personal identifiers, such identifiers are deleted before the information is made accessible to persons other than those of whom the subject was advised.

(c) If such deletion is not feasible, then before psychologists transfer such data to others or review such data collected by others, they take reasonable steps to determine that appropriate consent of personally identifiable individuals has been obtained.

5.08 Use of Confidential Information for Didactic or Other Purposes

(a) Psychologists do not disclose in their writings, lectures, or other public media, confidential, personally identifiable information concerning their patients, individual or organizational clients, students, research participants, or other recipients of their services that they obtained during the course of their work, unless the person or organization has consented in writing or unless there is other ethical or legal authorization for doing so.

(b) Ordinarily, in such scientific and professional presentations, psychologists disguise confidential information concerning such persons or organizations so that they are not individually identifiable to others and so that discussions do not cause harm to subjects who might identify themselves.

5.09 Preserving Records and Data

A psychologist makes plans in advance so that confidentiality of records and data is protected in the event of the psychologist's death, incapacity, or withdrawal from the position or practice.

5.10 Ownership of Records and Data

Recognizing that ownership of records and data is governed by legal principles, psychologists take reasonable and lawful steps so that records and data remain available to the extent needed to serve the best interests of patients, individual or organizational clients, research participants, or appropriate others.

6.06 Planning Research

(a) Psychologists design, conduct, and report research in accordance with recognized standards of scientific competence and ethical research.

(b) Psychologists plan their research so as to minimize the possibility that results will be misleading.

(c) In planning research, psychologists consider its ethical acceptability under the Ethics Code. If an ethical issue is unclear, psychologists seek to resolve the issue through consultation with institutional review boards, animal care and use committees, peer consultations, or other proper mechanisms.

(d) Psychologists take reasonable steps to implement appropriate protections for the rights and welfare of human participants, other persons affected by the research, and the welfare of animal subjects.

6.07 Responsibility

(a) Psychologists conduct research competently and with due concern for the dignity and welfare of the participants.

(b) Psychologists are responsible for the ethical conduct of research conducted by them or by others under their supervision or control.

(c) Researchers and assistants are permitted to perform only those tasks for which they are appropriately trained and prepared.

(d) As part of the process of development and implementation of research projects, psychologists consult those with expertise concerning any special population under investigation or most likely to be affected.

6.08 Compliance With Law and Standards

Psychologists plan and conduct research in a manner consistent with federal and state law and regulations, as well as professional standards governing the conduct of research, and particularly those standards governing research with human participants and animal subjects.

6.09 Institutional Approval

Psychologists obtain from host institutions or organizations appropriate approval prior to conducting research, and they provide accurate information about their research proposals. They conduct the research in accordance with the approved research protocol.

6.10 Research Responsibilities

Prior to conducting research (except research involving only anonymous surveys, naturalistic observations, or similar research), psychologists enter into an agreement with the participants that clarifies the nature of the research and the responsibilities of each party.

6.11 Informed Consent to Research

(a) Psychologists use language that is reasonably understandable to research participants in obtaining their appropriate informed consent (except as provided in Standard 6.12, Dispensing With Informed Consent). Such informed consent is appropriately documented.

(b) Using language that is reasonably understandable to participants, psychologists inform participants of the nature of the research; they inform participants that they are free to participate or to decline to participate or to withdraw from the research; they explain the foreseeable consequences of declining or withdrawing; they inform participants of significant factors that may be expected to influence their willingness to participate (such as risks, discomfort, adverse effects, or limitations on confidentiality, except as provided in Standard 6.15, Deception in Research); and they explain other aspects about which the prospective participants inquire.

(c) When psychologists conduct research with individuals such as students or subordinates, psychologists take special care to protect the prospective participants from adverse consequences of declining or withdrawing from participation.

(d) When research participation is a course requirement or opportunity for extra credit, the prospective participant is given the choice of equitable alternative activities.

(e) For persons who are legally incapable of giving informed consent, psychologists nevertheless (1) provide an appropriate explanation, (2) obtain the participant's assent, and (3) obtain appropriate permission from a legally authorized person, if such substitute consent is permitted by law.

6.12 Dispensing With Informed Consent

Before determining that planned research (such as research involving only anonymous questionnaires, naturalistic observations, or certain kinds of archival research) does not require the informed consent of research participants, psychologists consider applicable regulations and institutional review board requirements, and they consult with colleagues as appropriate.

6.13 Informed Consent in Research Filming or Recording

Psychologists obtain informed consent from research participants prior to filming or recording them in any form, unless the research involves simply naturalistic observations in public places and it is not anticipated that the recording will be used in a manner that could cause personal identification or harm.

6.14 Offering Inducements for Research Participants

(a) In offering professional services as an inducement to obtain research participants, psychologists make clear the nature of the services, as well as the risks, obligations, and limitations. (See also Standard 1.18, Barter [With Patients or Clients].)

(b) Psychologists do not offer excessive or inappropriate financial or other inducements to obtain research participants, particularly when it might tend to coerce participation.

6.15 Deception in Research

(a) Psychologists do not conduct a study involving deception unless they have determined that the use of deceptive techniques is justified by the study's prospective scientific, educational, or applied value and that equally effective alternative procedures that do not use deception are not feasible.

(b) Psychologists never deceive research participants about significant aspects that would affect their willingness to participate, such as physical risks, discomfort, or unpleasant emotional experiences.

(c) Any other deception that is an integral feature of the design and conduct of an experiment must be explained to participants as early as is feasible, preferably at the conclusion of their participation, but no later than at the conclusion of the research. (See also Standard 6.18, Providing Participants With Information About the Study.)

6.16 Sharing and Utilizing Data

Psychologists inform research participants of their anticipated sharing or further use of personally identifiable research data and of the possibility of unanticipated future uses.

6.17 Minimizing Invasiveness

In conducting research, psychologists interfere with the participants or milieu from which data are collected only in a manner that is warranted by an appropriate research design and that is consistent with psychologists' roles as scientific investigators.

6.18 Providing Participants With Information About the Study

(a) Psychologists provide a prompt opportunity for participants to obtain appropriate information about the nature, results, and conclusions of the research, and psychologists attempt to correct any misconceptions that participants may have.

(b) If scientific or humane values justify delaying or withholding this information, psychologists take reasonable measures to reduce the risk of harm.

6.19 Honoring Commitments

Psychologists take reasonable measures to honor all commitments they have made to research participants.

6.20 Care and Use of Animals in Research

(a) Psychologists who conduct research involving animals treat them humanely.

(b) Psychologists acquire, care for, use, and dispose of animals in compliance with current federal, state, and local laws and regulations, and with professional standards.

(c) Psychologists trained in research methods and experienced in the care of laboratory animals supervise all procedures involving animals and are responsible for ensuring appropriate consideration of their comfort, health, and humane treatment.

(d) Psychologists ensure that all individuals using animals under their supervision have received instruction in research methods and in the care, maintenance, and handling of the species being used, to the extent appropriate to their role.

(e) Responsibilities and activities of individuals assisting in a research project are consistent with their respective competencies.

(f) Psychologists make reasonable efforts to minimize the discomfort, infection, illness, and pain of animal subjects.

(g) A procedure subjecting animals to pain, stress, or privation is used only when an alternative procedure is unavailable and the goal is justified by its prospective scientific, educational, or applied value.

(h) Surgical procedures are performed under appropriate anesthesia; techniques to avoid infection and minimize pain are followed during and after surgery.

(i) When it is appropriate that the animal's life be terminated, it is done rapidly, with an effort to minimize pain, and in accordance with accepted procedures.

6.21 Reporting of Results

(a) Psychologists do not fabricate data or falsify results in their publications.

(b) If psychologists discover significant errors in their published data, they take reasonable steps to correct such errors in a correction, retraction, erratum, or other appropriate publication means.

6.22 Plagiarism

Psychologists do not present substantial portions or elements of another's work or data as their own, even if the other work or data source is cited occasionally.

6.23 Publication Credit

(a) Psychologists take responsibility and credit, including authorship credit, only for work they have actually performed or to which they have contributed.

(b) Principal authorship and other publication credits accurately reflect the relative scientific or professional contributions of the individuals involved, regardless of their relative status. Mere possession of an institutional position, such as Department Chair, does not justify authorship credit. Minor contributions to the research or to the writing for publications are appropriately acknowledged, such as in footnotes or in an introductory statement.

(c) A student is usually listed as principal author on any multiple-authored article that is substantially based on the student's dissertation or thesis.

6.24 Duplicate Publication of Data

Psychologists do not publish, as original data, data that have been previously published. This does not preclude republishing data when they are accompanied by proper acknowledgment.

6.25 Sharing Data

After research results are published, psychologists do not withhold the data on which their conclusions are based from other competent professionals who seek to verify the substantive claims through reanalysis and who intend to use such data only for that purpose, provided that the confidentiality of the participants can be protected and unless legal rights concerning proprietary data preclude their release.

6.26 Professional Reviewers

Psychologists who review material submitted for publication, grant, or other research proposal review respect the confidentiality of and the proprietary rights in such information of those who submitted it.

Appendix B: Bibliographic Databases

Searching the literature in psychology or related fields can be made easier by the use of bibliographic databases (i.e., collections of references to articles, books, book chapters, technical reports, and other sources of information about a topic). Most readers will be familiar with the print form of such databases. Examples include *Psychological Abstracts* and *Sociological Abstracts*. These are generally in the reference section of school libraries and are searched by hand, using key words or phrases. A list of print databases relevant to psychology is presented in Table B.1. These are not meant to be exhaustive, and there are many others that could have been included.

In addition to print databases, many libraries today have available very large database collections on computer disk. The availability of compact disc—read only memory (commonly known as CD-ROM) technology has made it possible to store extensive amounts of written material on compact discs. Libraries need only purchase a CD-ROM player or reader, a small personal computer, a printer, and appropriate software, and they are ready to subscribe to a service that furnishes CDs with the latest database updates. Rather than having to rely on library staff to perform your search for you, you merely sit before the computer keyboard, follow simple commands, and conduct your own search of the literature. When you find articles that are relevant, you can have the complete reference printed out or you can have the reference and its associated abstract printed. You can even download the references you are interested in looking at further to a computer disk and take it back to your own computer. Once there, the information can be read into files using your favorite word processing software and subsequently manipulated just as you would any text. This can make it unnecessary for you ever to have to type in a reference yourself!

Table B.1

Selected Databases Relevant to Psychology: Print Media

Database	Source
Biological Abstracts	BIOSIS 2100 Arch Street Philadelphia, PA 19103-1399 800-523-4806
Dissertation Abstracts International	UMI 300 N. Zeeb Road Ann Arbor, MI 48106 800-521-0600
Index Medicus	National Library of Medicine 8600 Rockville Pike Bethesda, MD 20894 800-638-8480
Linguistics & Language Behavior Abstracts	Sociological Abstracts, Inc. P.O. Box 22206 San Diego, CA 92192-0206 619-695-8803 800-752-3945
Mental Measurements Yearbook	University of Nebraska Press 901 North 17th Street Lincoln, NE 68588-0592 402-472-3581
Monthly Catalog of U. S. Government Publications	U. S. Government Printing Office North Capitol & H Streets, NW Washington, DC 20401 202-783-3238
Psychological Abstracts	American Psychological Association 750 First Street, NE Washington, DC 20002-4242 202-336-5650 800-374-2722
Research in Child Abuse and Neglect (This and other, more focused literature searches on child abuse and neglect are available from the source.)	Clearinghouse on Child Abuse and Neglect Information P.O. Box 1182 Washington, DC 20013 703-385-7565

continued

Table B.1, continued

Database	Source
Sociological Abstracts	Sociological Abstracts, Inc. P.O. Box 22206 San Diego, CA 92192-0206 619-695-8803 800-752-3945
Social Sciences Citation Index	Institute for Scientific Information 3501 Market Street Philadelphia, PA 19104 800-523-1857

The best known and most useful of the CD-ROM databases for psychologists is *PsycLIT*. Produced by the American Psychological Association, it contains the same journal information contained in *Psychological Abstracts*, dating back to 1974. *PsycLIT* is updated quarterly and in 1992 began including *PsycBOOKS* as well. A list of databases in CD-ROM format that might be of some relevance to psychologists is provided in Table B.2.

The third, and possibly the most useful type of database is the on-line database. Though they are a relatively recent development, today there are literally thousands of such databases with information on everything from airline schedules to soap operas. Of most interest to potential dissertation doers are the so-called reference databases. These contain citations or other information that refer the reader to another source for the complete text. Until recently, it was necessary to have a librarian perform a search of such on-line gold mines and pay the library a fee

Table B.2

Selected Databases Relevant to Psychology: CD-ROM Media

Database	Period covered
ABI/Inform	1971–present
Biological Abstracts	1990–present
Dissertation Abstracts International	1961–present
ERIC (Educational Resources Information Center)	1966–present
GPO (Government Printing Office) Monthly Catalog	1976–present
MEDLINE	1966–present
NTIS (National Technical Information Service)	1983–present
PsycLIT	1974–present
SSCI (Social Sciences Citation Index)	1986–present

Table B.3

Selected Databases Relevant to Psychology: On-line Computer Media

Database	On-line service	Source
ABI/Inform	B, D	UMI/Data Courier 620 South 3rd Sreet Louisville, KY 40202-2475 800-626-2823
Academic American Encyclopedia	P	Grolier Electronic Publishers, Inc. Sherman Turnpike Danbury, CT 06816 800-356-5590
AIDSLINE	B, D	National Library of Medicine 8600 Rockville Pike Bethesda, MD 20894 800-638-8480
BIOSIS Previews	B	BIOSIS, Inc. 2100 Arch Street Philadelphia, PA 19103 800-523-4806
CANCERLIT	B, D	National Institutes of Health National Cancer Institute International Cancer Research Data Bank R. A. Bloch International Cancer Information Center, Building 82 Bethesda, MD 20892 301-496-7403
Dissertation Abstracts Online	B, D	UMI 300 North Zeeb Road Ann Arbor, MI 48106 800-521-0600
Druginfo and Alcohol Use and Abuse	B	University of Minnesota Drug Information Services 3-160 Health Science Center, Unit F 308 Harvard Street, SE Minneapolis, MN 55455 612-624-6492

continued

Table B.3, continued

Database	On-line service	Source
Drug Information Fulltext	B, D	American Society of Hospital Pharmacists Database Services Division 4630 Montgomery Avenue Bethesda, MD 20814 301-657-3000
EPIC Service		Online Computer Library Center, Inc. 6565 Frantz Road Dublin, OH 43017-0702 800-848-5878
ERIC	B, D	ERIC Processing and Reference Facility 2440 Research Blvd., Suite 400 Rockville, MD 20850 301-258-5500
ETS Test Collection Database	B	Educational Testing Service Test Collection Center Rosedale Road Princeton, NJ 08541 609-734-5737
FACTS ON FILE World News Digest	D	Facts on File, Inc. 460 Park Avenue, South New York, NY 10016 212-683-2244
Family Resources Database	B, D	National Counsel on Family Relations Inventory of Marriage and Family Literature 3989 Central Avenue, NE, Suite 550 Minneapolis, MN 55421 612-781-9331
GPO Monthly Catalog	B, D	U.S. Government Printing Office North Capitol & H Streets, NW Washington, DC 20401 202-783-3238
Health and Psychosocial Instruments	B	Behavioral Measurement Database Services P.O. Box 110287 Pittsburgh, PA 15232-0787

continued

Table B.3, continued

Database	On-line service	Source
Life Collection	B, D	Cambridge Scientific Abstracts 7200 Wisconsin Avenue, Suite 601 Bethesda, MD 20814 800-843-7751
Linguistics and Language	B, D	Social Abstracts, Inc. Behavioral Abstracts P.O. Box 22206 San Diego, CA 92192-0206 619-695-8803 800-752-3945
Magazine Index	B, D	Information Access Co. 362 Lakeside Drive Foster City, CA 94404 800-227-8431
MEDLINE	B, D	National Library of Medicine 8600 Rockville Pike Bethesda, MD 20894 800-638-8480
Mental Health Abstracts	D	IFI/Plenum Data Co. 302 Swann Avenue Alexandria, VA 22301 800-368-3093
Mental Measurement Yearbook	B	Buros Institute of Mental Measurements University of Nebraska—Lincoln 135 Bancroft Hall Lincoln, NE 68588-0348 402-472-6203
NEWSEARCH	B, D	Info Access Company 362 Lakeside Drive Foster City, CA 94404 800-227-8431
PsycINFO	D, B	American Psychological Association 750 First Street, NE Washington, DC 20002-4242 202-336-5630 800-374-2722

continued

Table B.3, continued

Database	On-line service	Source
REHABDATA	B	National Rehabilitation Information Center Mairo Systems, Inc. 8455 Colesville Road, Room 935 Silver Spring, MD 20910
SCISEARCH		Institute of Science Information 3501 Market Street Philadelphia, PA 19104 800-523-1857
SMOKING AND HEALTH	D	US DHHS, CDC Office on Smoking and Health Technical Information Center Park Building, Room 1-16 5600 Fisher Lane Rockville, MD 20857 301-443-1690
Social SCISEARCH	B, D	Institute of Science Information 3501 Market Street Philadelphia, PA 19104 800-523-1857
Social Abstracts	B, D	Social Abstracts, Inc. P.O. Box 22206 San Diego, CA 92192-0206 619-695-8803 800-752-3945
The Software Directory	D	Black Box Corp. Mayview Road & Park Drive Pittsburgh, PA 15241 412-746-6368
UnCover	T	CARL Systems, Inc. 3801 E. Florida Bldg. D., Suite 300 Denver, CO 80222 303-758-3030

Note. B = BRS; D = Dialog; P = Prodigy; T = accessed directly or through Telenet. Most of the information in this table was obtained from the *Directory of On-line Databases* (1991), available in libraries or from the publisher, Gale Research, Inc., 835 Penobscot Building, Detroit, MI 48226-4094; 800-347-GALE.

that varied, depending on the number of items retrieved, the length of time the librarian was on-line conducting the search, or some combination of both.

With the advent of home computers and modems to connect them through phone lines to other computers, it has now become quite feasible to access databases from the comfort of your home. This can be done without cost in some cases, as in searching the more than 8 million volumes in the "Melvyl" catalog of the University of California system. In this case, you are accessing the computerized catalog of this university's system directly. In other cases, you might gain access to a particular database through an on-line service. Such services make databases available from various producers under licensing arrangements. To use their databases, you join or subscribe to the service and are charged a fee. Usually, this fee covers the administrative costs of entering you into the system, assigning you an account number and password, and providing you with a manual describing what the service has to offer and how you can go about accessing it. You may also be charged a fee for the time you are actually connected to the host computer conducting your search. These fees are generally quite reasonable. You will also incur charges for using the phone line while hooked into the service's computer. In most cases, this is a local call, but if you live somewhere that does not have local access to a computer network (e.g., DIALNET or TELENET), you might have to pay long-distance charges as well.

Two of the most important on-line services for scholars are Dialog Knowledge Index (DIALOG Information Services, Inc., 3460 Hillview Avenue, Palo Alto, CA 94304; 800-334-2654) and BRS/After Dark/Colleague (BRS Information Technologies, Maxwell Online, 8000 Westpark Drive, McLean, VA 22102; 800-955-0906). The databases included in each service are numerous and overlap a good deal. They include information on the latest movies and airline schedules as well as scientific literature. Another on-line service worth examining is Prodigy™ (Prodigy Services Co., 445 Hamilton Avenue, White Plains, NY 10601; 800-776-0840). A listing of some databases you can access from your own computer is provided in Table B.3.

Appendix C: Statistical Software

Below we list the names and sources of some of the most commonly used statistical software for personal computers. The list is biased toward programs that do a broad variety of tasks. For a more extensive listing of software, see Stoloff and Couch (1988). Be aware that software developers update their programs regularly and that the information we present applies at the date this book was published but may change in the future.

We do not offer our own opinions in listing these packages because we have not used all of them. Nonetheless, we have observed that some programs and their manuals are more user-friendly than others. If possible, try out competing programs that will do the same things to see how easy they are to use and how comprehensible the manuals are.

Except as noted, all of the following will do a broad variety of statistical tests. Most include options for evaluating whether data meet the assumptions of particular tests.

BMDP Statistical Software
BMDP Statistical Software, Inc.
1440 Sepulveda Blvd., Suite 316
Los Angeles, CA 90025
Available for IBM and compatibles;
  MAC

Crunch (Crunch Interactive
  Statistical Package)
Crunch Software Corporation
5335 College Avenue
Suite 27
Oakland, CA 94518
Available for IBM and compatibles;
  MAC

SPSS-PC+
SPSS, Inc.
444 N. Michigan Ave.
Chicago, IL 60611
Available for IBM and compatibles;
  MAC

Statistical Navigator Professional
The Idea Works, Inc.
607 Jackson Street
Columbia, MO 65203
Available for IBM and compatibles
Note: Helps user select appropriate
  statistics, locate references, etc.
  Does no calculations.

CSS: Statistica
StatSoft
2325 E. 13th Street
Tulsa, OK 74104
Available for IBM and compatibles;
  MAC

Minitab, Inc.
3081 Enterprise Drive
State College, PA 16801-3008
Available for IBM and compatibles;
  MAC

SAS
SAS Institute
SAS Campus Drive
Carey, NC 27513
Available for IBM and compatibles;
  MAC

Statistical Power Analysis:
  A Computer Program
(by M. Bornstein & J. Cohen)
Lawrence Erlbaum Associates
365 Broadway
Hillsdale, NJ 07642
Available for IBM and compatibles
Note: Does power analyses only

SYSTAT
SYSTAT, Inc.
1800 Sherman Avenue
Evanston, IL 60201-3793
Available for IBM and compatibles;
  MAC

Appendix D: Bibliography for Research Design, Measurement, Statistics, and Writing Style

Research Design

Barlow, D. H., Hayes, S. C., & Nelson, R. O. (1984). *The scientist practitioner*. Elmsford, NY: Pergamon Press.

Barlow, D. H., & Hersen, M. (1984). *Single-case experimental designs: Strategies for studying behavior change* (2nd ed.). Elmsford, NY: Pergamon Press.

Campbell, D. T., & Stanley, J. C. (1963). *Experimental and quasi-experimental designs for research*. Chicago: Rand McNally.

Cook, T. D., & Campbell, D. T. (1979). *Quasi-experimentation: Design and analysis issues for field settings*. Boston: Houghton Mifflin.

Kazdin, A. E. (1991). *Research design in clinical psychology* (2nd ed.). New York: HarperCollins.

Kerlinger, F. N. (1986). *Foundations of behavioral research* (3rd ed.). New York: Holt, Rinehart & Winston.

McBurney, D. H. (1990). *Experimental psychology* (2nd ed.). Belmont, CA: Wadsworth.

Miller, D. C. (1991). *Handbook of research design and social measurement* (5th ed.). Newbury Park, CA: Sage.

Ray, W. J., & Ravizza, R. (1988). *Methods*. Belmont, CA: Wadsworth.

Solso, R. L., & Johnson, H. H. (1989). *An introduction to experimental design in psychology: A case approach*. New York: HarperCollins.

Weisberg, H. F., Krosnick, J. A., & Bowen, B. D. (1989). *An introduction to survey research and data analysis*. New York: HarperCollins.

Measurement

Anastasi, A. (1988). *Psychological testing* (6th ed.). New York: Macmillan.

Bakeman, R., & Gottman, J. M. (1986). *Observing interaction: An introduction to sequential analysis*. Cambridge, England: Cambridge University Press.

Campbell, D. T., & Fiske, D. (1959). Convergent and discriminant validation by the multitrait–multimethod matrix. *Psychological Bulletin, 56*, 81–105.

Cronbach, L. J. (1990). *Essentials of psychological testing* (5th ed.). New York: HarperCollins.

DeVellis, R. F. (1991). *Scale development: Theories and applications*. Newbury Park, CA: Sage.

Edwards, A. L. (1970). *The measurement of traits by scales and inventories*. New York: Holt, Rinehart & Winston.

Foster, S. L., & Cone, J. D. (1986). Design and use of direct observation. In A. R. Ciminero,

K. S. Calhoun, & H. E. Adams (Eds.), *Handbook of behavioral assessment* (2nd ed.; pp. 253–324). New York: Wiley.

Kaplan, R. M., & Saccuzzo, D. P. (1989). *Psychological testing: Principles, applications, and issues* (2nd ed.). Pacific Grove, CA: Brooks/Cole.

Nunnally, J. C. (1967). *Psychometric theory.* New York: McGraw-Hill.

Oppenheim, A. N. (1966). *Questionnaire design and attitude measurement.* New York: Basic Books.

Suen, H. K., & Ary, D. (1989). *Analyzing quantitative behavioral observation data.* Hillsdale, NJ: Erlbaum.

Webb, E. J., Campbell, D. T., Schwartz, R. D., & Sechrest, L. (1966). *Unobtrusive measures: Nonreactive research in the social sciences.* Chicago: Rand McNally.

Weedman, C. (1975). *A guide for the preparation and evaluation of the dissertation or thesis.* San Diego, CA: Omega.

Wiggins, J. S. (1959). Interrelationships among MMPI measures of dissimulation under standard and social desirability instructions. *Journal of Consulting Psychology, 23,* 419–427.

Wiggins, J. S. (1973). *Personality and prediction: Principles of personality assessment.* Reading, MA: Addison-Wesley.

Statistics

Andrews, F. M., Klem, L., Davidson, T. N., O'Malley, P. M., & Rodgers, W. L. (1981). *A guide for selecting statistical techniques for analyzing social science data* (2nd ed.). Ann Arbor, MI: Survey Research Center, Institute for Social Research, University of Michigan.

Bakeman, R., & Gottman, J. M. (1986). *Observing interaction: An introduction to sequential analysis.* Cambridge, England: Cambridge University Press.

Bruning, J. L., & Kintz, B. L. (1987). *Computational handbook of statistics* (3rd ed.). Glenview, IL: Scott, Foresman.

Cohen, J. (1988). *Statistical power analysis for the behavioral sciences* (2nd ed.). Hillsdale, NJ: Erlbaum.

Cohen, J., & Cohen, P. (1983). *Applied multiple regression/correlation analysis for the behavioral sciences* (2nd ed.). Hillsdale, NJ: Erlbaum.

Connell, J. P., & Tanaka, J. S. (Eds.). (1987). Special section on structural equation modeling. *Child Development, 58,* 1–175.

Gorsuch, R. L. (1983). *Factor analysis.* Hillsdale, NJ: Erlbaum.

Gottman, J. M. (1981). *Time series analysis.* Cambridge, England: Cambridge University Press.

Gottman, J. M., & Roy, A. K. (1990). *Sequential analysis.* Cambridge, England: Cambridge University Press.

Huitema, B. E. (1980). *The analysis of covariance and alternatives.* New York: Wiley.

Jaccard, J., Becker, M. A., & Wood, G. (1984). Pairwise multiple comparison procedures: A review. *Psychological Bulletin, 96,* 589–596.

Keppel, G. (1991). *Design and analysis* (3rd ed.). Englewood Cliffs, NJ: Prentice-Hall.

Kirk, R. E. (1982). *Experimental design* (2nd ed.). Pacific Grove, CA: Brooks/Cole.

Kraemer, H. C., & Thiemann, S. (1987). *How many subjects? Statistical power analysis in research.* Newbury Park, CA: Sage.

Maxwell, S. E., & Delaney, H. D. (1990). *Designing experiments and analyzing data.* Belmont, CA: Wadsworth.

McNemar, Q. (1962). *Psychological statistics.* New York: Wiley.

Pedazhur, E. J. (1982). *Multiple regression in behavioral research: Explanation and prediction* (2nd ed.). New York: Holt, Rinehart & Winston.

Siegel, S. (1956). *Nonparametric statistics for the behavioral sciences*. New York: McGraw-Hill.

Suen, H. K., & Ary, D. (1989). *Analyzing quantitative behavioral observation data*. Hillsdale, NJ: Erlbaum.

Tabachnick, B. F., & Fidell, L. S. (1989). *Using multivariate statistics* (2nd ed.). New York: HarperCollins.

Tukey, J. W. (1977). *Exploratory data analysis*. Reading, MA: Addison-Wesley.

Winer, B. J. (1971). *Statistical principles in experimental design* (2nd ed.). New York: McGraw-Hill.

Writing Style

American Psychological Association. (1983). *Publication manual of the American Psychological Association* (3rd ed.). Washington, DC: Author. (Note: This book also provides a bibliography on writing style on pp. 184–185.)

Committee on Gay and Lesbian Concerns. (1991). Avoiding heterosexual bias in language. *American Psychologist, 46*, 973–974.

Follett, W. (1966). *Modern American usage: A guide*. New York: Farrar, Straus & Giroux.

Gelfand, H., & Walker, C. J. (1990). *Mastering APA style: Student's workbook and training guide*. Washington, DC: American Psychological Association.

Strunk, W., Jr., & White, E. B. (1979). *The elements of style* (3rd ed.). New York: Macmillan.

References

Ambady, N., & Rosenthal, R. (1992). Thin slices of expressive behavior as predictors of interpersonal consequences: A meta-analysis. *Psychological Bulletin, 111*, 256–274.

American Psychological Association, Committee for the Protection of Human Participants in Research. (1982). *Ethical principles in the conduct of research with human participants*. Washington, DC: Author.

American Psychological Association. (1992). *Ethical principles of psychologists and code of conduct. American Psychologist, 47*, 1597–1611.

American Psychological Association. (1994). *Publication manual of the American Psychological Association* (4th ed.). Washington, DC: Author.

American Psychological Association Ethics Committee. (1983). *Authorship guidelines for dissertation supervision*. Washington, DC: Author.

Anastasi, A. (1988). *Psychological testing* (6th ed.). New York: Macmillan.

Andrews, F. M., Klem, L., Davidson, T. N., O'Malley, P. M., & Rodgers, W. L. (1981). *A guide for selecting statistical techniques for analyzing social science data* (2nd ed.). Ann Arbor, MI: Survey Research Center, Institute for Social Research, University of Michigan.

Barlow, D. (1988). *Anxiety and its disorders*. New York: Guilford Press.

Barlow, D. H., Hayes, S. C., & Nelson, R. O. (1984). *The scientist practitioner*. Elmsford, NY: Pergamon Press.

Beck, A. T., Rush, A. J., Shaw, B. F., & Emery, G. (1979). *Cognitive therapy of depression*. New York: Guilford Press.

Bellack, A. S., & Hersen, M. (1977). Self-report inventories in behavioral assessment. In J. D. Cone & R. P. Hawkins (Eds.), *Behavioral assessment: New directions in clinical psychology* (pp. 52–76). New York: Brunner/Mazel.

Bell-Dolan, D. J., Foster, S. L., & Sikora, D. M. (1989). Effects of sociometric testing on children's behavior and loneliness in school. *Developmental Psychology, 25*, 306–311.

Billingsley, F., White, O. R., & Munson, R. (1980). Procedural reliability: A rationale and an example. *Behavioral Assessment, 2*, 229–241.

Bruning, J. L., & Kintz, B. L. (1987). *Computational handbook of statistics* (3rd ed.). Glenview, IL: Scott, Foresman.

Buros, O. K. (Ed.). (1974). *Tests in print II: An index to tests, test reviews, and the literature on specific tests*. Highland Park, NJ: Gryphon Press.

Cairns, R. B., & Green. J. A. (1979). How to assess personality and social patterns: Observations or ratings. In R. B. Cairns (Ed.), *The analysis of social interactions* (pp. 209–226). Hillsdale, NJ: Erlbaum.

Campbell, D. T. (1960). Recommendations for APA test standards regarding construct, trait, and discriminant validity. *American Psychologist, 15,* 546–553.

Campbell, D. T., & Fiske, D. (1959). Convergent and discriminant validation by the multitrait–multimethod matrix. *Psychological Bulletin, 56,* 81–105.

Campbell, D. T., & Stanley, J. C. (1963). *Experimental and quasi-experimental designs for research.* Chicago: Rand McNally.

Clarke, G. N., Lewinsohn, P. M., Hops, H., & Seeley, J. R. (1992). A self- and parent-report measure of adolescent depression: The Child Behavior Checklist Depression Scale (CBCL-D). *Behavioral Assessment, 14,* 443–463.

Cohen, J. (1983). The cost of dichotomization. *Applied Psychological Measurement, 7,* 249–253.

Cohen, J. (1988). *Statistical power analysis for the behavioral sciences* (2nd ed.). Hillsdale, NJ: Erlbaum.

Cohen, J. (1992). A power primer. *Psychological Bulletin, 112,* 155–159.

Cohen, J., & Cohen, P. (1983). *Applied multiple regression/correlation analysis for the behavioral sciences* (2nd ed.). Hillsdale, NJ: Erlbaum.

Cone, J. D. (1977). The relevance of reliability and validity for behavioral assessment. *Behavior Therapy, 8,* 411–426.

Cone, J. D. (1978). The Behavioral Assessment Grid (BAG): A conceptual framework and a taxonomy. *Behavior Therapy, 9,* 882–888.

Cone, J. D., (1992). Accuracy and curriculum-based measurement. *School Psychology Quarterly, 7,* 22–26.

Cook, T. D., & Campbell, D. T. (1979). *Quasi-experimentation: Design and analysis issues for field settings.* Boston: Houghton Mifflin.

Cooper, H. M. (1989). *Integrating research: A guide for literature reviews* (2nd ed.). Newbury Park, CA: Sage.

Corcoran, K. J., & Fischer, J. (1987). *Measures for clinical practice: A sourcebook.* New York: Free Press.

Cronbach, L. J. (1990). *Essentials of psychological testing* (5th ed.). New York: HarperCollins.

Cronbach, L. J., Gleser, G. C., Nanda, H., & Rajaratnam, N. (1972). *The dependability of behavioral measurements.* New York: Wiley.

Crowne, D. P., & Marlowe, D. (1960). A new scale of social desirability independent of psychopathology. *Journal of Consulting Psychology, 24,* 349–354.

Davinson, D. (1977). *Theses and dissertations as information sources.* London: Clive Bingley.

Davis, G. B., & Parker, C. A. (1979). *Writing the doctoral dissertation: A systematic approach.* Woodbury, NY: Barron's.

DeMaster, B., Reid, J., & Twentyman, C. (1977). The effects of different amounts of feedback on observer's reliability. *Behavior Therapy, 8,* 317–329.

DiLorenzo, T. M. (1984). *A functional assessment of heterosocial initiation behaviors in adults.* Unpublished doctoral dissertation, West Virginia University, Morgantown, WV.

Dionne, R. R. (1992). *Effective strategies for handling teasing among fifth and sixth grade children.* Unpublished doctoral dissertation, California School of Professional Psychology, San Diego, CA.

Dumas, M. D., Dionne, R. R., Foster, S. L., Chang, M. K., Achar, M. S., & Martinez, C. M., Jr. (1992, November). *A critical incidents analysis of strategies for handling peer provocation among second-, fifth-, and eighth-grade children.* Paper presented at the annual meeting of the Association for Advancement of Behavior Therapy, Boston, MA.

Edwards, A. L. (1957). *The social desirability variable in personality assessment and research.* Hinsdale, IL: Dryden Press.

Edwards, A. L. (1970). *The measurement of traits by scales and inventories*. New York: Holt, Rinehart & Winston.

Edwards, A. L. (1990). Construct validity and social desirability. *American Psychologist, 45,* 287–289.

Einstein, A. (1974). *The universe and Dr. Einstein*. New York: Lincoln Barnett.

Ellis, A., & Harper, R. A. (1961). *A guide to rational living*. North Hollywood, CA: Wilshire.

Foster, S. L., Bell-Dolan, D. J., & Burge, D. A. (1988). Behavioral observation. In A. S. Bellack & M. Hersen (Eds.), *Behavioral assessment: A practical handbook* (3rd ed.; pp. 119–160). Elmsford, NY: Pergamon Press.

Foster, S. L., & Cone, J. D. (1986). Design and use of direct observation. In A. R. Ciminero, K. S. Calhoun, & H. E. Adams (Eds.), *Handbook of behavioral assessment* (2nd ed.; pp. 253–324). New York: Wiley.

Goldstein, R. (1989). Power and sample size via MS/PC-DOS computers. *American Statistician, 43,* 253–260.

Gorsuch, R. L. (1983). *Factor analysis* (2nd ed.). Hillsdale, NJ: Erlbaum.

Grusec, J. (1991). The socialization of altruism. In M. S. Clark (Ed.), *Prosocial behavior* (pp. 9–33). Newbury Park, CA: Sage.

Guilford, J. P. (1956). *Fundamental statistics in psychology and education*. New York: McGraw-Hill.

Hartmann, D. P. (1982). Assessing the dependability of direct observational data. In D. P. Hartmann (Ed.), *New directions for methodology of social and behavioral science: Using observers to study behavior* (pp. 51–65). San Francisco: Jossey-Bass.

Hersen, M., & Bellack, A. S. (Eds.). (1988). *Dictionary of behavioral assessment techniques*. Elmsford, NY: Pergamon Press.

Hoier, T. S. (1984). *Target selection of social skills for children: An experimental investigation of the template matching procedure*. Unpublished doctoral dissertation, West Virginia University, Morgantown, WV.

Hoier, T. S., & Cone, J. D. (1987). Target selection of social skills for children: The template matching procedure. *Behavior Modification, 11,* 137–163.

Horowitz, M. J., Wilner, N., & Alvarez, W. (1979). Impact of Event Scale: A measure of psychosomatic stress. *Psychosomatic Medicine, 41,* 209–218.

House, A. E., House, B. J., & Campbell, M. D. (1981). Measures of interobserver agreement: Calculation formulas and distribution effects. *Journal of Behavioral Assessment, 3,* 37–57.

Huberty, C. J., & Morris, J. D. (1989). Multivariate analysis versus multiple univariate analyses. *Psychological Bulletin, 105,* 302–308.

Huitema, B. E. (1980). *The analysis of covariance and alternatives*. New York: Wiley.

Hunter, J. E., & Schmidt, F. L. (1990). *Methods of meta-analysis*. Newbury Park, CA: Sage.

Inderbitzen-Pisaruk, H., & Foster, S. L. (1990). Adolescent friendships and peer acceptance: Implications for social skills training. *Clinical Psychology Review, 10,* 425–439.

Jaccard, J., Becker, M. A., & Wood, G. (1984). Pairwise multiple comparison procedures: A review. *Psychological Bulletin, 96,* 589–596.

Johnston, J. M., & Pennypacker, H. S. (1980). *Strategies and tactics of human behavioral research*. Hillsdale, NJ: Erlbaum.

Kaplan, R. M., & Saccuzzo, D. P. (1989). *Psychological testing: Principles, applications, and issues* (2nd ed.). Pacific Grove, CA: Brooks/Cole.

Kent, R. N., O'Leary, K. D., Diament, C., & Dietz, A. (1974). Expectation biases in observational evaluation of therapeutic change. *Journal of Consulting and Clinical Psychology, 42,* 774–780.

Keppel, G. (1991). *Design and analysis* (3rd ed). Englewood Cliffs, NJ: Prentice-Hall.

Kerlinger, F. N. (1986). *Foundations of behavioral research*. (3rd ed.). New York: Holt, Rinehart & Winston.

Keyser, D. J., & Sweetland, R. C. (Eds.). (1984). *Test critiques*. Kansas City, MO: Test Corporation of America.

Kirk, R. E. (1982). *Experimental design* (2nd ed.). Pacific Grove, CA: Brooks/Cole.

Koyre, A. (1965). *Newtonian studies*. Cambridge, MA: Harvard University Press.

Kraemer, H. C., & Thiemann, S. (1987). *How many subjects? Statistical power analysis in research*. Newbury Park, CA: Sage.

Kramer, J. J., & Conoley, J. C. (Eds.). (1992). *The eleventh mental measurements yearbook*. Lincoln, NE: Buros Institute of Mental Measurements.

Kuhn, T. (1970). *The structure of scientific revolutions* (2nd ed.). Chicago: University of Chicago Press.

Lang, P. J. (1971). The application of psychophysiological methods to the study of psychotherapy and behavior modification. In A. E. Bergin & S. L. Garfield (Eds.), *Handbook of psychotherapy and behavior change* (pp. 75–125). New York: Wiley.

Maher, B. A. (1978). A reader's, writer's, and reviewer's guide to assessing research reports in clinical psychology. *Journal of Consulting and Clinical Psychology, 46*, 835–838.

Mahoney, M. J., & Mahoney, B. K. (1976). *Permanent weight control*. New York: Norton.

Maxwell, S. E., & Delaney, H. D. (1990). *Designing experiments and analyzing data*. Belmont, CA: Wadsworth.

McBurney, D. H. (1990). *Experimental psychology* (2nd ed.). Belmont, CA: Wadsworth.

McNemar, Q. (1962). *Psychological statistics*. New York: Wiley.

Meehl, P. E. (1978). Theoretical risks and tabular asterisks: Sir Karl, Sir Ronald, and the slow progress of soft psychology. *Journal of Consulting and Clinical Psychology, 46*, 806–834.

Mischel, W. (1968). *Personality and assessment*. New York: Wiley.

Myers, J. L., DiCecco, J. V., White, J. B., & Borden, V. M. (1982). Repeated measurements on dichotomous variables: Q and F tests. *Psychological Bulletin, 92*, 517–525.

Nangle, D., Foster, S. L., & Ellis, J. T. (1991, April). *The effects of a positive behavioral context on the social impact of aggressive behavior*. Paper presented at the Society for Research in Child Development, Seattle, WA.

Nelson, G. L., Cone, J. D., & Hanson, C. R. (1975). Training correct utensil use in retarded children: Modeling vs. physical guidance. *American Journal of Mental Deficiency, 80*, 114–122.

Nunnally, J. C. (1967). *Psychometric theory*. New York: McGraw-Hill.

O'Leary, K. D., Kent, R. N., & Kanowitz, J. (1975). Shaping data congruent with experimental hypotheses. *Journal of Applied Behavior Analysis, 8*, 463–469.

Parsonson, B. S., & Baer, D. M. (1978). The analysis and presentation of graphic data. In T. R. Kratochwill (Ed.), *Single subject research* (pp. 101–165). San Diego, CA: Academic Press.

Paul, G. L. (1966). *Insight vs. desensitization in psychotherapy*. Stanford, CA: Stanford University Press.

Paul, G. L. (1969). Behavior modification research: Design and tactics. In C. M. Franks (Ed.), *Behavior therapy: Appraisal and status* (pp. 29–62). New York: McGraw-Hill.

Peterson, L., Homer, A. L., & Wonderlich, S. A. (1982). The integrity of independent variables in behavior analysis. *Journal of Applied Behavior Analysis, 15*, 477–492.

Poppen, R. (1988). *Behavioral relaxation training and assessment*. Elmsford, NY: Pergamon Press.

Radcliff, B. M., Kawal, D. E., & Stephenson, R. J. (1967). *Critical path method*. Chicago: Cahners.

Ray, W. J., & Ravizza, R. (1988). *Methods*. Belmont, CA: Wadsworth.

Reed, J. G., & Baxter, P. M. (1992). *Library use: A handbook for psychology*. Washington, DC: American Psychological Association.

Research and Education Association. (1981). *Handbook of psychiatric rating scales*. New York: Author.

Roberts, R. E., Lewinsohn, P. M., & Seeley, J. R. (1991). Screening for adolescent depression: A comparison of depression scales. *Journal of the American Academy of Child and Adolescent Psychiatry, 30*, 58–66.

Robinson, J. P., Shaver, P. R., & Wrightsman, L. S. (Eds.). (1991). *Measures of personality and social psychological attributes*. San Diego, CA: Academic Press.

Romanczyk, R. G., Kent, R. N., Diament, C., & O'Leary, K. D. (1973). Measuring the reliability of observational data: A reactive process. *Journal of Applied Behavioral Analysis, 6*, 175–184.

Rosenthal, R. (1969). Interpersonal expectations: Effects of the experimenter's hypothesis. In R. Rosenthal & R. L. Rosnow (Eds.), *Artifact in behavioral research* (pp. 181–277). San Diego, CA: Academic Press.

Rossi, J. S. (1990). Statistical power of psychological research: What have we gained in 20 years? *Journal of Consulting and Clinical Psychology, 58*, 646–656.

Sanchez-Hucles, J., & Cash, T. F. (1992). The dissertation in professional psychology programs: 1. A survey of clinical directors on requirements and practices. *Professional Psychology: Research and Practice, 23*, 59–61.

Shuller, D.Y., & McNamara, J. R. (1976). Expectancy factors in behavioral observation. *Behavior Therapy, 7*, 519–527.

Sikora, D. M. (1989). *Divorce, environmental change, parental conflict, and the peer relations of preschool children*. Unpublished doctoral dissertation, West Virginia University, Morgantown, WV.

Skinner, B. F. (1950). Are theories of learning necessary? *Psychological Review, 57*, 193–216.

Sobell, M. B., Bogardis, J., Schuller, R., Leo, G. I., & Sobell, L. C. (1989). Is self-monitoring of alcohol consumption reactive? *Behavioral Assessment, 11*, 447–458.

Sternberg, D. (1981). *How to complete and survive a doctoral dissertation*. New York: St. Martin's Press.

Stoloff, M. L., & Couch, J. V. (1988). *Computer use in psychology: A directory of software* (2nd ed.). Washington, DC: American Psychological Association.

Stuart, R. B. (Ed.). (1977). *Behavioral self-management: Strategies, techniques and outcome*. New York: Brunner/Mazel.

Sweetland, R. C., & Keyser, D. J. (Eds.). (1983). *Tests: A comprehensive reference for assessments in psychology, education and business*. Kansas City, MO: Test Corporation of America.

Sweetland, R. C., & Keyser, D. J. (Eds.). (1990). *Tests* (3rd ed.). Austin, TX: PRO-ED.

Tabachnick, B. F., & Fidell, L. S. (1989). *Using multivariate statistics* (2nd ed.). New York: HarperCollins.

Taplin, P. S., & Reid, J. B. (1973). Effects of instructional set and experimental influence on observer reliability. *Child Development, 44*, 547–554.

Webb, E. J., Campbell, D. T., Schwartz, R. D., & Sechrest, L. (1966). *Unobtrusive measures: Nonreactive research in the social sciences*. Chicago: Rand McNally.

Webster's new international dictionary (2nd ed.). (1950). Springfield, MA: G & C Merriam.

Webster's new world dictionary of the American language (2nd college ed.). (1970). New York: World Publishing.

Weedman, C. (1975). *A guide for the preparation and evaluation of the dissertation or thesis*. San Diego, CA: Omega.

Wiggins, J. S. (1959). Interrelationships among MMPI measures of dissimulation under standard and social desirability instructions. *Journal of Consulting Psychology*, *23*, 419–427.

Wiggins, J. S. (1973). *Personality and prediction: Principles of personality assessment*. Reading, MA: Addison-Wesley.

Winer, B. J. (1971). *Statistical principles in experimental design* (2nd ed.). New York: McGraw-Hill.

Wolfe, V. V. (1986). *Paternal and marital factors related to child conduct problems*. Unpublished doctoral dissertation, West Virginia University, Morgantown, WV.

Wolfe, V. V., Gentile, C., Michienzi, T., Sas, L., & Wolfe, D. A. (1991). The Children's Impact of Traumatic Events Scale: A measure of post-sexual-abuse PTSD symptoms. *Behavioral Assessment*, *13*, 359–383.

Yale University. (1975). *Yale University catalog, 1975–76*. New Haven, CT: Author.

Yates, B. T. (1982). *Doing the dissertation: The nuts and bolts of psychological research*. Springfield, IL: Charles C Thomas.

Index

A

ABAB design, 120, 230
ABI/Inform, 311, 312
Abstracts, 279–282
Academic American Encyclopedia, 312
Accuracy of observation, 151
Achar, M. S., 204
Acquired immune deficiency syndrome
    (AIDS), 147
Age, as variable, 178
AIDSLINE, 312
Alpha level, 246
    and statistical power, 125
Alternate form reliability, 152, 154–155
Altruism, as research subject, 153–154,
    157
Alvarez, W., 33
Ambady, N., 32
American Psychological Association, 94,
    169, 278, 279, 280, 285, 292. *See
    also Publication Manual of the Ameri-
    can Psychological Association*
    ethics guidelines, 134–136, 299–308
    Membership Register, 69
American Psychological Society, 96, 169,
    279
Analyses of covariance (ANCOVA)
    assumptions of, 182
    controlling for social desirability, 165
    definition, 185
    possible difficulties with, 186–187
    reporting results of, 85
    role of, 124, 185–186
Analyses of variance (ANOVA)
    and ANCOVA, 185, 186

assumptions of, 182
and causality, 188
final review of results, 246
methodology, 123, 182
nonparametric alternatives to, 188–
    189
one-way, 120, 123, 126
and planned comparisons, 183–184
power analysis in, 126
reporting results of, 85
2×2 design, 120
with two groups, 179
and Type I errors, 187–188
vs. MANOVA, 187
Anastasi, A., 151
ANCOVA. *See* Analyses of covariance
Andrews, F. M., 198
Animal studies
    ethical guidelines for, 135–136, 306–
        307
    planning, 206
    reporting methodology in, 122–123
    surgery in, 128
Annual Review of Psychology, 33
ANOVA. *See* Analyses of variance
Anxiety, oral defense, 269–270
    cognitive component of, 270–271
    motor component of, 272–274
    physical component of, 272–274
    related to depression, 158
    serious cases of, 274
Apparatus, research. *See also* Computer-
    ized tools
    planning for, 206–207
    reporting use of, 126–127

Apparatus, research (*Cont.*)
  safety of, 138
Appendixes
  debriefing script in, 133
  measurement instruments described in, 129
  in proposal, 87–88
  raw data in, 220
Applied research, 192–193
  assistants in, 209
Assent forms, 141–143
Assessment. *See* Measures
Association for the Advancement of Behavior Therapy, 279, 280
Attention-deficit hyperactivity disorder, 175–176
Audiovisual materials, in defense, 262, 263, 264–265
Authorship issues, 62, 287–288, 307–308

B

Backward chaining, 47
Baer, D. M., 228, 230, 232
Barlow, D. H., 121, 158
Baxter, P. M., 96
Beck, A. T., 165
Becker, M. A., 184
Behavior, as subject matter, 156
Behavior research
  instrument validity in, 157–158
  manipulation checks in, 127
  measurement in, 149–150, 156, 159
  publishing, 286
  self-reports in, 150–151, 168–169, 245–246
Behavioral Measurement Database Service, 161
Bell-Dolan, D. J., 130, 137, 144
Bellack, A. S., 150, 159
Between-subjects design, 120, 121, 178–179
  alternatives to ANOVA in, 188
Bias
  experimenter, 32, 131, 205, 209
  from heterogeneity of variance, 181–183
  research subject, 131
Bibliography
  compiling, 94

  reference sources for, 94–95, 309–316
Billingsley, F., 127
Biological Abstracts, 310
BIOSIS Previews, 312
Bivariate correlations, 189–190
Blind experimenters, 127–128, 131, 205
Bogardis, J., 121
Bonferroni procedure, 185, 188, 246
Booz, Allen, & Hamilton, 51
Borden, V. M., 177
Brevity, x, 104–105
  in conference presentations, 280–282
BRS/After Dark/Colleague, 316
Bruning, J. L., 174–175
Burge, D. A., 130
Buros. See Mental Measurements Yearbook
Buros, Oscar K., 159

C

Cairns, R. B., 150
Campbell, D. T., 120, 121, 130, 165, 166, 168, 187, 245
Campbell, M. D., 130
CANCERLIT, 312
Captions, figure, 232–233
Cash, T. F., 4
Causation
  language of, misused, 248–249
  reverse, 244–245
  types of, 244–245
Chairperson
  availability of, 66–67
  checklist for selecting, 79
  and committee selection, 74
  criteria for selecting, 61, 79
  and dissemination of research, 62, 288
  expertise of, 63–65
  interviewing potential, 69–71
  investigating, 67–69
  in oral defense, 267–268
  personal qualities of, x, 63, 64–65, 67
  potential problems with, 75–77
  in proposal meeting, 257, 258
  and publishing research results, 285
  relations with committee, 72–73
  and research authorship, 287
  role of, 61, 62–63, 65
  standards of, 65–66, 69–70
Chang, M. K., 204
Chi square, 126, 223

with categorical data, 189
Children, as subjects, 202
  consent issues, 140–144
  scheduling, 207–208
Citation style, for secondary sources, 98
Clarke, G. N., 142
Clinical Psychology Review, 114, 286
Clinical research, 242–243
  measures for, 159–160
Coefficient alpha procedures, 155
Coefficients
  bivariate correlation, 189–190
  intraclass correlation, 154, 189
  phi, 190
Cohen, J., 126, 177, 190, 191, 192, 193
Cohen, P., 190, 191, 192, 193
Collateral data sources, 166
Colorado Alliance of Research Libraries, 96
Committee. *See also* Chairperson; Defense
  changes in methodology reported to, 203
  checklist for selecting, 79
  expertise of, 65, 72
  grandstanding by, 266–267
  interpreting reactions of, 267
  interviewing candidates for, 74
  investigating candidates for, 73–74
  potential problems with, 75–77
  proposal meeting with, 255–259
  recruiting, 65
  relations with chairperson, 72–73
  relationships within, 77
  role of, 4, 71–72
  rules of, 22–23, 72–73
  suggestions from, 258
Committee meetings, managing, 275
Completions, energy from, 55
Computerized tools
  for bivariate correlations, 190
  for creating figures, 233
  data analysis by, 212
  data collection, 209–212
  data entry, 208
  familiarity with, 20–21
  format of summaries from, 212–213
  grammar-checking programs, 14
  for literature searches, 95–96, 309, 311, 312–316

for planning work, 48, 50
for power analysis, 126
raw data from, 213
in regression analysis, 192
in selecting assessment instruments, 161
in selecting statistics, 198
spell-checking software, 14
for statistical work, 211, 317–318
for testing homogeneity of variance, 183
Cone, J. D., 98, 127, 129, 130, 131, 149, 151, 158, 228
Conferences/conventions, xi
  access to current research in, 97
  oral presentation at, 282–283
  poster presentations at, 283–285
  presenting research at, 279–280
Confidentiality, 135, 138, 205, 207, 301–303
Confounding variables, 18, 124, 128–129, 245
  and ANCOVA, 185–186
Conoley, J. C., 159
Consent
  forms, 138–140
  passive procedures, 142–143
Constructs, research on
  differentiated from behavior, 156
  measurement in, 148–149, 165–166
  self-report measures for, 164–165
  setting generalizability in, 167
  validity in, 130, 153, 156, 157, 165–166
Consultants, 86–87, 195–198
Content validity, 157–158
Context-dependent stochastologicals, 153
Continuous data, 177
Control groups, 131
  for temporal effects, 163
Convergent validity, 130, 157, 164–166
Cook, T. D., 120, 121, 187, 245
Cooper, H. M., 97, 103, 107, 112
Copyright issues
  assessment instrument, 169
  in proposal, 87–88
  in publishing of research, 289
Corcoran, K. J., 161
Correlational designs, 120
  bivariate, 189–190

Correlational designs (*Cont.*)
  causal language in discussion of, 248–249
  discriminant function analysis in, 194–195
  function analysis, 195
  internal validity issues in, 244–245
  nonparametric regression in, 194
  nonsignificant results in, 249
  parametric regression in, 190–194
  power analysis in, 126
  presentation of results from, 222
  research populations in, 123
  role of, 176–177
  statistical techniques for, 189–195
  vs. group comparison, 176–177, 178
Covariate analysis. *See* Analyses of covariance (ANCOVA)
Cricket Graph™, 233
Criterion validity, 130, 157
Critical reading
  in literature review, 112–113, 262
  techniques, 18–19, 98–103
  of your work, anticipating, 248, 278–280
Criticism, avoiding overstatement in, 113
Cronbach, L. J., 129, 151, 152, 155
Crowne, D. P., 165
Current Contents, 94

D

Data entry, 208
Data transformation, 179
Databases, 96
  bibliographic, 309–316
  reviews of assessment instruments in, 161
Davidson, T. N., 198
Davinson, D., 4
Davis, G. B., 5, 19
Debriefing subjects, 133
  confidentiality in, 138
  monitoring, 138
Deceptions, in research, 135, 136, 305–306
Deductive methods, 37
Defense
  audiovisual materials in, 262, 263, 264–265
  checklist for, 269, 275

  committee role in, 72
  definition of, 4
  failing, 271
  format of, 257, 259–261
  humor in, 261, 266
  of literature review, 262
  managing anxiety in, 269–274
  materials to bring to, 267
  of methodology, 262
  minidefense model, 255
  presentation in, 261–264
  problem-solving model, 255
  purpose of, 256
  questioning in, 260, 265–267
  rehearsing, 267–269
  of research design, 263
  speculation in, 266
  suggestions from committee in, 260
  verbal style in, 263
Delaney, H. D., 179, 181, 183, 184, 186, 187, 188, 246
DeMaster, B., 208
Demographic data
  gathering, 124
  in method section, 122
  and parametric statistics, 178
  in regression strategies, 190
  supplemental analysis of, 240
  as variables, 175
Dependent variables, 35–36, 127, 186
  adequacy of, 127
  conceptually related, 188
  literature review organized by, 108
  and MANOVA, 187–188
  in methodology section, 129–131
  operationalizing, 147
  and parametric statistics, 177, 178
  in regression strategies, 190
  reliability of, 129–130
  in results section, 222, 223
  results section organized by, 221
  and statistical needs, 175–176
  step-down procedures for, 187
Depression
  correlated with anxiety, 158
  correlated with social desirability, 165
Developmental PsycSCAN, 94
Developmental Review, 33, 114, 286
Diagnostic and Statistical Manual of Mental Disorders, 122
Dialog Knowledge Index, 316

Diament, C., 32, 131
DiCecco, J. V., 177
Dictionary of Behavioral Assessment Techniques, 159
Dietz, A., 32
Dionne, R. R., 8, 204
Direct observation, 149–151
  monitoring, 130–131
  observer agreement in, 152, 162, 220
  recording as, 151, 162
  videotaping and, 151
Directness, as quality of measures, 148
Directory of Behavioral Assessment Techniques, 159
Discriminant function analysis, 125, 194–195
  assumptions of, 182
Discriminant validity 130, 157, 162, 164
Discriminative validity, 128, 157
Discussion section
  anticipating critical reading of, 248
  avoiding nonsignificant results in, 248, 249
  causal language in, misuse of, 248–249
  checklist for, 252
  clinical implications in, 242–243
  comparative analysis in, 240–241
  contents of, 249
  future directions noted in, 247–248
  generalizability problems noted in, 245
  imperfections of research noted in, 243–247
  implications of results noted in, 241–243
  interpreting findings in, 238–240
  lack of significant findings in, 239–240
  last paragraph of, 25
  measurement problems noted in, 245–246
  oral presentation of, 261, 263
  organization of, 249–25
  research design of, 242
  role of, 237
  speculation in, 243
  statistical research noted in, 246–247
  summary of findings in, 237–238
  supplemental analyses in, 239–240
  unexpected results noted in, 238
  validity issues noted in, 244–245

writing style in, 248–251
Dissertation
  defense, 72, 256
  definition of, 2–3
  empirical research in, 4–5
  investments of time in, 19
  length of, 5
  literature review, 83–84
  literature review in, 115
  origins of, 4
  proposal in, 83–84
  role of, 3–4, 6–7, 67, 241
  table of contents in proposal for, 88–90
  vs. thesis, 2–4
Dissertation Abstracts International, 5, 35, 62, 94, 310
Dissertation Abstracts Online, 312
Dissertations, research ideas in existing, 34–35
Doctor of Psychology degree, 3, 4, 5
Double-blind design, 131
Drafts
  chairperson review of, 66
  editing software, 14
  role of, 109
Drug Information Fulltext, 313
Druginfo and Alcohol Use and Abuse, 312
DSM. *See Diagnostic and Statistical Manual of Mental Disorders*
Dumas, M. D., 204

E

Editing
  hiring help for, 14
  for publication, 286–287, 289–290
  software for, 14
Educational Resources Information Center (ERIC), 94, 313
Edwards, A. L., 165
Effects, size of, 174
  identifying significant, 248, 249
  and power analysis, 125, 126
Einstein, A., 45
Ellis, A., 270
Ellis, J. T., 282
Emery, G., 165
Empirical research
  alternatives to, 4–5

Empirical research (*Cont.*)
  guidelines for evaluating, 98–103
Employment opportunities
  interview for, 283
  and presentation of research results, 279–280
  and publication in popular press, 292–293
EPIC Service, 313
ERIC, 94, 313
Ethical Principles in the Conduct of Research with Human Participants, 136
Ethics. *See also* Informed consent
  in animal research, 135–136, 306–307
  authorship issues, 287–288
  in clinical research, 138
  confidentiality issues, 135, 138, 205, 207, 301–303
  guidelines, 134–136, 299–308
  managing research subject data, 138
  and research assistants, 137, 205, 299–300
  in research design, 136–138
Ethnicity. *See* Race/ethnicity
ETS Test Collection database, 313
External validity, 18, 24–25, 245
  and direct assessment, 149

F

F tests, 183, 188
Factor analysis, 41, 125, 164, 168, 195
  role of, 167
FACTS ON FILE World News Digest, 313
Faculty. *See also* Committee
  role in topic selection, 28–30, 33
Failed predictions, 240
Family Resource Database, 313
Farrell, A., 266
Fellowships, xi
Fidell, L. S., 185, 187, 193, 194, 195, 198
Figures
  captions for, 232–233
  checklist for, 233
  content of, 222
  conventions for presentation of, 227–233
  data between phases in, 231
  deciding whether to use, 228
  labeling, 230
  multiple dependent variables in, 231

  numbers of, 226
  percentages in, 229–230
  research design depicted in, 120–121
  software for, 233
  symbols in, 230–231
  tick marks in, 230
  time as measure in, 230
Financial issues
  compensating assistants, 53, 203
  consultation, 196
  ethical guidelines, 300
  funding, informed consent practices and, 143
  hiring blind experimenters, 128
  in use of figures, 228
Fischer, J., 161
Fisher, R., 39
Fishing expeditions, 38
Fiske, D., 165, 168
Follow-up studies, 134
  recommending, 247–248
Format
  of appendixes in proposal, 87–88
  of audiovisual presentation in defense, 264–265
  for computer summaries, 212–213
  for conference presentation, 280
  of defense presentation, 261–264
  of discussion section, 249–251
  of figures, 228–233
  guidelines for, 5–6
  for introducing research question, 114–115
  for introduction to proposal, 83–84
  for journal submissions, 285–287, 288–290
  of literature review, 104–105, 110–112
  of method section in proposal, 84–85
  one-chapter, in literature review, 83–84, 104, 114
  of oral defense meeting, 259–261
  for poster presentation, 283–285
  of proposal meeting, 255, 257–259
  of references section in proposal, 87
  of results section, 219–221, 238
  of results section in proposal, 85–87
  of table of contents, 88–90
  of tables, 224–227
  two-chapter, in literature review, 83–84, 104, 114

Forms
  for chairperson collaboration, 62
  documenting proposal acceptance, 82
  informed consent, 133, 134, 138–144
  organizing, 207
  for recruiting assistants, 203
Forward chaining, 47
Foster, S. L., 98, 111, 130, 137, 144, 151,
    204, 282
Four-group comparisons, 224
Friedman's test, 189

G
Games and Howell test, 185
Gantt charts, 48
  in planning work, 48–49
Gender
  and parametric statistics, 178
  as variable, 179–182
Generalizability, 129, 131, 148, 151. *See
    also* Reliability; Validity
  alternate form, 154–155
  assessing instruments for, 155–156
  internal consistency, 163–164
  no evidence of, for chosen measure,
    161
  as results topic, 241
  scorer, 152–153, 161–163
  setting, 157–158, 167
  temporal, 129–130, 153–154, 163
  theory of reliability, 152
Gentile, C., 33
Gleser, G. C., 129
Goal setting
  increments in, 47, 51
  product vs. process goals in, 110
  time considerations in, 45–48
  visual representations in, 48–50
  in writing process, 110
Goldstein, R., 126
Gorsuch, R. L., 195
GPO Monthly Catalog, 313
Graduating, 137
Grammar, 13–14
Grammatik™, 14
Graphics. *See* Audiovisual materials, in
    defense; Figures; Tables
Graphs. *See* Figures
Great Britain, post-graduate education
    in, 4

Green, J. A., 150
Group comparison designs, 176
  ANCOVA tests in, 185–187
  ANOVA tests in, 178–183, 188
  evaluating computer analyses in, 214
  MANOVA tests in, 187–188
  nonparametric statistics in, 188–189
  planned comparisons in, 183–184
  post hoc tests in, 184–185
  presentation of results from, 222
  role of, 176–177
  t tests in, 179–182
  with two groups, 179
Grusec, J., 157
Guilford, J. P., 151

H
Handbook for Psychiatric Rating Scales,
    159–161
Hanson, C. R., 228
Harper, R. A., 270
Hartmann, D. P., 130
Harvard Graphics™, 233
Harvard University, 3
Hawthorne effect, 131
Hayes, S. C., 121
Health and Human Services, Department
    of, 143
Health and Psychosocial Instruments, 160,
    161, 313
Hersen, M., 151, 159
Hoier, T. S., 127
Homer, A. L., 127
Homogeneity of variance, 123, 164,
    179–182
  and post hoc tests, 184–185
  testing, 183
Homoscedasticity, 193
Hops, H., 142
Horowitz, M. J., 33
Hospital records, as research data, 162–
    163
House, A. E., 130
House, B. J., 130
Huberty, C. J., 187, 188
Huitema, B. E., 186, 187
Human subjects review, 137
Humor in oral defense, 261, 266
Hunter, J. E., 112
Hypotheses

Hypotheses (*Cont.*)
  checklist for, 41
  defense of, 262
  definition of, 37
  developing, 37–42
  experimenters blind to, 127–128, 131, 205
  failed predictions, 238–240
  identifying statistical needs of, 175
  importance of having, 37
  introducing, 114–115
  null, 39, 240
  number of, 40–41
  and planned comparisons, 183–184
  and presentation of results, 221, 238
  in proposal, 40–41, 83, 84
  research, 39
  role of, 37–38
  types of, 39
  variables in, 37, 40, 41
  wording of, 37, 39–41
Hypothetical construct, differences with behavior, 149

I

Idea log, 35
Ideas, best, worst sources of, 31
Impact of Event Scale, 33
Independent variables, 35–36
  and ANCOVA effects, 185
  in correlational designs, 177
  in group-comparison designs, 176, 177
  integrity of, 127–128
  literature review organized by, 108
  manipulation checks, 127, 134
  measurement techniques, 130
  in method section, 127–130
  and methodological validity, 244–245
  operationalizing, 127, 147
  and research population size, 123–124
  and statistical needs, 175–176, 178–179, 180
Inderbitzen-Pisaruk, H., 111
Index Medicus, 310
Individual differences research
  measurement theory in, 18
  temporal stability in, 153
Inductive methods, 37
Information management
  confidentiality issues, 135, 138, 205, 207, 301–303

consent forms, 138
  ethical guidelines for, 300, 302–303
Informed consent, 131, 133, 134, 135, 137–138
  and children, 140–144
  in ethical guidelines, 304–305, 306
  and institutional review boards, 143–144
  minimum requirements, 138–141
  passive, 142–143
Insight-oriented therapy, 181, 186
Institutional requirements, 22–23
  for chairperson selection, 62
  for format, 5–6
  for informed consent, 138, 143–144
  length of oral defense, 261
  for literature review, 115
  for meetings, 257
  regarding committee, 72–73
Institutional review boards, 119
  changes in methodology reported to, 203
  and informed consent/assent issues, 143–144
  on recruitment of subjects, 201
Instruments. *See* Measures
Integrity of data, 127–128
  and experimenter behavior, 130–131
  in self-reports, 150
Intentions, lists of, 47
Internal validity, 18, 24, 129–130, 152, 155, 163–164
Interobserver agreement, 152, 162, 220
  correlating differences in, 189
  monitoring, 130–131
  placing data on, 220
  reactivity of, 130
  slippage of, 163
Interpersonal relations, 20
  with chairperson, x, 63, 64–65, 67
  chairperson–committee, 72–73
  within committee, 77
  and dissemination of research, 288
  ethical guidelines for, 299
  with faculty, choosing chairperson and, 75–76
  multiple regression analysis of, 191
  skills in, 21–22
Interrater agreement, 130–131, 152, 162, 163, 220
Interviews, assessment, 131

scorer generalizability of, 162
training assistants for, 204–205
vs. self-reports, 150–151
Introduction to proposal, 83–84
IQ data, 122, 176–177, 185

J

Jaccard, J., 184, 185
Johnston, J. M., 151, 156
Joint ranking tests, 188–189
Journals. *See* Publication of research
Judges, 122, 127, 163
 assessing agreement between, 130–131
 data agreement, 163
 describing use of, 130–131
 in pilot testing, 202–203

K

Kanowitz, J., 209
Kaplan, R. M., 151, 155
Kappa coefficient, 162
Kawal, D. E., 51
Kent, R. N., 32, 131, 209
Keppel, G., 125, 126, 181
Kerlinger, F. N., 35, 36, 37, 38
Keyser, D. J., 159
Kintz, B. L., 174–175
Kirk, R. E., 181, 184
Klem, L., 198
Koyre, A., 21
Kraemer, H. C., 125, 126
Kramer, J. J., 159
Kruskal-Wallis test, 188, 189
Kuder-Richardson procedures, 155, 164
Kuhn,T., 25

L

Laboratory. *See* Research setting
Lang, P. J., 270
Language, decisive, 47
Legal issues, 304
 parental consent, 141–143
Length of dissertation/thesis, x, 5
 in conference presentations, 282–283
 introduction to literature review, 110
 introductory section in proposal, 83–84
 as journal article, 286
 literature review section, 104–105, 105–108

in oral presentation, 261, 264
in presentation to colleagues, 280–282
in proposal meeting, 255, 257
Leo, G. I., 121
Levity, importance of, 47
Lewinsohn, P. M., 142
Life Collection, 314
Linguistics and Language Behavior Abstracts, 310, 314
LISREL, 86
Literature review
 critical analysis in, 18–19, 98–103, 112–113
 identifying major sources for, 93–94
 locating authors, 96–97
 obtaining reprints, 96–97
 in related disciplines, 97
 for research ideas, 33–34
 scanning key journal contents, 97
 shortage of material for, 107–108
Literature review section
 bibliographic reference sources for, 94–95, 309–316
 checklist for, 117
 defense of, 262
 degree of criticism in, 113
 in discussion of results, 240–241
 format, one chapter vs. two, 83–84, 104, 114
 goals of, 113
 introduction to, 110, 114
 length of, 104–105
 limiting contents of, 105–108
 meta-analysis in, 112
 outline for, 105
 preparing to write, 109–110
 in proposal, 83–84
 publication of, 105, 286, 291–292
 revising, 214–215
 secondary sources in, 98
 statement of problem in, 114–115
 subgroupings in, 108–109, 111–112
 summary in, 114
Log-linear analysis, 189
Logit analysis, 189, 194

M

MacProject™, 50
Magazine Index, 314
Mahoney, B. K., 23

Mahoney, M. J., 23
Manipulation checks, 127, 134
Mann-Whitney *U* test, 188
MANOVA. *See* Multivariate analyses of variance (MANOVA)
Manuscript format, 286–287
Manuscript Manager™, 14
Marital relations, research in, 148, 149, 150, 181
Marlowe, D., 165
Martinez, C. M., 204
Master's degree. *See* Thesis, vs. dissertation
Maxwell, S. E., 179, 181, 184, 186, 187, 188, 246
McBurney, D. H., 147
McNamara, J. R., 32
McNemar, Q., 123
Mean scores, 126
    correlated with temporal stability, 154
    stability of, 130
    systematic differences in, 189
Measures. *See also* Self-report measures
    academic preparation for use of, 18
    accuracy of, 151
    altering, 167
    alternate-form reliability of, 154–155
    in behavior research, 149–150
    checklist for, 171
    in clinical research, 159–161
    copyright issues, 169
    correlated with social desirability, 165
    data checking, 130–131
    de novo, 131
    describing in paper, 129–131
    developing, 42
    direct, 149–151
    experimenter agreement, 130–131
    factor analysis in, 41, 125, 167, 168, 195
    getting copies of, 169
    good qualities in, 148–151
    and homogeneity of variances, 123, 164, 181
    identified in proposal, 85–87
    and independent variables, 130
    internal consistency in, 155, 163–164
    interviews, 150
    locating, 158–161
    manipulation checks, 127, 134

names of, vs. content, 168
operationalizing variables, 147–148
potential problems with, 245–246
power analysis, 125–126
of psychological construct, 164–165
psychometric adequacy of, 129–130
reference works on, 319–320
reliability of, 151–156
in results section, 220
reviewed for flaws, 239
scoring, 129, 152–153, 161–163
significant, vs. high, correlation in, 168
single-item, 169
and size of effect, 125, 126, 174
and social desirability effects, 165, 191
temporal stability in, 129–130, 152, 153–154, 163
test–retest, 129–130, 152
validity of, 157–158
MEDLINE, 314
Meehl, P. E., 153
Melvyl catalog, 316
Mental Health Abstracts, 314
Mental Measurements Yearbook, 159, 310
Meta-analysis, in literature review, 112
Method section. *See also* Methodology
    addressing instrument reliability in, 155–156
    apparatus described in, 126–127
    checklist for, 132–133, 145
    contents of, 84–85, 119, 220
    control procedures described in, 128–129
    independent variables described in, 127–129
    informed consent procedures in, 131, 133–134
    judging procedures documented in, 130–131
    measures described in, 129–131
    oral presentation of, 261, 262–263
    procedures described in, 131–134
    in proposal, 84–85
    research assistants described in, 130–131
    research design described in, 120–121
    revising, 215
    self-assessment of weaknesses in, 243–247
    setting described in, 126–127
    subjects described in, 121–126

Method variance, 168
Methodology. *See also* Measures; Method
    section; Research design
  abstracting, 282
  chairperson expertise in, 64
  comparative analysis of, 240–241
  control procedures, 128–129
  data analysis, 212–214
  data checking, 130–131
  data collection, 209–212, 211–212
  data management checklist, 216
  defense of, 262
  defining variables, 148–149
  in discussion section, 244–245
  ethical issues in, 134–144
  implications of results, 242
  importance of, x-xi
  in literature, critical analysis of, 99,
      112–114
  literature review materials grouped by,
      108–109, 111–112
  major changes in, 203
  perfection in, 24, 246
  pilot testing, 201–203
  review of, in proposal meeting, 257–
      258
  reviewed for flaws, 239–240
  and risk to subjects, 137
  and setting, 126–127
  skills for, 12, 17–19, 42, 119
  supplemental review of, 246–247
  verifying accuracy of data, 212
Michienzi, T., 33
Minnesota Multiphasic Personality Inven-
    tory, 129, 165, 167
Mischel, W., 150
Monitoring
  computer summaries, 213
  data collection, 208–209
  scoring, 212
*Monthly Catalog of U. S. Government Publi-
    cations*, 310
Morris, J. D., 187, 188
Multicollinearity, 193
Multiple-baseline design, 120
Multiple regression, 125–126, 182, 190–
    194
Multitrait-multimethod matrix, 166
Multivariate analyses of variance (MAN-
    OVA), 125, 185
  assumptions of, 182

decision tree for application of, 198
and discriminant function analysis,
    194–195
number of subjects needed in, 124–
    125
role of, 187
and Type I errors, 187–188
Munson, R., 127
Myers, J. L., 177
Myths of research, 24, 25, 45

N
Nanda, H., 129
Nangle, D., 282
National Aeronautics and Space Admin-
    istration, 54
Natural science perspective, 156, 157–
    158
Need for approval, 165
Nelson, G. L., 228
Nelson, R. O., 121
NEWSEARCH, 314
Newton, Isaac, 21
Nobel laureate error, 24, 27
Note taking
  idea log, 35
  in oral defense, 260
  in proposal meeting, 259
  in reviewing literature, 94, 99–102
  techniques, 46–47
Null hypothesis, 39, 240
Nunnally, J. C., 151, 164

O
Observation codes, 149, 162
  drift in use of, 162, 208
  training in, 204–205
Observers
  agreement slippage, 163
  coding procedures, 149, 162, 204–205,
      208
  direct assessment by, 149–150
  interobserver agreement, 130–131,
      152, 153, 162–163, 189, 220
  in pilot testing, 202–203
  single, 162
  training, 162, 163, 204–205
Occam's razor, 41
O'Leary, K. D., 32, 131, 209
O'Malley, P. M., 198

Omega squared, 126
One-chapter format of literature review, 83–84, 104, 114
Originality, x
  in choosing a topic, 28
  emphasis on, 3–4
  in writing proposal, 82
Outlines
  discussion section, 250–251
  literature review section, 105–109
  oral defense, 261

P

Pairwise ranking tests, 188–189
Parametric statistics. *See also* Analyses of covariance (ANCOVA); Multivariate analyses of variance (MANOVA)
  assumptions of, 182–183
  bivariate, 189–190
  flowchart for choosing, 178–179, 180
  nonparametric alternatives, 188–189
  planned comparisons in, 183–184
  post hoc tests in, 184–185
  power analysis in, 126
  power of, 179
  regression strategies, 190–194
  role of, 177–178
  t test, 179–182
  vs. nonparametric, 179
Parental consent, 140–143
Parker, C. A., 5, 19
Parsonson, B. S., 228, 230, 232
Partial correlation procedures, 165
Passive consent, 142–143
Path analysis, 174
Patient files, as research data, 162–163
Paul, G. L., 108, 274
Pearson product-moment correlation, 189
  assumptions of, 183
Peer review, 34
  role of, in research, 278
Pennypacker, H. S., 151, 156
Percentages, in figures, 229–230
Peritz test, 185
Personal life
  and planning work, 51–52, 57
  and research question, 31–32
PERT analysis, 48, 51

Peterson, L., 127
Phi coefficients, 190
Pilot studies
  for assessing generalizability, 163
  ethical guidelines for, 144
  observers in, 202–203
  research subjects for, 202
  role of, 167, 201–202
Place of study, 19–20
Plagiarism, 102, 115–116, 307
Planned comparisons, 183–184
Planning. *See also* Time management; Work habits
  authorship credits, 62, 288
  backward chaining in, 47
  checklist for, 58
  for committee meetings, 257–259
  computerized data collection, 210–211
  for defense, 259–269
  dissemination of research, 288
  ethics considerations in, 303
  flexibility in, 50
  forward chaining in, 47
  instrument needs, 86–87
  literature review, 93–94
  methodological practice, checklist for, 205–206
  outline for literature review, 105–109
  place of study, 19–20
  proposal, 88
  realism in, 23–24
  for research assistants, 53–54, 203–205
  for research subjects, 36–37, 52–53, 207–208
  role of, 50–52
  visual representations of, 48–50
Point-biserial correlation, 190
Poppen, R., 272
Post hoc tests, 184–185
  with ANCOVA, 187
Poster presentations, 283–285
Power, statistical
  analysis of, 125–126
  in parametric, vs. nonparametric, statistics, 179
  and planned comparisons, 183–184
Pragmatic school, 36
Premack principle, 57, 110
Principal components analysis, 195
Probability levels, 223

Problem-solving therapy, 182–183, 186
Procrastination, 54–57, 102, 110
Prodigy™, 316
Professional associations
    directories of, 169
    meetings of, xi, 97, 279–280, 282–285
Professional development
    and presentation of research, 278–280
    and publication of research, 278, 292–293
    recommendations for, xi
    and thesis/dissertation, 7
Program Evaluation and Review Technique (PERT), 48, 51
Project scheduling software, 48
Proofreading, 14
Proposal
    appendixes in, 87
    checklists for, 90, 275
    committee meeting, 255–259, 275
    and committee procedures, 72–73
    committee suggestions for improving, 258–259
    as contract, 82
    copyright issues in, 87–88
    de novo instruments in, 131
    grounds for rejection of, 259
    introduction section in, 83–84
    methodology section in, 84–85
    number of hypotheses in, 40–41
    organization of, 83–90
    references section in, 87
    results section in, 85–87
    role of, 81–82
    table of contents in, 88–90
PsycBOOKS, 94, 96, 311
Psychological Abstracts, 94, 96, 97, 161, 310
Psychological Bulletin, 33, 114, 286
Psychological Review, 286
Psychometric properties of measures, where to find, 158
PsycINFO, 96, 314
PsycLIT, 96, 97, 161, 311
PsycSCAN, 94
PsyD degree, 3, 4, 5
Publication Manual of the American Psychological Association, 6, 14–15, 87, 119, 223, 226, 227, 228, 232–233, 286, 287
Publication of research

authorship issues, 287–288, 307–308
    benefits of, 277–278
    checklist for, 294
    ethical guidelines for, 307–308
    literature review section, 105, 291–292
    manuscript preparation, 286–287
    planning for, 105, 288
    in popular press, 292–293
    rejection, 289–291
    selecting a journal for, 285–286
    soliciting comments before, 278–280
    subdividing project for, 291–292
    submission of manuscript, 288–291
    timing of, 277, 285
Publications, professional. *See also* Literature review section
    to locate assessment instruments, 158–161, 169
    obtaining reprints from, 96–97
    refereed, xi
    as sources for research ideas, 33–34
    for statistical work, 174–175, 181, 198

Q

Questions, responding to, 197, 258–259, 265–267
Quotations, using, 102

R

Race/ethnicity, 148, 178
    defining, 148
Radcliff, B. M., 51
Rajaratnam, N., 129
Random assignment, 122, 131
    and ANCOVA, 186
Ratings by others, 150
Ravizza, R., 39, 131, 147
Raw data, 209, 213, 220
Ray, W. J., 39, 131, 147
Reactivity, subject, 246
Readiness for research, 24–25
    checklist, 11–13, 45
    computer skills, 20–21
    interpersonal skills, 21–22
    methodological skills, 17–19, 119
    realism in assessing, 23–24
    specific project, 42
    statistical knowledge, 174–175
    writing skills, 13–15
Recalibration, 208

Recorded evidence
  as direct observation, 150, 151, 162
  drift in coding of, 208
  in oral presentation, 264–265
  of subject debriefing, 138
Recruiting
  assistants, 203–204
  subjects, 122, 131, 201
Reed, J. G., 96
References, in proposal, 87
Regression strategies, 190
  backward deletion procedures in, 192
  conditions for, 193–194
  forward entry procedures in, 192
  forward stepwise procedures in, 192
  hierarchical, 191, 193
  logistic, 194
  and multicollinearity, 193
  nonparametric, 194
  parametric multiple, 190–194
  in proposal, 86
  stepwise procedures in, 191–193
REHABDATA, 315
Rehearsal, oral presentation, 267–269, 283
Reid, J., 208
Reid, J. B., 202
Relaxation techniques, 272
Reliability
  addressing in paper, 155–156
  alternate form, 154–155
  assessing, 155–156
  of dependent variables, 129–130
  evaluating, 151–156
  forms of, 151–152
  generalizability theory of, 152
  internal consistency, 130, 155
  interrater, 152
  reviews of, 159–160
  scorer, 152–153, 163
  and Spearman–Brown formula, 155
  temporal stability, 153–154
  and validity, 156
Replication of research, x
  failed attempt at, 241
  and stepwise procedures, 192
Replication of study
  as element of proposal, 84–85
  as research topic, 34, 241
Reprints, 96–97
Research assistants

in applied research, 209
assessing interrater agreement, 130–131
blind experimenters, 127–128, 131, 205
communicating with, 209
compensation for, 53
educational benefits for, 205
ethical guidelines for, 137, 205, 299–300
good qualities in, 204
in methodology section, 122, 128
monitoring, 53–54, 171, 208–209
potential problems with, 53–54
recruiting, 203–204
research bias in, 32, 205
in statistical work, 197–198
training, 53, 54, 128, 201–203, 204–205, 207
Research design. See also Correlational design; Group comparison design; Methodology
between-subjects, 120, 121, 178–179
classes in, 18
controlling for temporal effects in, 163
dependent variables in, 130
description of, 120–121
ethical practices in, 137–138
external validity in, 245
and figure formats, 230
identifying limitations of, 243–244
implications of results for, 242
mixed, 245
nonexperimental, 244–245
nonhomogeneous variances in, 184–185
and number of research subjects, 124–126
oral presentation of, 263
and post hoc tests, 184–185
quasi-experimental, 244, 245, 247
reference works on, 147, 151, 319
review of, in proposal meeting, 257–259
and screening procedures, 123–124
Solomon four-group, 120, 155
and statistical needs, 75–76
and stepwise procedures, 192–193
within-subjects, 120, 121
Research in Child Abuse and Neglect, 310
Research populations. See also Informed consent

access to, 36
animal, 122–123, 135–136, 206, 306–307
assessing availability of, 36–37
assessing characteristics of, 124
bias effects, 131
children as, 140–144, 202, 207–208
classification of, 121–122
clinical samples in, 138
data collection, 131–134, 207, 209–211, 212
data management, 138, 207–208
deceiving, 136
demographic data from, 122, 124
describing, in methodology section, 121–126
ethical research issues, 135–136, 138
factor analysis requirements, 164, 195
feedback from, 202
follow-up procedures, 134
homogeneous, 123
identified in hypothesis, 39
instructions to, 134
levels of, 176
manipulation checks for, 127, 134
number of subjects needed, 124–126, 164, 195
in pilot study, 202
potential problems with, 52–53
recruiting, 122, 131, 201
representativeness of, 123
rights of, 135
risk to, 135, 137
scheduling, 207–208
screening procedures for, 123–124
sending results to, 134
subsets of, effects in, 240
voluntary participation of, 137–138
Research question. *See also* Topic selection
abstract of, 280–282
animal surgery in, 128
criteria for framing, 35–36
description of, in defense, 262
developing hypothesis for, 37–42
experimental confederates in, 128
form of, 30–31
and generalizability of data, 170
identifying statistical needs of, 175–178

and instrument stability needs, 153–154
and instrument validity needs, 157
interventions in, 128
in literature review section, 114–115
no basis for predictions in, 115
relevance of, 31
Research Readiness Checklist, 11–13, 45
Research setting, 126–127
for direct observation, 149–150, 151
generalizability, 157–158, 167
planning, 206
Results. *See also* Discussion section; Publication of research
abstract of, 280–282
alternative explanations for, 239
clinical implications of, 242–243
comparative analysis of, 240–241
ethical guidelines for reporting, 307
forums for presentation of, 278–280
identifying significance in, 248, 249
implications of, 241–243
lack of significant, 239–240
literature review organized by, 112
oral defense presentation of, 263–264
oral presentation to colleagues, 282–283
poster presentation of, 283–285
related to theory, 242
supplemental analyses of, 246–247
and type of causality, 244–245
unexpected, x–xi, 238
Results section
checklist for preparation of, 234
contents of, 85–87, 219–220
mock-up of, 85–87, 216
oral presentation of, 261
order of, 221
presentation of figures in, 227–233
in proposal, 85–87
repetition in, 222, 227
statistics in, 221–222, 223–224
tables in, 224–227
writing style of, 222–223
Retesting, 129–130
Reverse causation, 244–245
Rights, research subject, 135–138
RightWriter™, 14
Risk assessment, 137
apparatus, 38
ethical guidelines for, 299

Risk assessment (*Cont.*)
  ethical responsibilities, 135
Rite of passage, 8
Roberts, R. E., 142
Robinson, J. P., 161
Robustness, test, 179, 181
Rodgers, W. L., 198
Romanczyk, R. G., 131, 162, 163, 208
Rosenthal, R., 32, 205
Rossi, J. S., 124
Rule of threes, 23, 45
Rules
  for chairperson selection, 62
  committee, 72–73
  informal, 22–23
  school, 22–23
Rush, A. J., 165

S

Saccuzzo, D. P., 151, 155
Sampling strategy, 122
Sanchez-Hucles, J., 5
Sas, L., 33
Scatterplots, 213
Schmidt, F. L., 112
Schuller, R., 121
Schwartz, R. D., 166
Scientific method
  choice of measures in, 148
  deductive approach, 37
  hypotheses in, 37–38
  inductive approach, 37
  role of failed predictions in, 240
  in wording research question, 35–36
SCISEARCH, 315
Scorer generalizability
  of archival data, 162–163
  in direct observation, 162
  in interview assessments, 162
  on practice, vs. real, material, 163
  role of, 152–153, 161–162
  unproven, for chosen measure, 161–163
Scoring
  accuracy of, 151
  computers for, 209–210
  drift in, 208
  frequency distribution in, 181
  generalizability in, 152–153, 161–163
  monitoring of, 162, 212
  recalibration of, 208

residual differences in, 193
  of self-reports, 152
  validity in, 156–158
Screening of subjects, 123–124
Sechrest, L., 166
Seeley, J. R., 142
Self-fulfilling prophecies, 32
Self-monitoring, 121
Self-report measures, 130, 150–151, 162
  collateral data sources with, 166
  and construct validity, 164–165
  correlations between, 168–169
  internal consistency of, 164
  potential problems in use of, 245–246
  reporting results from, 249
  scoring in, 152
Sequential analysis, 174
Setting generalizability, 158, 167
Sexually anatomically correct dolls, 35, 37, 39
Shaver, P. R., 161
Shaw, B. F., 165
Shuller, D. Y., 32
Sikora, D. M., 137, 238, 242
Single-item measures, 169
Single-subject designs, 220
Skinner, B. F., 37
  work habits of, 20
Slides, 264–265
Sobell, M. B., 121
Social Abstracts, 315
Social desirability measures, 165, 191
Social Sciences Citation Index, 94–95, 311
Social SCISEARCH, 315
Social support, 128
Society for Research in Child Development, 279
Society for Research on Child Development, 282
Socioeconomic status, 124, 147, 165
Sociological Abstracts, 311
Software Directory, The, 315
Solomon four-group design, 120, 155, 163
Spearman-Brown prophecy formula, 155
Spearman rank order procedure, 190
Spelling, 14
Split-half procedures, 155
Stanley, J. C., 245
Statement of the Problem, 114
Statistical Navigator, 198

Statistical techniques
  academic preparation for, 17–18, 42,
    173–175
  Analyses of covariance (ANCOVA), 85,
    124, 165, 182, 185–187
  Analyses of variance (ANOVA), 26, 85,
    120, 123, 179, 181, 182, 183–
    184, 187–189, 246
  for assessing interjudge agreement,
    130
  computational formulas, 175
  computers for, 211, 317–38
  consultation for, 195–198
  conventions for presentation, 223–224
  in correlational research designs, 176–
    177, 189–195
  covariate analysis, 124
  data transformation in, 179
  defense of, 196–198
  in discussion section, 246–247
  fear of, 173
  fishing expeditions, 38
  and homogeneity of variances, 181–
    183
  identifying needs, 175–178
  MANOVA, 125, 182–183, 185, 187–
    188, 194–195
  mock results of, 85–87, 219
  nonparametric, 188–189
  and number of subjects needed, 124–
    126
  parametric, 177–179, 180
  planned comparisons, 183–184
  post hoc tests, 184–185
  power analysis, 125–126
  power of, 179
  in presentation of results, 221–222
  in proposal, 85–87
  reference works on, 320–321
  robustness of, 179
  selecting, 199
  supplemental review of, 246–247
  teaching of, 173
  and use of assistants, 197–198
  writing about results of, 223–224
Stephenson, R. J., 51
Stepwise procedures, 191–193
Sternberg, D., 82, 86
Structural equation modeling, 174
Stuart, R. B., 20
Style. *See also* Writing style

  intellectual, ix-x
  in oral defense presentation, 263–264
  in responding to committee questions,
    266
Subjects, research. *See* Research popula-
    tions
Super Project™, 50
Support groups, dissertation, 57
Survival analysis, 174
Sweetland, R. C., 159

T

t test
  assumptions of, 179–182
  role of, 179
Tabachnick, B. F., 185, 187, 193, 194,
    195, 198
Table of contents
  in proposal, 88–90
  scanning, in literature review, 97
Tables
  for audiovisual display, 265
  checklist for, 227
  content of, 222
  conventions for presentation of, 224–
    227
  number of, 224, 226
  placement of, in manuscript, 226
  titles for, 227
Talk, and relation to other behavior, 47
Tape recording. *See also* Recorded evi-
    dence
  instructions to subjects, 134
Taplin, P. S., 202
Temporal stability, 129–130, 152, 153–
    154
  controlling for effects of, 163
  correlated with mean scores, 154
  establishing, for chosen measure, 163
Test–retest technique, 129–130, 152
*Tests in Print II. See Mental Measurements
    Yearbook*
Theory
  literature review materials grouped by,
    108
  relating results to, 242
Theses, research ideas from existing, 34–
    35
Thesis, vs. dissertation
  choosing topic for, 30, 63

Thesis, vs. dissertation (*Cont.*)
  defense, 72, 255, 256
  definition of, 2–3
  empirical research in, 4–5
  as learning experience, 67
  length of, 5
  origins of, 4
  publication of, 278
  replicating existing study for, 34
  role of, 3–4, 6–7, 241
Thiemann, S., 125, 126
Time-line charts, 48
Time management
  chairperson availability and, 66–67
  checklist, 58
  definition of time, 45
  estimates of, 19, 23–24, 46–48
  increments of work in, 47
  and institutional review board schedule, 144
  of oral defense, 259, 261, 264
  pilot testing for, 201
  in publication of research, 277, 285, 289
  in recruiting assistants, 203–204
  scheduling, 19, 205–208
  school rules and, 22–23
  setting goals in, 45–46
  and unexpected disruptions, 53
  visual representations for, 47–50
Time-series procedures, 174
Timed Behavioral Checklist for Performance Anxiety, 273
Tolerance for ambiguity, ix-x
Topic selection. *See also* Research question
  access to research population and, 36–37
  advantages of early start in, 28–29
  bad qualities in, x
  chairperson in, 63–64
  checklist for, 43
  criteria for, 29
  ethical considerations in, 137
  existing dissertations/theses for ideas on, 34–35
  existing literature for ideas on, 33–34
  first step, 29
  idea log for, 35
  identifying area of interest, 29
  intellectual style and, ix-x
  personal considerations, 7, 31–32
  realism in, 27–28
  role of faculty in, 28–30, 33
  sources of ideas for, 31–35
  undergraduate experience in, 28
Training
  animal researchers, 135–136
  assistants, 53, 54
  coding procedures, 204–205
  confidentiality procedures, 205, 207
  describing procedures for, 128
  ethical research, 137, 205, 299–300
  observers, 162, 163
  of observers, 130
  pilot testing for, 201–203
Trait assessment, 166
Transparencies, 264–265
Treatment validity, 130
"Trying" to do things, 47
Tukey honestly significant difference test, 185
Tukey–Kramer test, 185
Twentyman, C., 208
Two-chapter format, 83–84, 104, 114
Two-group experimental design, 120
2 X 2 design, 120
Type I errors, xi, 246
  and controlling for nonhomogeneous variances, 181
  and MANOVA, 187–188

U

UnCover, 96, 315
Undergraduate experience. *See also* Readiness for research and topic selection, 28
Unequal-*n* designs, 184
Unexpected outcomes, x–xi, 238
University of California, 316
University of Washington, 3
Unobtrusive measures, 166

V

Vail model, 5
Validity
  concurrent, 157
  construct, 130, 156, 157, 165–166
  content, 157–158

convergent, 130, 157, 164–166
criterion-related, 130, 157
defining, 156–157
of dependent variables, 129–130
discriminant, 130, 157, 164–166
discriminative, 157
external, 18, 25, 149, 245
face, 156–157
internal, 18, 24, 129–130, 152, 155, 163–164
methodological, 18, 25, 244–246
predictive, 157
and reliability, 156
reviews of, 159–160
supplemental analysis of, 239
treatment, 130
types of, 156–157
Variability, related to different designs, 123, 124
Variables. *See also* Dependent variables; Independent variables; Measures
computer analyses of, 213
in correlational designs, 176–177
criterion, 190, 191–192
defining, 35–36, 148–149
dichotomous, 190–191
direct assessment of, 151
in factor analysis, 195
in figures, 228–231
in hypotheses, 37, 40, 41
and methodological validity, 244–245
operationalizing, 36, 40, 147–148
outcome, 190
in regression analysis, 191–192, 193–194
and research design, 123–124
in self-report measures of construct, 165
social desirability, 165, 191
and statistical needs, 175–176
subjects per, in factor analysis, 164
supplemental analysis of, 239–240
in tables, 224–226
and temporal stability, 153–154
Verb use
in avoiding causal language, 249
tense, 39, 215
Videotape. *See* Recorded evidence
Volunteers, for research, 137–138
vs. nonvolunteers, 123

W

W tests, 183, 188
Webb, E. J., 166
Wechsler Adult Intelligence Test—Revised, 129
White, J. B., 177
White, O. R., 127
Wiggins, J. S., 152, 165
Wilcoxin Rank Sum test, 188
Wilner, N., 33
Winer, B. J., 189, 246
Within-subjects designs, 120, 121, 163, 176, 178–179
non-robust, 184
and post hoc tests, 184, 185
Wolfe, D. A., 33
Wolfe, V. V., 33, 108
Wonderlich, S. A., 127
Wood, G., 184
Work habits, 19–20, 21. *See also* Time management
avoiding procrastination in, 54–57, 110
of chairperson, 63, 66–67
in literature review, 99–102
rewarding good, 57
role of planning in, 50–52
Workplace, 19–20
Wrightsman, L. S., 161
Writer's Tool Kit™, 14
Writes Right™, 14
Writing process
literature review, 109–115
outline for literature review, 105
procrastination in, 55–56, 110
role of drafts in, 109
Writing style. *See also* Format
for abstracts, 282–282
causal language misused in, 248–249
and computers, 14
conventions for statistics, 223–224
in discussion section, 237, 248–251
for figure captions, 232–233
goals of, 104
good qualities of, 261
journal requirements, 286–287, 289–290
in literature review, 110–115
for methodology section, 215

Writing style (*Cont.*)
  for poster presentations, 283–284
  proposal, 82, 84, 85, 88
  reference works on, 321
  references to authors in, 287–288
  in results section, 222–223
  for self-report results, 249
  skills assessment, 12, 13–16
  for table titles, 227
  wording of hypothesis, 37, 39–41

Y

Yale University, 3
Yates, B. T., 30, 97, 131, 138, 198, 220, 223, 233, 261, 266

Z

z tests, 189

About the Authors

John D. Cone, professor of clinical psychology at United States International University, earned his BA in psychology from Stanford University and his MS and PhD from the University of Washington. He has taught at the University of Puget Sound, West Virginia University, and the University of Hawaii. He is a fellow of both the American Psychological Association and the American Psychological Society. His research interests include the development of idiographic assessment methodology; childhood sexual abuse; and the development, implementation, and evaluation of large scale service delivery systems, especially for persons with developmental disabilities. A frequent organizational consultant, he is past editor of *Behavioral Assessment* and currently teaches courses in behavior therapy, research design, assessment methodology, dissertation planning, and child abuse. When not being professionally active, John spends his time jogging, windsurfing, and sailing the waters of the blue Pacific.

Sharon L. Foster is a professor and director of the PhD Program in Clinical Psychology at the California School of Professional Psychology in San Diego. She received her PhD in clinical psychology from the State University of New York at Stony Brook and completed a clinical internship at the University of Washington. She has served on the editorial boards of numerous professional journals, including *Journal of Consulting and Clinical Psychology, Psychological Assessment*, and *Behavior Therapy*. Her research revolves around children's peer relations and parent–adolescent conflict.